Voices of the Civil War

Voices of the Civil War · Gettysburg

By the Editors of Time-Life Books, Alexandria, Virginia

Contents

8 The Gathering Storm

36 Clash at Dawn: July 1

66 In Hell's Terrain: July 2

Little Round Top

The Peach Orchard and Wheat Field

Cemetery Ridge and Cemetery Hill

106 The Great Rebel Charge: July 3

140 Aftermath in Blood

172 *Glossary*

173 *Acknowledgments*

173 *Picture Credits*

174 *Bibliography*

176 *Index*

THE FIELD AT GETTYSBURG
The pivotal encounters of the three-day Battle of Gettysburg unfolded on the hills, fields, and ridges south of the town. An artist's rendering depicts the geographical features where the fiercest fighting took place.
McPherson's Ridge
Hagerstown Road
Seminary Ridge
Sherfy Farm
Emmitsburg Road
Peach Orchard
Wheat Field Road
Rose Farm
Rose Woods

utheran Theological Seminary
Gettysburg
Culp's Hill
Cemetery Hill
Bliss Farm
The Angle
Ziegler's Grove
Grove of Trees
Codori Farm
Taneytown Road
Trostle Farm
Weikert Farm
Wheat Field
Little Round Top
Plum Run
Big Round Top
Devil's Den
Slaughter Pen

The Gathering Storm

The road to Gettysburg began at the tiny Virginia crossroads of Chancellorsville. There, shortly after noon on May 3, 1863, as the sulfurous smoke of battle clung to the ground, General Robert E. Lee rode forth to savor his army's triumph. The stalwart general and his mounted entourage guided their horses around the mangled dead and writhing wounded, past demolished cannon and exploded limber chests that flanked the burning Chancellor house. At the sight of their beloved commander, thousands of powder-stained soldiers in uniforms of butternut and gray erupted in wild shouts of enthusiasm. Lee's aide, Major Charles Marshall, noted, "One long, unbroken cheer, in which the feeble cry of those who lay helpless on the earth blended with the strong voices of those who still fought, hailed the presence of the victorious chief."

In three days of bloody combat amid the scrub oak and pine forest called the Wilderness, Lee's Confederate Army of Northern Virginia—just under 61,000 strong—had outmaneuvered and outfought a Federal force of nearly 134,000 men. Major General Joseph Hooker, the vainglorious Union commander, became the fourth leader of the Army of the Potomac to fall victim to Lee's tactical expertise. Many of Hooker's disgruntled soldiers, slogging back to their camps across the Rappahannock River, placed the blame for their defeat on Fighting Joe's well-known fondness for the bottle. "The failure at Chancellorsville was due to the incompetency which comes from a besotted brain," grumbled Private Robert G. Carter of the 22d Massachusetts Infantry. "The Army of the Potomac had marched, fought and endured, and was there at Chancellorsville, as it always had been, superior to the genius of any commander yet appointed."

Although the Army of the Potomac had been soundly beaten, the massive Union force was far from crippled. Moreover, while Hooker had lost 13 percent of his force at Chancellorsville, Lee's smaller army had sustained a 22 percent casualty rate. Among the casualties was a particularly devastating loss, the brilliant General Thomas J. "Stonewall" Jackson, Lee's most trusted subordi-

Artillerymen of the VI Corps pause near pontoon bridges over the Rappahannock River south of Fredericksburg, Virginia, during the Federal reconnaissance of early June 1863.

nate, who succumbed to his wounds on May 10. In the wake of this problematic victory, the question loomed for Lee: What now to do? The Confederate commander realized that his victory had achieved little more than a postponement of the day when the Army of the Potomac would again press his outnumbered army back toward Richmond. In considering his prospects, Lee concluded that he had only two alternatives. The first was to retire to Richmond and defend the city, a course of action that he suspected would end in a Confederate surrender. The other choice was audacious and full of risk—the kind of option that seemed to suit Lee's style of command. It was an invasion of the North, a march across the Potomac River and a strike into Pennsylvania.

In a series of meetings with Confederate president Jefferson Davis and his cabinet, Lee built a persuasive case for taking the offensive. Moving north would solve one of Lee's critical problems—a chronic supply shortage. Hampered by an inadequate railroad system, and operating in a war-ravaged region partly occupied by the enemy, Lee was unable to provide sufficient food and clothing for his army or forage for his horses. An invasion of Pennsylvania would afford his soldiers access to rich farmlands and give the people of Virginia time to stockpile supplies.

But Davis and his advisers had other ideas about what to do with the Army of Northern Virginia. For one thing, they were preoccupied with the deteriorating situation in the western theater, where General Ulysses S. Grant's Federals were laying siege to the Mississippi River bastion of Vicksburg. Some wanted Lee to send forces west to relieve Vicksburg. They also feared that if Lee moved north, Hooker might take advantage of the opportunity to strike south, toward the Confederate capital at Richmond. All were agreed, however, that something had to be done to shift the fighting away from war-torn northern Virginia.

And the Confederate leaders knew well that a successful invasion might win prizes of incalculable value. The Northern Peace Democrats surely would be encouraged to demand an end to the conflict under terms reasonably favorable to the South; a victory might also persuade Britain and France to intervene on behalf of the Confederacy.

In the weeks following Chancellorsville, to adjust for the loss of Stonewall Jackson, Lee reorganized the Army of Northern Virginia into three corps commanded by his most able generals: James Longstreet, Richard Stoddert Ewell, and Ambrose Powell Hill. The force was resupplied as best it could be, reinforced to more than 75,000 strong, and readied for the great invasion.

Despite their losses at Chancellorsville, Lee's soldiers were supremely confident of their fighting prowess and the military judgment of their commander. Lee had led the Southern army in a string of victories since taking over command: the Seven Days' Battles around Richmond, and a second triumph on the banks of Bull Run. His first invasion of the North was turned back at Antietam, but he had withstood the Federals at Fredericksburg and then defeated them at Chancellorsville. His men were with him heart and soul. "The troops of Lee were now at the zenith of their perfection and glory," South Carolina lieutenant D. Augustus Dickert recalled. "They looked upon themselves as invincible, and that no General the North could put in the field could match our Lee." Artillery Colonel Edward Porter Alexander professed, "Nothing gave me much concern so long as I knew that General Lee was in command. We looked forward to victory under him as confidently as to successive sunrises." For his part, Lee considered his devoted soldiers "the finest body of men that ever tramped the earth."

A month after Chancellorsville, with Hooker apparently still reluctant to resume the offensive, Lee prepared to move his army by stages 30 miles northwest to the vicinity of Culpeper. "I propose to do so cautiously," Lee wired Davis on June 2, "watching the result, and not to get beyond recall until I find it safe." By June 7 both Longstreet's and Ewell's corps had encamped near Culpeper, and A. P. Hill's corps was preparing to follow. The next day Lee attended a grand review put on by his swashbuckling cavalry commander, Major General James Ewell Brown (Jeb) Stuart, whose 9,500 troopers were stationed six miles northeast of Culpeper near the hamlet of Brandy Station. "It was a splendid sight," Lee wrote his wife, Mary; "Stuart was in all his glory."

Alerted to increased Confederate activity, but uncertain of what it portended, on June 5 General Hooker expressed his suspicions to President Abraham Lincoln that Lee "must have it either in mind to cross the Upper Potomac, or to throw his army between mine and Washington." Unaware that two-thirds of Lee's army had already concentrated at Culpeper, Hooker believed the Rebel forces there consisted largely of Stuart's cavalry, perhaps poised for a raid against Union supply lines. In an effort to preempt a Confederate attack, Hooker ordered his chief of cavalry, Brigadier General Alfred Pleasonton, "to disperse and destroy the rebel force assembled in the vicinity of Culpeper."

In the early morning darkness of June 9, 1863, Pleasonton's 8,000 troopers, with 3,000 infantrymen in support, splashed across the fog-shrouded Rappahannock River at Beverly's and Kelly's Fords, and overran Stuart's outlying pickets. Surprised by the sudden onslaught, Stuart desperately shifted his forces to confront the advancing Yankee columns. For the next 14 hours, charge and countercharge thundered across the ridges near Brandy Station in the largest cavalry engagement ever waged on American soil. By day's end Stuart's horsemen held the field, with Pleasonton in retreat across the Rappahannock. But the self-confident Rebel horsemen had been forced to accept the fact that the once ridiculed Union cavalry were now their equals in fighting ability.

Following the inconclusive battle at Brandy Station, the Army of Northern Virginia continued its epic trek northward. In the vanguard, the 21,000 troops of Ewell's corps moved down the valley of the Shenandoah toward that river's confluence with the Potomac. From June 13 through June 15, Ewell attacked Major General Robert H. Milroy's Union troops at Winchester, capturing 3,000 prisoners and 23 cannon, and virtually annihilating the last Yankee obstacle to the fords of the Potomac River. On the evening of the 15th, Major General Robert E. Rodes' division tramped across a pontoon bridge and gained the north bank of the Potomac just south of Williamsport, Maryland.

Having gained a foothold in Maryland, Lee was now fully determined to press his invasion of the North. Longstreet's and Hill's forces were ordered to march with all haste from their positions at Culpeper and Fredericksburg. The Blue Ridge Mountains shielded the Confederate columns from Federal observation, while Stuart's horsemen effectively fended off Yankee cavalry probes east of the mountains. In a series of mounted clashes at Aldie, Middleburg, and Upperville, Pleasonton's Union troopers fought courageously but failed to penetrate Stuart's cavalry screen.

When word of a Confederate onslaught in the lower Shenandoah Valley reached Army of the Potomac headquarters at Falmouth—across the Rappahannock from Fredericksburg—Hooker's worst fears were realized. As yet uncertain whether Lee intended to invade the North, to threaten Washington, or to strike at the principal Federal supply line—the Orange & Alexandria Railroad—the Union commander began shifting his seven army corps northward to Manassas Junction and Centreville, 20 miles outside the defenses of Washington.

The Rebels had stolen several days' march on the Federals, and the Northern troops were pushed to the breaking point in the attempt to catch up with their enemy. Marching for 15 hours at a stretch, clad in woolen uniforms and weighed down with muskets, ammunition, and knapsacks, the Yankee foot soldiers found their endurance sorely tested. "The air was almost suffocating," recalled Private John Haley of the 17th Maine. "The soil of Virginia was sucked into our throats, sniffed into our nostrils, and flew into our eyes and ears until our most intimate friends would not have recognized us." Nauseated and temporarily blind, Haley was one of hundreds who collapsed by the wayside.

"All day long we tugged our weary knapsacks in the broiling sun, and many fell out to fall no more," Private Wilbur Fisk of Vermont wrote his wife during a brief halt near Fairfax. "We expect more hard marching, but shall either get toughened to it, or, as the boys say, die toughening."

Plodding northward in the ranks of the Fifth Corps, Robert Carter observed that even veteran troops abandoned all discipline in their quest for water. When officers attempted to maintain order at roadside springs—most little more than "slimy mud-holes"—mobs of thirsty soldiers shoved them aside while "the scooping and filtering of mud and grit went on." As the tramp continued, Carter discovered how callous human nature could become when subjected to such an ordeal. The amputated arm of a Federal cavalryman wounded in the fighting near Upperville "became a football for every one, and had to run the gauntlet, from the head of the brigade to the rear."

While the Federals were struggling to catch up, the bulk of the Army of Northern Virginia was crossing the Potomac into Maryland. On June 24 A. P. Hill's corps forded the river at Shepherdstown, and over the next two days Longstreet crossed his corps at Williamsport. The crossing took on the air of a celebration. Gray-clad soldiers tossed their hats aloft and cheered, while regimental bands played "Maryland! My Maryland" and "The Bonnie Blue Flag." Though nearly as tired as their Federal pursuers, the Rebels were jubilant to be once again on Northern soil. Captain Charles Minor Blackford of Longstreet's corps heard one Confederate laughingly exclaim, "Well, boys, I've been seceding for two years and now I've got back into the Union!" Another soldier told a somber group of Maryland women, "Here we are, ladies, as rough and ragged as ever but back again to bother you."

Aware that the prosperous farms of Maryland and Pennsylvania offered an irresistible temptation to his hungry soldiers, Lee issued orders to prevent the theft of crops and livestock. All confiscated supplies, he declared, would be paid for at "the market price." The soldiers mostly ignored their commander's directive, however. Pilfering was widespread, and many Confederate officers turned a blind eye to their soldiers' indiscretions. "Some of the boys have been 'capturing' chickens," Corporal Edmund D. Patterson of Alabama wrote his wife; "It is against positive orders, but I would not punish one of them." Colonel Clement A. Evans of the 31st Georgia expressed a desire for revenge that motivated many of his comrades-in-arms: "The rascals are afraid we are going to overrun Pennsylvania," he noted. "That would indeed be glorious, if we could ravage that state making her desolate like Virginia. It would be a just punishment."

Thus far Lee's daring gamble had exceeded all expectations, and the path to Pennsylvania appeared wide open. In an effort to keep his dazed opponents off balance, the Confederate commander instructed General Jeb Stuart to "pass around" Hooker's forces with three of his four cavalry divisions, "doing them all the damage you can." Eager to repeat the success of his two previous circumventions of the Yankee army, Stuart struck eastward and embarked on a characteristically daring raid. But it would prove to be a costly foray. Without the aid of Stuart's troopers, Lee would be unable to track the Federal movements for a crucial week of the campaign.

As Hill's and Longstreet's forces made their way rapidly north through Maryland, Ewell's vanguard corps was already across the Mason-Dixon line. One of Ewell's divisions, led by gruff, hard-fighting Major General Jubal A. Early, forged ahead toward the Susquehanna River, easily overcoming the hastily mustered contingents of local militia that stood in his path. Lee had advised Ewell, "If Harrisburg comes within your means, capture it," and by June 27, with the rest of Lee's army massing near Chambersburg, Ewell had occupied the towns of York and Carlisle and was poised to cross the Susquehanna and converge on Pennsylvania's capital from the south and east.

Lee was confident that not only Harrisburg but also the strategic railroad line linking that city with Philadelphia would soon be in Confederate hands. But on the evening of June 28, Robert E. Lee's optimism abruptly gave way to alarm when one of Longstreet's scouts brought word that Hooker's army was on the march. Indeed, the Federals had crossed the Potomac at Edward's Ferry and were massing near Frederick, Maryland, less than 40 miles south of the Confederate headquarters at Chambersburg. Lee immediately recognized the danger—if the Yankees continued their rapid advance, they might well interpose themselves between the widely scattered Rebel columns. He immediately called off the movement against Harrisburg and ordered his corps commanders to concentrate their forces at the village of Cashtown, some 25 miles east of Chambersburg.

The scout who brought the word of Yankee movements also passed along, almost incidentally, another interesting piece of news. Joseph Hooker was no longer directing Federal operations. In the predawn darkness of June 28, grizzled, hot-tempered Major General George Gordon Meade—commander of the Union Fifth Corps—was abruptly summoned to a meeting at Hooker's headquarters. When he emerged, Meade turned to his son, Lieutenant George Meade, Jr., and said, "Well, George, I am in command of the Army of the Potomac."

Recognizing that a clash was imminent, General Meade continued the army's relentless march northward, dispatching Brigadier General John Buford's cavalry division to determine the exact position of the Rebel columns. "I am moving at once against Lee," the new commander informed his wife; "a battle will decide the fate of our country and our cause. Pray earnestly, pray for the success of my country."

With Major General John F. Reynolds' First Corps in the vanguard, and the Eleventh Corps close behind, the weary troops of the Army of the Potomac trekked across the Mason-Dixon line. Many units had been covering 35 or more miles a day and marching well into the night. "We tramped over the dusty road with blistered feet and heavy loads," recalled Robert Stewart of the 140th Pennsylvania; "the only solid food available was mouthful of 'hardtack,' now and then, which we munched as we marched along."

Robert Carter saw "hundreds falling exhausted by the roadside," many of them the victims of heatstroke. "Every face looked like a piece of leather, bestreaked with sweat, and besprinkled with dust." Despite cheers and encouragement from the local populace, 5th New Hampshire officer Charles Livermore found that fatigue and knowledge of impending battle instilled grim silence in the trudging column: "There was little heard in the ranks but the tread of feet, the clanking of arms and equipment, and an occasional oath or grumble from some tired mortal."

As Meade's forces were entering Pennsylvania, the first of Lee's troops—Major General Henry Heth's division of Hill's corps—

arrived at Cashtown, the designated staging area. On June 30 Heth ordered one of his brigade commanders, Brigadier General James Johnston Pettigrew, to conduct a reconnaissance of the town of Gettysburg, which lay eight miles to the southeast. There was known to be a shoe factory in Gettysburg. Pettigrew was instructed to search the town for any usable supplies, especially shoes, but he was to pull back if Gettysburg was found to be occupied by Yankee troops.

When Pettigrew's 2,700 North Carolinians neared Gettysburg on the late afternoon of June 30, they spotted blue-clad horsemen heading for the ridges northwest of the town. Pettigrew dutifully withdrew toward Cashtown as ordered, and that night he and Heth conferred with Third Corps commander Hill, in charge at Cashtown pending Lee's arrival. Hill was convinced that any Federals in Gettysburg must be nothing more than local militia. Heth responded: "If there is no objection, General, I will take my division tomorrow and get those shoes." Hill replied: "None in the world."

Hill could not have been more wrong. The Yankees in Gettysburg were in fact the 2,700 troopers of General John Buford's cavalry division. With the trained eye of a veteran campaigner, Buford immediately recognized the town's strategic importance. Twelve roads converged at Gettysburg like the spokes of a wheel, making the town a logical point of concentration for both the Union and Confederate armies. Buford sent word to General Reynolds to bring up his infantry as quickly as possible, and dispersed his troopers to defend the high ground to the north and west of Gettysburg until the reinforcements arrived. The great bloodletting would begin at dawn.

CHRONOLOGY

Prelude	*May 1–3*	*Chancellorsville*
	May 10	*Death of Stonewall Jackson*
	June 3	*Lee moves north*
	June 9	*Brandy Station*
	June 9–17	*Middleburg, Aldie, Centreville*
	June 10–28	*The Shenandoah Valley*
	June 25–30	*Stuart's Raid*
	June 24–28	*Lee invades Pennsylvania*
	June 28	*Meade takes command of Army of Potomac*
First Day, July 1	*McPherson's Ridge*	
	The Railroad Cut and McPherson's Woods	
	Seminary Ridge	
	Ewell breaks Federal line	
	Federals dig in at Cemetery Hill and Culp's Hill	
Second Day, July 2	*Sickles moves forward*	
	Longstreet attacks	
	Devil's Den	
	Little Round Top	
	Slaughter Pen	
	The Wheat Field	
	The Peach Orchard	
	Trostle House	
	Cemetery Ridge	
	Culp's Hill	
Third Day, July 3	*Culp's Hill*	
	Pickett's Charge	
	The Angle	
	Farnsworth's Charge	
Aftermath July 4 – November	*Confederates retreat*	
	Falling Waters	
	Gettysburg Address	

ORDER OF BATTLE

ARMY OF THE POTOMAC

Meade 85,500 men

I Corps Reynolds

1st Division Wadsworth
Meredith's Brigade
Cutler's Brigade

2d Division Robinson
Paul's Brigade
Baxter's Brigade

3d Division Rowley
Biddle's Brigade
Stone's Brigade
Stannard's Brigade

II Corps Hancock

1st Division Caldwell
Cross' Brigade
Kelly's Brigade
Zook's Brigade
Brooke's Brigade

2d Division Gibbon
Harrow's Brigade
Webb's Brigade
Hall's Brigade

3d Division Hays
Carroll's Brigade
Smyth's Brigade
Willard's Brigade

III Corps Sickles

1st Division Birney
Graham's Brigade
Ward's Brigade
De Trobriand's Brigade

2d Division Humphreys
Carr's Brigade
Brewster's Brigade
Burling's Brigade

V Corps Sykes

1st Division Barnes
Tilton's Brigade
Sweitzer's Brigade
Vincent's Brigade

2d Division Ayres
Day's Brigade
Burbank's Brigade
Weed's Brigade

3d Division Crawford
McCandless' Brigade
Fisher's Brigade

VI Corps Sedgwick

1st Division Wright
Torbert's Brigade
Bartlett's Brigade
Russell's Brigade

2d Division Howe
Grant's Brigade
Neill's Brigade

3d Division Newton
Shaler's Brigade
Eustis' Brigade
Wheaton's Brigade

XI Corps Howard

1st Division Barlow
Von Gilsa's Brigade
Ames' Brigade

2d Division Von Steinwehr
Coster's Brigade
Smith's Brigade

3d Division Schurz
Schimmelfennig's Brigade
Krzyzanowski's Brigade

XII Corps Slocum

1st Division Williams
McDougall's Brigade
Lockwood's Brigade
Ruger's Brigade

2d Division Geary
Candy's Brigade
Cobham's Brigade
Greene's Brigade

Cavalry Corps Pleasonton

1st Division Buford
Gamble's Brigade
Devin's Brigade
Merritt's Brigade

2d Division Gregg
McIntosh's Brigade
Huey's Brigade
Gregg's Brigade

3d Division Kilpatrick
Farnsworth's Brigade
Custer's Brigade

ARMY OF NORTHERN VIRGINIA

Lee 75,000 men

I Corps Longstreet

McLaws' Division
Kershaw's Brigade
Semmes' Brigade
Barksdale's Brigade
Wofford's Brigade

Pickett's Division
Garnett's Brigade
Kemper's Brigade
Armistead's Brigade

Hood's Division
Law's Brigade
Robertson's Brigade
G. T. Anderson's Brigade
Benning's Brigade

II Corps Ewell

Early's Division
Hays' Brigade
Smith's Brigade
Gordon's Brigade
Avery's Brigade

Johnson's Division
Steuart's Brigade
Walker's Brigade
Williams' Brigade
Jones' Brigade

Rodes' Division
Daniel's Brigade
Iverson's Brigade
Doles' Brigade
Ramseur's Brigade
O'Neal's Brigade

III Corps Hill

R. H. Anderson's Division
Wilcox's Brigade
Wright's Brigade
Mahone's Brigade
Lang's Brigade
Posey's Brigade

Heth's Division
Pettigrew's Brigade
Brockenbrough's Brigade
Archer's Brigade
Davis' Brigade

Pender's Division
Perrin's Brigade
Lane's Brigade
Thomas' Brigade
Scale's Brigade

Cavalry Stuart

Hampton's Division
F. Lee's Brigade
Robertson's Brigade
Jenkins' Brigade
Jones' Brigade
W. H. F. Lee's Brigade

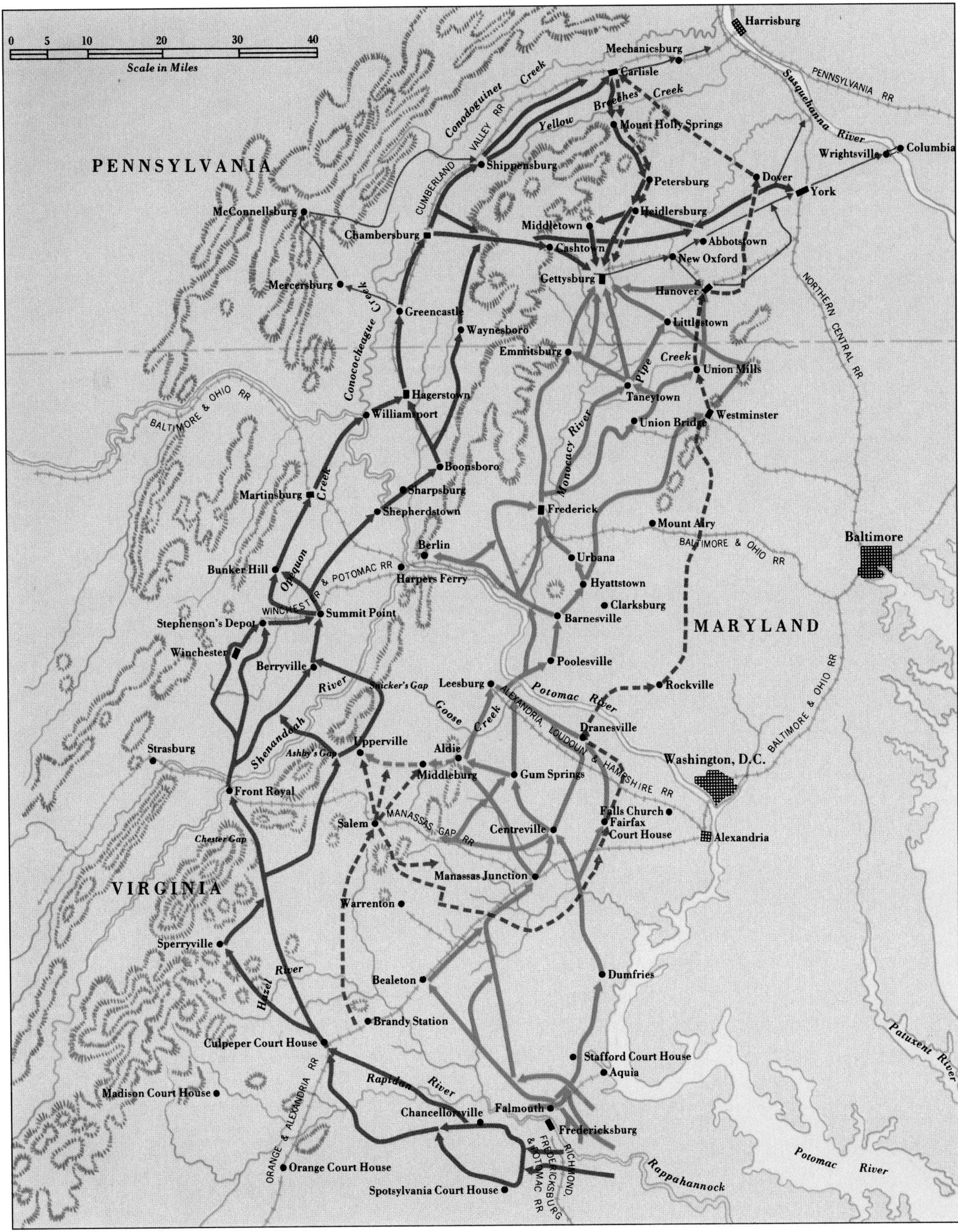

On June 10, 1863, General Robert E. Lee ordered Major General Richard Ewell to march his corps north toward Pennsylvania, taking a route (red line) down the Shenandoah Valley. Ewell was followed by the corps of Longstreet and Hill. On June 13, General Joseph Hooker began to shift the Army of the Potomac (blue line) to pursue Lee. The Confederate cavalry under Jeb Stuart (broken red line) screened the army's route before leaving Salem, Virginia, on a raid that placed them out of contact with Lee.

SERGEANT ALEXANDER T. BARCLAY

4th Virginia Infantry, Walker's Brigade
In 1861 Barclay and 57 classmates from Washington College joined the Liberty Hall Volunteers, Company I of the 4th Virginia. Barclay, later commissioned a lieutenant for gallantry at Mine Run, was captured at Spotsylvania in May 1864.

June 12th
Dear Sister,

We have just received orders to cook all our rations, strike tents very quietly and be ready to move at any time, which all, we think, means that we are going to move against the Yankees across the river, who, by the way, have been exhibiting signs of uneasiness for some days past.

I wrote for fear I may not have an opportunity again shortly. So if you do not receive letters for some time, do not be uneasy. You can still write regularly to me as we have a mail carrier who brings our mail to us. I enclose my certificate of membership with the church which please give to Dr. White.

I am quite well and am prepared to move with the rest. I think before you hear from me again we will in all probability have had a battle. I fear not the result, am confident that we through God will be victorious. Fear not for my safety, God can protect me amidst the storm of battle as well as at home, and if I shall fall I trust that I will go to a better world and is that not gain? In haste

Good bye, Ted

Batteries of the Federal VI Corps shell Confederate rifle pits across the Rappahannock River near Franklin's Crossing south of Fredericksburg on June 5, 1863.

"We are going to move against the Yankees across the river."

"Our town had a great fright last night between 12 and 1 o'clock."

SARAH M. BROADHEAD

Resident of Gettysburg

Sarah Broadhead lived with her husband, Joseph, and four-year-old daughter, Mary, in a house on Chambersburg Street. From their windows the family had a fine view of Seminary Ridge with its Lutheran Theological Seminary buildings. In Gettysburg, as in other Pennsylvania communities, fears of a Rebel invasion fostered rumor and panic.

June 16

Our town had a great fright last night between 12 and 1 o'clock. I had retired, and was soundly asleep, when my child cried for a drink of water. When I got up to get it, I heard so great a noise in the street that I went to the window, and the first thing I saw was a large fire, seemingly not far off, and the people were hallooing, "The Rebels are coming, and burning as they go." Many left town, but, having waited for the fire to go down a little, I returned to bed and slept till morning. Then I learned that the fire was in Emmettsburg, ten miles from here just over the Maryland line, and that the buildings were fired by one of her townsmen. Twenty-seven houses were burned, and thirty-six families made homeless, all effort to stop the flames being useless, as, owing to everything being so dry, they spread with great rapidity.

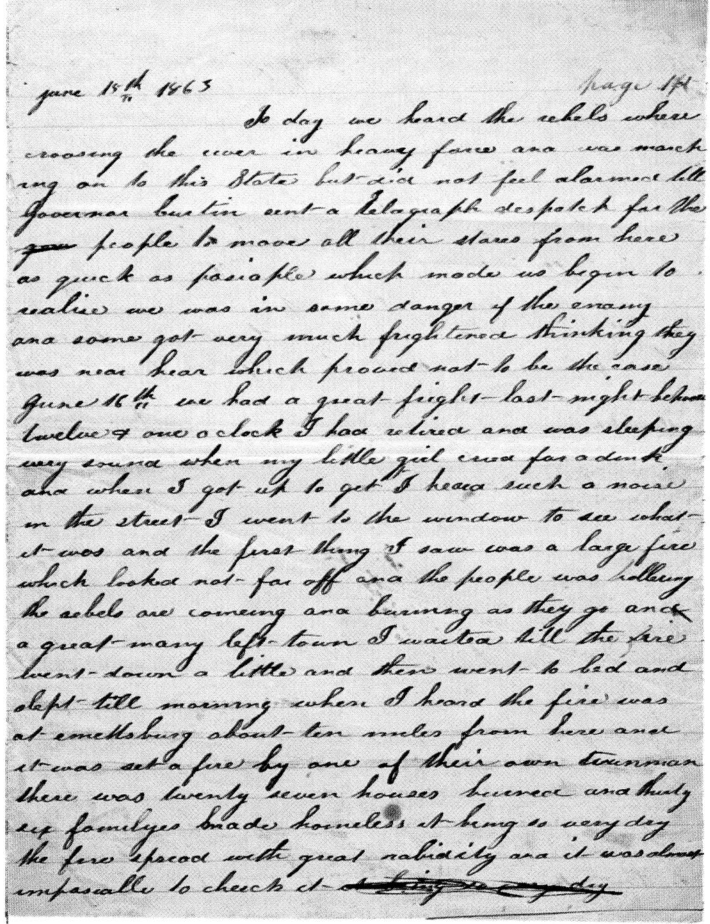

june 15th 1863 page 1st
To day we heard the rebels where crossing the river in heavy force and was marching on to this State but did not feel alarmed till Governor Curtin sent a telegraph despatch for the people to move all their stores from here as quick as possiable which made us begin to realise we was in some danger of the enamy and some got very much frightened thinking they was near hear which proved not to be the case
June 16th we had a great fright last night between twelve & one o clock I had retired and was sleeping very sound when my little girl cried for a drink and when I got up to get it I heard such a noise in the street I went to the window to see what it was and the first thing I saw was a large fire which looked not far off and the people was hollering the rebels are comeing and burning as they go and a great many left town I waited till the fire went down a little and then went to bed and slept till morning when I heard the fire was at emettsburg about ten miles from here and it was set a fire by one of their own townsman there was twenty seven houses burned and thirty six familyes made homeless it being so very dry the fire spread with great rabidity and it was almost impossable to check it [illegible] day

Gettysburg resident Sarah Broadhead kept her diary (left) "to aid in whiling away time filled up with anxiety, apprehension, and danger." Some months after the battle, she had an edition of 200 copies of the entries for June and July printed for private distribution.

The Wagon Hotel, a Gettysburg inn that catered to teamsters, fronts on Baltimore Street in this 1863 photograph. The small but thriving market town had rail connections to Baltimore and Harrisburg and was home to Pennsylvania College and the Lutheran Theological Seminary. Gettysburg had a population of about 2,400 people, with small-scale manufacture of goods such as carriages and shoes. The town's location at the intersection of several major roads made a visit from the invading Rebels a distinct possibility.

Trumpeter Charles W. Reed of the 9th Massachusetts Light Artillery sketched a column of weary Federal soldiers on this letter to his mother written from Centreville, Virginia. Reed illustrated all of his letters home and kept sketchbooks to record his adventures. At Gettysburg he won the Medal of Honor for rescuing his commanding officer.

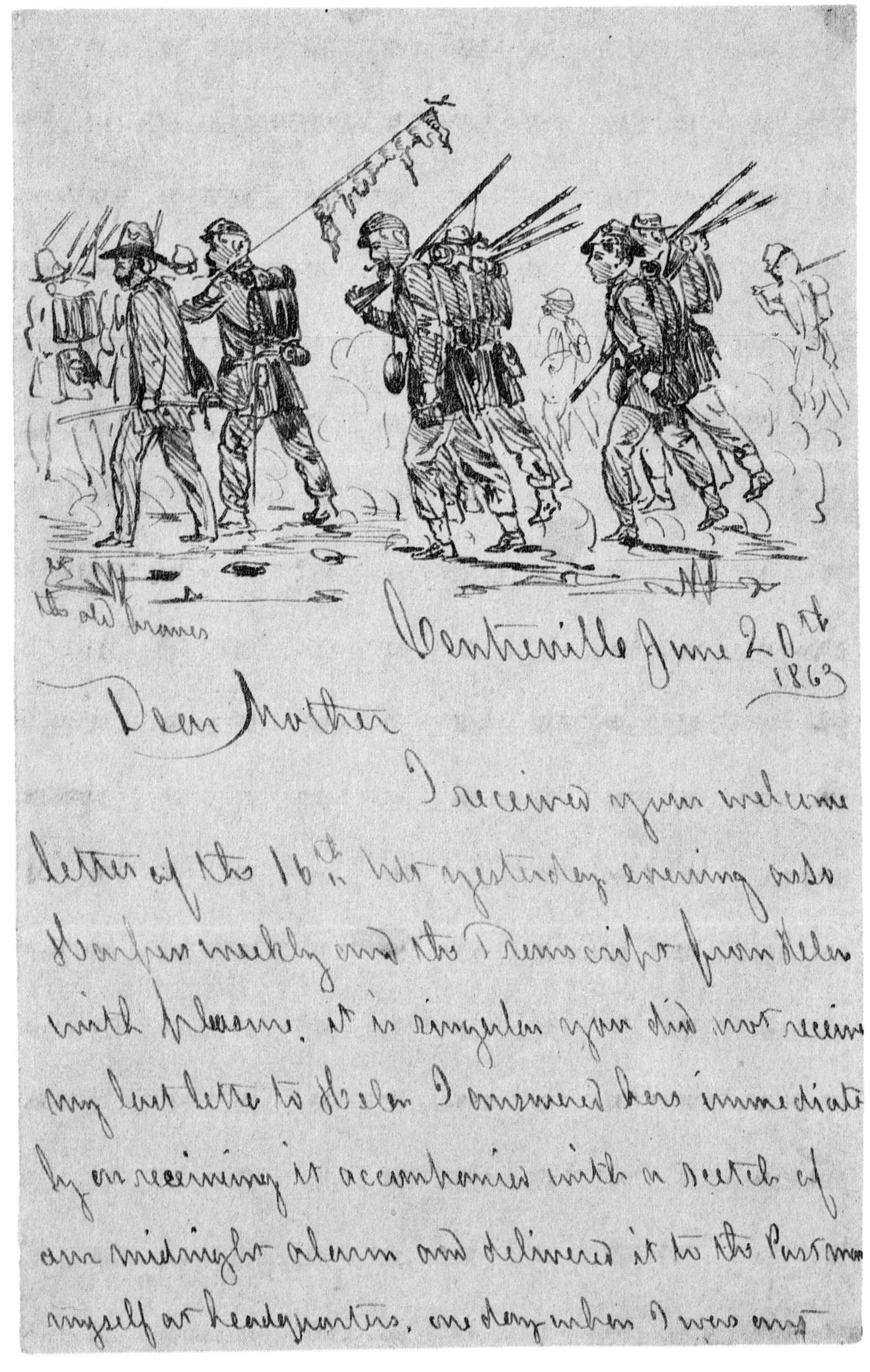

the old braves

Centreville June 20th
1863

Dear Mother

I received your welcome letter of the 16th inst yesterday evening also Harpers weekly and the Transcript from Helen with thanks. it is singular you did not receive my last letter to Helen I answered hers immediately on receiving it accompanied with a sketch of our midnight alarm and delivered it to the Post man myself at headquarters. one day when I was out

LIEUTENANT WILLIAM B. TAYLOR

11th North Carolina Infantry, Pettigrew's Brigade

In 1861 Taylor, a resident of Mecklenburg County, fought at Big Bethel, Virginia, the first land battle of the war. In 1862 he was promoted to lieutenant in the 11th North Carolina. Fresh from the victory at Chancellorsville, Taylor and his comrades were confident of their ability to carry the war to the North.

Bivouc on the road near Brryville Clark Co Va
June 22nd 1863
Dear Mother

I write a few lines but I dont know whether you will receive them or not but I hope you will but it is a bad chance from here we have been on the march since yesterday week we were 10 miles below Fredickburg we crossed the Blue Ridge and the Rappidan Rappahannock and both branches of the Shenendoah north and south and are within 21 miles of the Potomic and I would take any amount for the trip the most butiful scenery I ever beheld since I have been in the army witch is some time you know

It is suposed that we will go into Pensylvania and I hope we may and I hope the officers will devestate the territory and give the enemy a taste of the horrors of war and that is all that will close the war soon if anything will if this invasion dont do anything but relieve Vicksburg witch will be a great thing within itself the army is in fine spirits and anxious for the trip. . . .

You can write but I dont know when I will get it and direct it to Richmond and it will come. . . .

I remain your affectionate son
W B Taylor

CORPORAL EDMUND D. PATTERSON

9th Alabama Infantry, Wilcox's Brigade

An Ohio native, Patterson traveled south, settling in Waterloo, Alabama, as a dry-goods clerk. Insinuations that he was a Yankee spy prompted him to join the 9th Alabama as a show of loyalty to his adopted state. Patterson kept a journal and recorded the difficult crossing of the Shenandoah River.

Saturday 20th.

Last night I felt more like "cussing" than I did like writing. Yesterday morning we marched to Front Royal, where we remained until 4 o'clock in the evening, waiting, they said until the pontoons were laid across both branches of the Shenandoah. In due time we moved forward, and the head of the column commenced crossing just at dark, and about the same time it commenced raining. We found the pontoons still upon the wagons packed near the river, and as regiment after regiment came up they made sport of them, and "waded in." It was no pleasant task crossing the river at that time. I pulled off my boots, socks, pants and etc., thinking I might keep them a little dry, but by the time I had cut my feet on the sharp rocks, and fallen down a time or two, I regretted it. The bank on this side of the river is steep and by the time we crossed it had become perfectly slippery and I had to go up it on "all fours." Some of the boys would nearly reach the top and then an unlucky slip would send them "sousing" into the river again. The rain poured down in torrents and the cussing of some of the boys was fearfully serious.

After reaching this side of the river, we went out into an old field, where I fell into a gulley; ran over a briar patch, scratched my face and nearly broke my neck, so dark that I could see it, feel it, taste it, and smell it, and such thick darkness that a streak of lightning could not have cut through it. After wandering about in the darkness a while I ran against a fence, and taking about half a dozen rails I made me a comfortable bed, so as to keep me out of the mud, laying them side by side. After getting into an easy position, I slept well, with my rail bed, and with the darkness and rain for a covering, and awoke this morning feeling a little stiff, but after shaking myself a time or two, felt all right.

COLONEL DAVID W. AIKEN

7th South Carolina Infantry, Kershaw's Brigade

Aiken, a planter from Greenwood, South Carolina, described for his wife a clash with Federal forces at the summit of Ashby's Gap in Virginia's Blue Ridge Mountains. After the war, Aiken was elected to two terms in Congress before a fall on an icy street in 1886 cost him his life.

Shenandoah River June 22d 10 PM

I wrote to you a few days ago, my darling wife, from my tent then on the top of a mountain beyond the river. I told you some little of the beautiful scenery, which should have been seen to have been appreciated. That night there came up a very hard rain, & the next morning until noon we were enveloped in the clouds, though we heard that the view was clearing in the valley. . . . The next morning, (Sunday, yesterday) we were about proceeding on our march, when a courier arrived from the rear saying Stuarts cavalry was heavily pressed by the enemy. We were put under arms & by 3 PM ordered hurriedly back across this river, marched three miles, drew up in line of battle across the turn pike, each flank [reaching] up on the mountain. Here we allowed the cavalry to pass to our rear, & we waited for the enemy who had been pressing him with overwhelming numbers. The wounded were passing by us for some time. The fight had progressed all day & was very severe. Our men stood there trembling wet, up to their arms & the wind blowing from the mountains as cold as October. Poor fellows how I sympathized with them. After all we could see the thousands of Yankee camp fires in the valley about 3 miles in our front. We watched them with [ ] until morning & then advanced upon them, when lo they had gone. As soon as they discovered we had infantry they turned towards Manassas. That night on that mountain was one of the severest I ever [saw], I wrapt up in my overcoat & cape & laid down to sleep, which I did for about two hours, when I awoke almost freezing. I got up and walked up & down the mountain to get warm, & then laid down again, but it was only in chattering of teeth until morning. The men were allowed, this morning to build fires & dry the wet clothes in which they had shivered all night. At about 3 PM we again received orders to cross the river again & all the drying of clothes had to be done again this evening. Strange to say, all this exposure has not made half dozen sick men that I can hear of in all the division numbering about 7000. . . .

It is now after 10 PM and we have not yet recd any orders about moving tomorrow. So I can tell you nothing of our future movements. . . . Where we go none of us knows, but must certainly meet the foe before many more days, and when we do we intend to whip certain, regardless of what he intends to do with us. I may be among the number to be sacrificed. God grant I may not be, but if I should I believe I'll die with a full assurance of some day meeting you in Heaven. I will fall too in a noble cause, & leave to my beloved wife & dear little children the future consolation, that I fell battling for the liberty they may live to enjoy. We can only hope for the best, but it is the part of prudence to look sometimes on the dark side of things, not however with despondent feelings, but with the firm conviction that all will be well at last, May God protect & preserve us & ours, and give us both the strength & fortitude necessary to correctly endure whatever future awaits us. Kiss our dear little pets often for me. Oh for a short sojourn with you and them. But for this dreadful war how happy would we be! Give much love to everybody at home for me.

"Oh for a short sojourn with you. . . . But for this dreadful war how happy would we be!"

The 147th Pennsylvania Infantry carried this state color on the march to Gettysburg. The field once bore stars and a state crest.

CORPORAL JOSEPH A. LUMBARD

147th Pennsylvania Infantry, Candy's Brigade

Lumbard describes two favorite pastimes of Civil War soldiers: scouting out something to drink and speculating on changes in the high command. As it happened, General George Meade replaced Joseph Hooker as commander of the Federal army shortly after Lumbard penned his letter.

A short distance North of Frederick we passed a very large brewery, a detail of men had taken out the liquor and emptied the casks in the streets, and whilst passing this place a number of the boys got down on their knees and drank up the beer out of the gutters.

During the day several times we heard rumors that General McClellan was to be placed in command of the old army of the Potomac, and the announcement served to inspire the army with the utmost confidence for the soldiers of the gallant old army of the Potomac had not forgotten their formerly idolized commander, little Mack the hero of Antietam.

The band and a company of the 8th United States Regular Infantry mount guard over the tents (above) of Major General Joseph Hooker's headquarters near Fairfax Court House, Virginia, during the march north in June 1863. The 8th formed part of a mixed force of cavalry and infantry under the command of the army provost marshal, Brigadier General Marsena R. Patrick. The headquarters detachment provided security for the army commander and acted as military police.

CORPORAL THOMAS D. MARBAKER

11th New Jersey Infantry, Carr's Brigade

As the Federal army marched through Maryland in pursuit of the invading Rebels, its columns received a jubilant welcome from loyal Marylanders. Marbaker had been wounded at Chancellorsville but left the hospital and rejoined his unit, his wound still unhealed.

Later in the day we marched through Middletown, beyond which we soon halted for dinner, then past a hamlet called Jerusalem, and soon in the distance we saw the spires of Frederick. Before reaching the town the ranks were closed up and flags unfurled, and with bands playing and colors flying we marched through the city that gave birth to the author of the "Star Spangled Banner." The inhabitants greeted us with every demonstration of delight, but they seemed to be surprised at our numbers. One old gentleman who from an upper window was busily engaged in waving a flag, as he gazed down the long street and saw the blue-coated column come pouring steadily on, kept exclaiming, as if in wonder, "Still they come! still they come!" As the boys passed beneath his window they greeted him with hearty cheers. . . .

The transition from the pine forests and desolated fields of Virginia, from contact with a disloyal people, who meet you with open defiance or ill-concealed dislike, to the fruitful fields and overflowing loyalty of western Maryland was especially grateful to the army. It gave new courage to the heart and life to the lagging footstep.

Surrounded by members of his staff, Major General George G. Meade poses on the steps of a house near Bealton, Virginia, in the aftermath of the Gettysburg campaign. Appointed to replace Major General Joseph Hooker as commander of the Army of the Potomac on June 28, Meade was forced to take control of the army the hard way—while it was on the march.

Entered according to Act of Congress in the year 1863, by Frank Leslie, in the Clerk's Office of the District Court for the Southern District of New York.

No. 310.—Band XII. No. 24.] New York, Samstag, 18. Juli 1863. [Preis 8 Cents.

Land und Leute in Neapel.

Die Neapolitaner, oder das Volk beider Sicilien, sind jetzt frei, aber sie haben kein Werkzeug, von der Freiheit ordentlich Gebrauch zu machen, keine Bildung.

Von einer ordentlichen Schulbildung und Volksbildung, welche die Regierung in die Hand genommen hätte, war unter der Herrschaft der Bourbonen natürlich keine Rede. Außer in den größeren Städten gibt es in diesem Lande keine Schulen. Lesen und schreiben können nicht fünfzehn Procent der Bevölkerung. Wenn in einem deutschen Staate von hundert zehn Individuen außer Stande sind, zu lesen und zu schreiben, so ist dies eine seltene Ausnahme. Hier findet das umgekehrte Verhältniß statt. Selbst die Bildung in den höheren und reicheren Ständen der neapolitanischen Bevölkerung ist eine sehr unbedeutende. Ich kenne viele Familien in Neapel, Messina und Palermo, welche sich deutsche Hauslehrer und deutsche Gouvernanten haben kommen lassen, um ihre Kinder ordentlich unterrichten zu können; andere Familien haben ihre Söhne deshalb nach Deutschland und der Schweiz geschickt. Wie unrecht thun deshalb die Touristen dieser armen Bevölkerung in Neapel und Sicilien, wenn sie voll Entrüstung über deren Betteleien, Ueberforderungen und Plackereien nach Deutschland, England und Frankreich zurückkehren und davon nicht genug zu erzählen wissen! Wie kann man vom Standpunkt der Moralität Anforderungen an diese armen Lazzaroni machen, welche wie die Kinder eines Indianerstammes aufwachsen und denen niemals irgend Jemand gesagt hat, was Gut und was Böse ist? Niemand hat sich während ihres ganzen Lebens mit ihrer moralischen Bildung abgegeben; eine Schule haben sie nie besucht; sie sind in irgend einem schmutzigen Winkel geboren und auf der Straße in Schmutz, Lumpen und bei Maccaroni groß geworden. Nur der Priester hat sich ihrer angenommen, aber ihren Geist und ihr Herz hat auch er nicht gebildet. Daß sie Existenzmittel finden, darum kümmert sich natürlich Niemand. Manufakturen und Fabriken gibt es im ganzen Lande keine einzige. — Sie haben also keinen andern Erwerb als die Bettelei, das Lasttragen, den Fischfang und die Ausbeutung der Fremden. Der weißblaue Himmel Neapels ist gütiger gegen sie, als die Menschen. Sie brauchen außerordentlich wenig; mit dem Erwerb einiger Kupfermünzen bestreiten sie ihren täglichen Lebensunterhalt. Die Maccaroni und der Wein sind außerordentlich billig, sie kosten nur einige Gran. Eine Schlafstelle finden sie auf jeder Straße, unter dem Portal jeder Kirche; die wollene Jacke ist ihr Kopfkissen, oder, wenn sie keine wollene Jacke haben, legen sie den müden Kopf auf das Pflaster, um am andern Morgen zu demselben armseligen Leben wieder zu erwachen. Ich muß sagen, daß ich, angesichts dieser entsetzlichen Verkommenheit, zu einer ganz andern Ansicht über diese armen Menschen gekommen bin, als andere Touristen und Schriftsteller. Ich bin täglich mit ihnen in Berührung gekommen; wenn ich nicht im Hauptquartier vor Capua war, habe ich die Campagna nach allen Richtungen hin durchstreift und den Charakter dieser Menschen genau studirt. Ich habe auf ihren Barken den Golf und seine Küsten nach allen Richtungen hin bereist; ich habe mit dem zweirädrigen Wagen des Vetturino alle die kleinen Ortschaften besucht, welche am Posilipp bis zum Cap Misere und an der andern Seite sich bis zum Cap Sorrent in ununterbrochener Reihe ausdehnen; ich habe alle Inseln durchstreift, welche mit ihren Orangenwäldern und Citronenhainen, mit ihren Cactusfeldern und Palmen in zauberischer Schönheit aus den ewig blauen Flächen des Golfs aufsteigen — und ich wundere mich, daß diese Menschen noch so gut geblieben sind, als sie es sind. Diese Bettelei ist empörend, der Schmutz ist entsetzlich, das Ueberfordern ist unerträglich, aber schließlich sind alle diese Armen … dem Geringsten zufrieden, was man ihm … nachtragend, nie boshaft. Eine derbe … sie auf der Stelle zur Ruhe, und sie sind … Zurechtweisung, trotz dem, daß man von … und Forderungen auch nicht den klein… ebenso freundlich und gutmüthig, wie …

Bürger Baltimore's errichten Barricaden in den Straßen, am 29. Juni 1863. (Nach einer Skizze des Herrn Forbes.)

The front page of Frank Leslie's Illustrated Newspaper for July 18, 1863, displays an engraving depicting citizens of Baltimore helping Federal troops erect barricades in city streets against a possible attack as the Rebels marched north in June. The special German-language edition of Leslie's shown here circulated among the country's large German American population.

The Leslie's engraving at left was rendered from a sketch (above) drawn by special artist Edwin Forbes in Baltimore on June 28. Slow communications kept Leslie's from publishing the sketch until after the Battle of Gettysburg.

CORPORAL EDMUND D. PATTERSON

9th Alabama Infantry, Wilcox's Brigade

Confederate troops marching through Pennsylvania towns generally encountered a hostile reception. Since many of Patterson's comrades had scavenged Federal equipment after earlier battles, knapsacks marked with the numbers of Federal regiments were a common sight in their ranks.

Saturday the 27th.

On the march again. Passed through Marion [and] Chambersburg. While passing through the latter place Gen'l. Lee rode up the column speaking kindly to acquaintances and passed on. The boys never cheer him, but pull off their hats and worship. The females of Chambersburg seem to be very spiteful, make faces, sing "Rally round the flag," wave their little banners etc. I think if they had a hole burned out in their town about the size and extent of that which the Yankees burned in Florence or Athens, Alabama, these patriotic females would not be quite so saucy. A widow in the place discovered the knapsack of her deceased husband in the command, she wished it and the soldier gave it to her. He had picked it up on the battlefield of "Gaine's Mills," where we fought the "squirrel tail rifles." I suppose that her husband has gone to that home from whence etc., such is war. We reached this place, Fayetteville, a little before sun down, and Jim and I went out and took supper with a good old Pennsylvania farmer; plenty of everything, especially apple butter, the first I have tasted since I left Ohio.

BATTLE CRY OF FREEDOM

(Rallying Song)

Yes we'll rally round the flag, boys,
we'll rally once again,
Shouting the battle cry of Freedom,
We will rally from the hillside,
we'll gather from the plain,
Shouting the battle cry of Freedom.

Chorus:
The Union forever, Hurrah, boys, Hurrah!
Down with the traitor, Up with the star;
While we rally round the flag, boys, Rally
once again,
Shouting the battle cry of Freedom.

BATTLE CRY OF FREEDOM

(Southern Version)

Our flag is proudly floating
On the land and on the main,
Shout, shout, the battle cry of Freedom,
Beneath it oft we've conquered
And will conquer oft again,
Shout, shout, the battle cry of Freedom.

Chorus:
Our Dixie forever, she's never at a loss,
Down with the eagle and up with the cross,
We'll rally 'round the bonny flag, we'll rally
once again,
Shout, shout the battle cry of Freedom.

Chicago songwriter George F. Root composed one of his best songs, "Battle Cry of Freedom," in 1862. The spirited tune, with its call to rally to the defense of the Union, quickly became a favorite of Northern soldiers and civilians. When the tune became popular in the South, Baltimore composer Hermann L. Schreiner, a Confederate advocate, penned a Rebel version.

COLONEL DAVID W. AIKEN

7th South Carolina Infantry, Kershaw's Brigade

Lee issued strict orders prohibiting theft of private property. Everything was to be properly purchased, albeit with Confederate currency, and receipts were issued for all requisitioned items. Colonel Aiken wrote home describing the wealth of the enemy's country.

Chambersburg, June 28

Genl Lee is doing it all his own way, & is almost adored by his troops, which I believe would follow him to Boston. His army is in fine spirits, well armed, horses & mules fat, & everything ready to try to whip out Yankeedom. The Genl is very guarded in his advance & allows no depredations to be committed, not even a chicken to be taken unless paid for. He takes corn, flour, cattle, horses, & everything that the army needs, but pays for everything in Confed money. If the [farmer] takes the money, well, but if not, he just gives him a receipt for the article, so the Yankee may present this receipt to Lincoln's Govt as a claim for damages. Only this morning he issued an order congratulating the troops on their good behavior, and told them that while Providence would certainly smile on such conduct, He would as certainly frustrate our movements if conducted in the manner the Vandals conducted their warfare in Virg. He told them he had come here to fight armed men & not to plunder & frighten women & children.

Being in the rear we do not fare as well as the advance, but we are doing well. Meat & bread plentiful, and very little sickness. As for myself, Ive never enjoyed better health in my life.

LATEST NEWS FROM THE NORTH.

OPERATIONS OF OUR ARMY IN MARYLAND AND PENNSYLVANIA—HARRISBURG THREATENED—OUR WHOLE ARMY REPORTED NORTH OF THE POTOMAC—THE PANIC ALONG THE PENNSYLVANIA BORDER—THE CONFEDERATES AMONG THE YANKEES—GENERAL LEE'S PLANS—THE SCARE AT WASHINGTON—OPINIONS AND SPECULATIONS IN THE NORTH.

Through the kindness of Judge Ould, commissioner for the exchange of prisoners, we have a batch of Northern papers, bringing us dates down to the 27th, inclusive. We make up from them the following summary of news:

With the Army of Northern Virginia out of contact with Richmond, Southern journalists were dependent upon rumor and gleanings from the Northern press for news of Lee's operations. The Daily Richmond Examiner was unable to confirm that the army had entered Pennsylvania until July 2, by which time the outcome of the Confederate invasion was being decided at Gettysburg.

RACHEL CORMANY

Resident of Chambersburg

In the summer of 1863, Rachel Cormany lived with her infant daughter in a rented room in Chambersburg. Her husband, Samuel, a lieutenant in the 16th Pennsylvania Cavalry, in Brigadier General David M. Gregg's brigade, was with his unit shadowing the Rebel advance.

June 27, 1863—All day since 7 oclock they have been going through. Between 30 & 40 pieces of cannon—& an almost endless trail of waggons. While I am writing thousands are passing—such a rough dirty ragged rowdyish set one does not often see—Gen's Lee & Longstreet passed through today. A body would think the whole south had broke loose & are coming into Pa. It makes me feel too badly to see so many men & cannon going through knowing that they have come to kill our men—Many have chickens as they pass—There a number are going with honey—robed some man of it no doubt—they are even carrying it in buckets. . . .

They are poorly clad—many have no shoes on. As they pass along they take the hats off our citizens heads and throw their old ones in exchange. I was at the window up stairs with my baby nearly all day looking at them—at one time one of them said something that I did not like so I curled my lip as disdainful as I could & turned away just look at he[r] he said to another I saw a lot of looking up, so I just wheeled & left the window at which they set up a cheer. . . .

June 30, 1863—Nothing special transpired today. The Rebs are still about doing all the mischief they can. They have everything ready to set fire to the warehouses & machine shops—Tore up the railroad track & burned the crossties—They have cleared out nearly every store so they cannot rob much more—Evening—Quite a number of the young folks were in the parlor this evening singing all the patriotic & popular war songs. Quite a squad of rebels gathered outside to listen & seemed much pleased with the music—"When this cruel war is over" nearly brought tears from some. they sent in a petition to have it sung again which was done. they then thanked the girls very much & left—they acted real nicely.

June 27 Saturday
Received orders to leave at 8 A.M.
Cool & pleasant day. 15th Ga in the rear
soon in the pike & then we stopped for
2 hours & several the Quartermasters & Sergts
armed went ahead with the Pioneers
3 miles then brought us to the
beautiful town of "Greencastle" on the
"Harrisburg R.R. this is a fine town
larger than Washington Ga houses large
& fine shady streets this town like others
in this State have never felt the
affect of war. the R.R. runs down main
street. People strong unionist & looked
mad & sullen at our apperance a great
many closed doors; Stores all closed
the Streets & Hotels crowded with young
men just out of Service. Some nice
looking girls dressed very fine as every
thing is cheap, Several Federal flags were
seen the girls had them on their bonnets.
We marched through quick time with
music. the depot on the north side of town
was burnt & R.R. in several places,

Sergeant Thomas L. Ware of the 15th Georgia recorded his regiment's march through Greencastle, Pennsylvania, in his diary on June 27.

CHAPLAIN JAMES B. SHEERAN

14th Louisiana Infantry, Nicholl's Brigade

Father James Sheeran recorded his impressions of Pennsylvania in his diary. Born in Ireland, Sheeran emigrated to America at the age of 12, living in New York and Pennsylvania before taking priestly vows with the Redemptorist Order in Michigan. Assigned to a parish in New Orleans, he became an ardent secessionist.

June 24
This morning we commenced our march in the direction of Chambersburg, passing through Middletown formerly called Smoketown. I was sensibly struck by the difference between the people of this part of the country and the inhabitants of Virginia. Here you find none of that grace of manners, high-toned sentiment, or intellectual culture that you find in old Virginia. Indeed, with all their wealth they appear little advanced in civilization. . . .

I perceived the people of this country were most agreeably disappointed. Knowing what their army had done to us; that they had burned our towns, laid waste our lands, driven helpless women and children from their homes, destroyed our implements of husbandry, that we might not be able to cultivate our lands, they very naturally expected that our soldiers would treat them in a similar manner. Great then was their surprise when they saw the conduct of our men. Many of these people told me that by our kindness and good treatment of the people we had made many friends among them.

PRIVATE WILLIAM L. DANIEL

2d South Carolina Infantry, Kershaw's Brigade
As Lee's army moved through Pennsylvania, Confederate quartermasters scoured the region for desperately needed supplies. Private Daniel described the result of these foraging expeditions in a letter to his mother written from Chambersburg on June 28.

We passed through Hagerstown during this day, a town of some 7 or 8 thousand inhabitants and a very pretty town too it is. The people seemed mortified and downcast and, no doubt came to the conclusion that the rebellion lacked a good deal in being "crushed out." Every thing that could be of use to our Army was impressed by our authorities, such as wagons, horses, shoes, sugar, molasses, whiskey, flour, leather, beef, cattle & c. It is said that many hundreds of fine cattle have been driven across the Potomac to be used by our Army when we return to Virginia. I saw fine wagons and teams pass us in the road taken in Maryland and Pennsylvania by our Army. Some loaded with shoes. Some with leather and other things. Our Army is now entirely subsisted on its enemy. This day we crossed the boundary between Maryland and Pennsylvania and marched ten miles into Pennsylvania, passing through some pretty villages and towns, one called Greencastle, and at night stopped at Ducktown 5 miles from Chambersburg. Here our men feasted themselves on cherries of which the country affords the greatest abundance, mutton, chickens, turkeys, & c—they, no doubt, wishing to retaliate on the enemy for all their excesses committed in the South. At the same time such conduct is prohibited by the authorities. The flour we are now using costs about 8 Dollars per barrel. I suppose every thing is very cheap. Sugar 12 cents per pound, molasses 50 cts per gallon—but the people very few of them will take our Confederate money, and those that do, do so because they are afraid to refuse. In the Yankee towns, broad cloth and such like things are common as with us in times of peace.

"One fair lady asked General Lee for a lock of his hair."

Guards officer Arthur Fremantle, a British observer who was traveling with Major General James Longstreet, characterized General Robert E. Lee (right) as "a perfect gentleman in every respect," noting that Southerners pronounced him "as near perfection as a man can be."

LIEUTENANT FRANCIS W. DAWSON

Staff, Major General James Longstreet

Dawson, an Englishman, signed aboard the Confederate steamer Nashville and arrived in Beaufort, South Carolina, in 1862. He soon volunteered for the artillery service and was appointed to Longstreet's staff. Since Longstreet and his aides usually traveled with Lee's headquarters, Dawson had many opportunities to observe the army's commander.

When we reached the Maryland shore we found several patriotic ladies with small feet and big umbrellas waiting to receive the Confederates who were coming a second time to deliver downtrodden Maryland. As General Lee rode out of the water, one of the ladies, with a face like a door-knocker, stepped forward and said: "This is General Lee, I presume?" General Lee gave an affirmative reply, and the lady continued: "General Lee, allow me to bid you welcome to Maryland, and allow me to present to you these ladies who were determined to give you this reception—Miss Brown, General Lee; Miss Jones, General Lee; Miss Smith, General Lee." General Lee thanked them courteously for their attention, and introduced General Longstreet and General Pickett to Miss Brown, Miss Jones and Miss Smith. This was not the end of the affair, however, as one of the ladies had an enormous wreath which she was anxious to place on the neck of General Lee's charger. The horse objected to it seriously, and the wreath was turned over to one of the couriers. The next morning we went into Hagerstown, where more ladies were in waiting. There were more presentations to General Lee and more introductions for Generals Longstreet and Pickett. One fair lady asked General Lee for a lock of his hair. General Lee said that he really had none to spare, and he was quite sure, besides, that they would prefer such a souvenir from one of his younger officers, and that he was confident that General Pickett would be pleased to give them one of his curls. General Pickett did not enjoy the joke, for he was known everywhere by his corkscrew ringlets, which were not particularly becoming when the rain made them lank in such weather as we then had. The ladies did not press the request. When we resumed our march more ladies came to be presented, but this time there were no petitions for a lock of Pickett's hair.

Major General George E. Pickett graduated last in the West Point class of 1846 but was breveted twice for gallantry in the Mexican War. In the Civil War's Peninsula campaign he led a brigade with great dash before a wound forced him out of action until the fall of 1862. His division of Virginians missed the momentous victory at Chancellorsville. At Gettysburg, Pickett commanded the rear guard for Longstreet's corps and feared that his men might be left out of action again.

Robert E. Lee affectionately called Major General James Longstreet "my old war horse," while his men reserved the nickname "Old Pete." A brilliant battlefield tactician, Longstreet favored a defensive posture in any confrontation with the Federal armies in Pennsylvania, an idea that ran counter to Lee's aggressive plans.

CAPTAIN FREDERICK BARON VON FRITSCH

68th New York Infantry, von Gilsa's Brigade

A native of Weimar, Germany, von Fritsch was a soldier of fortune who served in the Saxon Cavalry and later in Mexico with forces opposing French intervention there. Expelled from Mexico in 1862, he gained a commission in the U.S. Army through the chance influence of Colonel Bourry d'Ivernois of the 68th New York, who drunkenly convinced himself that he had served with von Fritsch in Europe.

Next morning we tramped on again and camped at night on a slight elevation. The troops were very tired, and while I was sitting with Colonel von Gilsa and several officers, waiting for the coffee to boil, a Sergeant came and placed a big iron pail before us, saying: "With the compliments of the Commissary." I smelled the contents and reported: "Whiskey." "Let us taste it," said the Colonel, and each of us dipped his tin cup in; without intention, mine was filled to the brim.

"Here's to our new commander, General Meade," said the Colonel, and we all took a drink. The Colonel, noticing that I had only tasted mine, said: "That won't do; drain your cup to such a toast as this!" And foolishly I swallowed the entire contents. Soon the blood mounted to my head, and I began to feel quite dizzy. The Commissary arrived a few minutes after we had drunk the toast, and complained to the Colonel that he had some fresh meat in the valley below, and that the boys refused to get it on the plea of being too tired. "Please order them

Saint Joseph's Academy, a school for girls run by the Sisters of Charity of Saint Vincent de Paul, was located near Emmitsburg, Maryland, about 10 miles southwest of Gettysburg. Soldiers of the Federal I Corps marching past on their way to Gettysburg found the roadside lined with kneeling sisters and their young charges, praying for the soldiers' safety, and for their souls.

down, sir, as I must be off," he added. "I'll make them go," I said, and walking through the camps I waved a stick I had picked up and sang out: "Go for meat, boys, and quickly, too." Then feeling that my steps were becoming uncertain, and noticing Fränkel behind me, I exclaimed: "Fränkel, hold tight!" He grasped my jacket and kept me steady, and the boys laughed as they ran down the hill.

On the march to Emmetsburg, where we arrived on the thirtieth, I was trotting by the Brigade, and to my horror the drummer boys of the 68th cried out loudly: "Fränkel!" And all the regiments answered: "Hold tight!" This joke followed me through all the marches, but it always revived the spirits of the men, who invariably laughed at it, even though they grumbled and cursed through the tedious marches. This induced me never to stop it, but rather to encourage it with a smile.

CAPTAIN RICHARD IRBY

18th Virginia Infantry, Garnett's Brigade

As the Confederate army moved north, discipline became increasingly strict. Captain Irby, a planter from Nottoway County, Virginia, and an early practitioner of scientific farming, recalled the execution of a deserter shortly after crossing the Potomac at Williamsport.

Here, before going into camp, a sad and solemn scene was enacted—the shooting of a man by the name of Riley, who had deserted the Regiment several times. The Division was formed into a hollow square, and the poor man, according to military custom, was marched around with Chaplain Granbery as attendant, followed by a guard of twelve men, and preceded by the drum beating the "Dead March." He seemed perfectly calm. He was seated on his coffin, and at the word "fire," fell, pierced by six bullets—half the guns being loaded with blank cartridges.

CAPTAIN JOHN E. DOOLEY

1st Virginia Infantry, Kemper's Brigade

Dooley was born into a socially prominent Richmond household, the son of an Irish immigrant who had made a fortune in the clothing trade. In 1862 he left his studies at Georgetown College in the District of Columbia to join the elite 1st Virginia.

Terrible had been that march along the scorched and blazing plains of Virginia. Angry was the glare of the sun during those fearful days of June, as it flashed upon our ranks and fiercely smote again and again the burning temples of our fagged and fainting soldiers. Choking, blinding were the clouds of dust that rose from beneath the army's unsteady tread; parching was that unquenchable thirst which dried the tongue to its very roots. The men fell by tens, twenties, nay by hundreds along the dusty roadsides. Such days as these prove the true soldier, and he who falters not in the long and wearisome march will not be absent from the charge. . . .

Our Division (Pickett's) is the rearmost, and we are left in the vicinity of Chambersburg to cover the march of the main body advancing on Gettysburg, to protect the convoys of horses, cattle, etc., the spoils of our invasion, which with very frail guards were being constantly sent across the Potomac; and to be ready at a moment's warning to join the main army whenever the enemy might be found, for as yet we were ignorant of his position.

July 1
Clash at Dawn

At 5:30 on the morning of July 1, 1863, a detail of troopers from the 8th Illinois Cavalry noted ominous signs of movement in the fog-shrouded valley of Marsh Creek, some three miles west of Gettysburg. Soldiers in uniforms of gray were materializing in the mist, ghostly shapes marching down the Chambersburg Pike from the direction of Cashtown. Hastily dispatching a courier to alert his commanding officer, Lieutenant Marcellus Jones took a carbine from one of his sergeants and fired a shot at the enemy column. The Battle of Gettysburg had begun.

The advancing Rebels belonged to Major General Henry Heth's division of A. P. Hill's First Corps. Following Hill's instructions, Heth was marching to occupy the crossroads at Gettysburg, confident that his 7,500 men would easily brush aside the handful of local militia he believed to be guarding the town. But when Heth arrived on the high ground known as Herr Ridge, he saw formations of Federal cavalrymen deploying atop McPherson's Ridge, half a mile to his front, and blocking his advance.

The polished movements of the horsemen as they dismounted and fanned out to fight on foot—every man in his proper place and horses led quickly to the rear—marked these Yankees as veterans.

The Confederates were not going to get into Gettysburg without a fight. Heth ordered forward the brigades of Brigadier Generals James J. Archer and Joseph R. Davis. From the high ground, General John Buford's Federal cavalrymen opened fire with their breech-loading carbines. Buford had been forced to stretch his line precariously thin, but he was determined to cover the approaches to Gettysburg and buy time in order to allow Major General John F. Reynolds, commanding the Army of the Potomac's left wing, to hasten up the infantry.

Reynolds arrived on the field at 9:00 a.m., and soon troops of the First Corps were marching at a double-quick into line atop McPherson's Ridge, relieving Buford's hard-pressed troopers. Reynolds rode forward with the Iron Brigade, shouting encourage-

Ruined fences, stripped of rails to feed Confederate campfires, line the Chambersburg Pike west of Gettysburg. A. P. Hill's victorious Confederates pursued the retreating Federals along the road toward town on the afternoon of July 1.

ment to the black-hatted midwesterners who loaded their muskets and fixed bayonets on the run. As the general turned in the saddle to urge on his men, a bullet slammed into the back of his head, and Reynolds fell dead from his horse.

At that loss, Major General Abner Doubleday took charge of the First Corps and decisively blunted Heth's onslaught. Archer's brigade was driven out of McPherson's Woods and Archer himself hauled into captivity by Private Patrick Mahoney of the 2d Wisconsin. North of the Chambersburg Pike, General Davis' Mississippians breached the Yankee line along the cut of an unfinished railroad only to be counterattacked and trapped in the steep-sided excavation. The flag of the 2d Mississippi was captured in a frenzied melee, and scores of Rebels were forced to surrender.

Shortly after 11:00 a.m., a three-hour lull settled over the field as both sides regrouped and adjusted their lines. Major General Oliver O. Howard—the devout, one-armed "praying general"—arrived at the head of his Eleventh Corps and assumed command of the Union forces. Howard extended the Federal line north and east of Gettysburg with two of his divisions and placed another in reserve on Cemetery Hill, a commanding elevation just south of the town. "Tell Doubleday to fight on the left," Howard instructed an aide, "and I will fight on the right."

Robert E. Lee had also arrived at Gettysburg. Initially frustrated by Heth's premature and unsuccessful advance, he was soon heartened by news that Richard Ewell's Second Corps was coming into position north of town. Even without Longstreet's corps—still a day's march to the west—the army commander felt that a coordinated advance by Hill's and Ewell's forces held the promise of victory.

Unfortunately for the Confederates, when the fighting resumed at 2:30 p.m. Lee's plans almost immediately began to go awry. Major General Robert E. Rodes, the young and headstrong commander of Ewell's largest division, launched his men in a poorly timed assault along Oak Ridge northwest of Gettysburg. One brigade was brought to a standstill north of the railroad cut, and four North Carolina regiments commanded by Brigadier General Alfred Iverson were pinned down in a shallow swale by fire so intense that one survivor concluded that "every man who stood up was either killed or wounded." Shouting, "Up boys, and give them steel," Brigadier General Henry Baxter launched a counterattack that virtually annihilated Iverson's Carolinians.

As Rodes continued to press his attack, fresh Confederate brigades resumed the assault on McPherson's Ridge. Sweeping forward in parade-ground order, Brigadier General Johnston Pettigrew's regiments were savaged by the fire of the Iron Brigade, but they kept coming. "Their advance was not checked," noted Colonel Henry Morrow of the 24th Michigan, "and they came on with rapid strides, yelling like demons." Morrow's troops squared off with the 26th North Carolina in a brutal stand-up fight in which both units lost more than 70 percent of their number. Fourteen men went down in succession carrying the battle flag of the 26th North Carolina, among them 21-year-old Henry King Burgwyn, the youngest colonel in the Confederate army. Morrow likewise fell gravely wounded carrying his regiment's bullet-torn colors, as the tide began to turn against the Yankee defenders. At 3:45 p.m. two of Pettigrew's regiments struck the flank of the leftmost Federal brigade, and the hard-fighting First Corps line began to unravel.

The two divisions of the Eleventh Corps deployed north and east of Gettysburg were similarly beleaguered by the onslaught of Major General Jubal Early's Rebel division. Positioned on a knoll between the Carlisle and Harrisburg roads, on the far right of the Union line, Brigadier General Francis C. Barlow's brigades were caught in a deadly crossfire. Barlow was wounded while trying to rally his crumbling formations, and panic began to spread through the Eleventh Corps. "There was no alternative for Howard's men except to break and fly, or to throw down their arms and surrender," Confederate general John B. Gordon said later; "Under the concentrated fire from front and flank, the marvel is that any escaped."

By 4:30 p.m. both Union corps were in full retreat on Gettysburg. Elements of the First Corps managed to make a brief stand just west of town beside the buildings of the Lutheran Theological Seminary, but the Seminary Ridge position proved untenable when Major General William D. Pender's division joined the Southern juggernaut. As the sweating, powder-stained Union soldiers fell back into the streets of the town, the last vestiges of order gave way in inextricable confusion. "On every side our troops were madly rushing to the rear," confessed a Wisconsin volunteer; "My heart sank within me. I lost all hope."

Oliver Howard was striving to re-form his shattered forces on Cemetery Hill south of town when the arrival of a forceful and highly regarded Federal officer breathed new hope into the dispirited troops. Major General Winfield Scott Hancock, commander of the Second Corps, had been dispatched by Meade to assess the situation at Gettysburg. After a strained consultation with Howard—who seems to have interpreted Hancock's mission as a personal slight—the imposing officer set about bringing order out of chaos. "His bearing was courageous and hopeful," one staff officer recalled, "while his eyes flashed defiance." Lieutenant Sidney Cooke of the 147th New York noted that Hancock's imperturbable demeanor "almost led us to doubt whether there had been cause for retreat at all."

The Federals averted disaster, but only by a narrow margin. Had the onrushing Rebels managed to mount a unified assault on Cemetery Hill, the battle at Gettysburg likely would have ended on the first day—with a decisive Confederate victory. But the sudden success of the Rebels seems to have rendered them indecisive. When Lee advised General Ewell to take Cemetery Hill "if practicable," the corps commander chose not to risk an attack. The Army of Northern Virginia had carried the day, but the impending arrival of Meade's hard-marching columns meant that the battle for Gettysburg had only just begun.

Federal cavalry and units of the I Corps stubbornly held the area surrounding McPherson's Ridge, west of Gettysburg, against the advance of A. P. Hill's Confederate corps on July 1, 1863. Both armies rushed reinforcements to the field and by late afternoon an attack by Early's division of Ewell's corps routed the Federal XI Corps, forcing the Yankees to retreat to Cemetery Hill south of town.

MAJOR GENERAL HENRY HETH

Division Commander, Hill's Corps

At dawn on the morning of July 1, Heth marched his division to Gettysburg in search of shoes and found the Yankees instead. Heth was wearing a new hat that day—one that his clerk had thickly lined with folded paper in order to make it fit. It was a circumstance for which the general would be eternally grateful.

I now formed my division along Willoughby Run, in the McPherson . . . woods. . . . The engagement of Davis and Archer gave General Lee the first intimation that there was an infantry force within thirty miles of him. I saw General Lee several times between the 27th and 30th of June. The first thing he would say showed his anxiety about his cavalry. "Have you heard anything about my cavalry? I hope no disaster has overtaken my cavalry." The last time I saw him before the first of July he said, "Any news to give me about General Stuart? Well, General Heth, if General Hooker does not find us, we must find him." He had not learned that Hooker had been relieved by General Meade. . . .

Hearing the heavy firing on my left I rode where I had first placed my artillery in position and found there Generals Lee and Hill. I told General Lee that as Rhodes appeared to be heavily engaged, I thought I had better go in. He replied, "I do not wish to bring on a general engagement to-day; Longstreet is not up." I returned to my division; soon I went again where I had left General Lee and told him that I believed they were withdrawing troops from my front and pushing them against Rhodes, and again requested permission to attack. The General said, "Wait awhile and I will send you word when to go in." I returned to my division, and very soon an aide came to me with orders to attack.

I struck the Iron Brigade and had a desperate fight. I lost 2300 men in thirty minutes. I was struck by a minie ball on the head which passed through my hat and the paper my clerk had placed there, broke the outer coating of my skull and cracked the inner coating, and I fell senseless.

SERGEANT GEORGE A. BOWEN

12th New Jersey Infantry, Smyth's Brigade

Sergeant Bowen recalled the crowds of stragglers and civilians along the Emmitsburg road, the route taken by his brigade of the 2d Division, II Corps. Bowen was commissioned a lieutenant in 1864 and mustered out at the war's end as a captain.

We marched toward Gettysburg Pa. where there has been some fighting there today. As we marched along the road we met the stragglers and Coffee Coolers, niggers, servants, and all the noncombatants that follow an army, coming toward us getting away from the point of danger, they all had terrible stories to tell of what had happened at Gettysburg. The people along the road all are Union folks they come out to cheer us up and offer food of all kinds, but they do not have enough to half go round. It seems strange to be in a country where we are welcome and to feel we are among friends and well wishers. Arrived at Gettysburg some time in the night. Had a good supper of fresh bread, fried Eggs and milk, all given me by some ladies along the road.

A native of Maryland and a veteran of the Mexican War, James J. Archer resigned from the Regular Army in 1861 to serve with the Confederacy. Captured with most of his brigade on July 1 at Gettysburg, he was imprisoned and his health was shattered. He died in Richmond on October 4, 1864.

Major General John Reynolds, commander of Federal forces at Gettysburg, falls from his horse mortally wounded on being struck in the head by a Confederate bullet. Reynolds was killed at the edge of McPherson's Woods as he led the Iron Brigade into battle.

PRIVATE JOSEPH A. LUMBARD

147th Pennsylvania Infantry, Candy's Brigade

Among the Federal troops converging on Gettysburg were the men of Major General Henry W. Slocum's XII Corps, including the 147th Pennsylvania. Odd acoustics convinced Private Lumbard and his mates that the battle was a mere skirmish until evidence to the contrary became unmistakable.

We here experienced the strangest phenomenon of the war, being less than five miles from the scene of the engagement, and looking in the direction of the town of Gettysburg, we could see the smoke of exploding shells, but [we were] not able to catch the slightest report, whilst upon going a short distance south of where we were lying the sound of musketry and artillery was plainly audible.

At first when the boys brought the news to the company, we were loath to believe them and had it not been for the serious faces of those who gave us the information we would have been tempted to treat it as an attempt at a scare.

Quite a number of the members of the company started down the ravine to ascertain for themselves and soon returned with a report confirming the tidings already received. Soon afterwards a number of rebel prisoners, about 300, were marched past where we were resting.

As soon as we saw them we crowded up close to the road to get a good look at them. They all seemed to be in the best of spirits, evidently glad to escape the pending battle. Quite a number of very pertinent remarks were made by the "Johnnies," among which we distinctly remember:

"The Stars, we met you at Chancellorsville," "We arn't all, theirs a right smart chance left back for youen's to capture," "here goes Lee's advance for Baltimore," with many other similar expressions, which were good naturedly answered by our boys.

"I could have walked a half or three quarters of a mile on the dead soldiers of the enemy and not have put my feet on the ground."

PRIVATE ANDREW PARK

42d Mississippi Infantry, Davis' Brigade

At about 10:15 a.m. Davis' brigade of Mississippians and North Carolinians crossed Willoughby Run and collided with Brigadier General Lysander Cutler's Federal brigade alongside an unfinished railroad cut on McPherson's Ridge. In the pitched battle, the men of the 42d captured the colors of the 56th Pennsylvania. Park, a farmer from Panola County, Mississippi, enlisted in the spring of 1862 and served until he was captured in 1865—seven days before Appomattox.

After forming his command, Col. Hugh R. Miller walked down the line, and stated that if there was a man there who could not stand the smell of gunpowder he had better step out, for we were going into a fight. To my astonishment one poor felow went to him and said: "Colonel, I just cannot go into a fight today, for if I do I will get wounded or killed." The Colonel, with an oath, ordered him back into line. Just at this moment General Davis, and staff rode up and gave the command to move forward, and to let nothing stop us. . . .

I should have stated in the beginning that we were thrown into a fine field of wheat as I ever saw. We had not gone more than three or four hundred yards in this field until we met the enemy's skirmishers. We drove them in, and they fell back over their main line. This drew us up to within fifty or sixty yards of that line, where they were lying down in the wheat. They rose up and resting on one knee fired the first volley. But they shot too high, and but few of our men were hurt. We received orders to fire and charge. This broke their line, and they retreated down the railroad cut. . . . Our troops on the left were ordered to fire right oblique; and those on the right to fire left oblique. In this manner we poured volley after volley into them as they ran down this railroad cut. I think there never was such slaughter as we made on this occasion. I could have walked a half or three quarters of a mile on the dead soldiers of the enemy and not have put my feet on the ground. In some places they were lying three deep. The enemy now brought up more troops when we were about a half mile from the town. They were very strong now, while our forces consisted of only Heath's division; so we received orders to fall back and wait for reinforcements. We fell back about three hundred yards. We had been fighting about two hours and our loss was quite heavy, and right here I will say that among first of my company to get hurt was the man who in the outset told the Colonel he could not go into battle. His arm was broken by a ball.

When we arrived on the ground where we first began the fight in the morning we could see no Yankees. But about three hundred yards farther to our right we [saw] standing two flags; one of which was the flag of Pennsylvania and the other the National flag. There seemed to be no one about them; and Col. Miller called to his men and asked if he had a man in his regiment that could or would bring those flags to him. In an instant Willie Clarke, a fourteen year old lad, said: "I can," and started after them. At about the same time five others started, two them being from my regiment (42nd) and three from the Second regiment. Willie Clarke outran the rest, having had a little the start of them, and got there first, and threw his arms around the flag-staff. But, low and behold! the flags were not alone, for six Yankees were there, and a hand to hand fight began. Two men from the 42nd were wounded and two from the 2nd killed and the other wounded. Five of the Yankees were killed, and the sixth took the flags and started off with them. But Willie Clarke shot him before he got fifty yards and brought [the flags] to Colonel Miller without receiving a scratch.

SERGEANT JAMES P. SULLIVAN

6th Wisconsin Infantry, Meredith's Brigade

In 1861 Sullivan, an Irish immigrant working as a farm laborer, joined the 6th Wisconsin, a regiment of the acclaimed Iron Brigade. In a series of articles written for a Milwaukee newspaper, he recalled his unit's charge across the Chambersburg Pike toward the railroad cut that sheltered Davis' Mississippians.

On the road our fellows straightened up their lines and waited for all hands to get over the fence and opened fire on the Johnnies, and then I found my gun would not go off. . . . We climbed over the fence and I tried my gun again, and finding it had two loads in it I went to our Adjutant who was just in rear of our company and said: "Brooks, my gun won't go off." "Here, take this," he said, and handed me one he had picked up, and telling him not to lose mine, I went back into place in the line and fired it off, but when I loaded up and tried again it would not go, and then I knew my caps were bad. I went to Ticknor and told him my caps were bad. He said, "take Crawford's," pointing to a corporal of our company who had just dropped dead and we rolled him over and I took the cartridge box and buckled it on myself.

As I turned around I saw Capt. Ticknor start for the rear in a spread out, staggering sort of way a few feet he fell. . . .

We were then within a few feet of the railroad cut and were ordered to fix bayonets and charge, which we did. Some of the Johnnies threw down their guns and surrendered. Some would fire and then throw down their guns and cry, I surrender, and some of them broke for the rear. I jumped into the railroad cut and a rebel officer handed me his sword and passed through the cut with the intention of stopping the Johnnies, who were limbering to the rear. Just as I climbed up the side of the cut a big rebel broke and run for the rear, and I called on him to halt, to which he paid no attention, and I flung the rebel sword at him with all my might, but I never knew whether it hit or not, for just as I turned to throw the sword, a bullet hit me on the left shoulder and knocked me down as quick as if I had been hit with a sledge hammer. The first thought I had was that some rebel had hit me with the butt of his gun, for I felt numb and stunned, but I was not long in finding out what was the matter. . . .

After a while I began to feel better, and like a true Irishman I spoke to myself to see if I was dead or only speechless, and finding it was only the latter, I picked up my gun and tried to shoulder it, but I found that my left arm was powerless and so I went around to the other side of the cut where our fellows had a heavy line of prisoners, and a very thin skirmish line of themselves, and took my place outside the rebs, intending to help guard them, but I felt sick and faint and the blood was running down inside my clothes and dropping from my pants leg and my shoe was full and running over.

Five colorbearers of this 6th Wisconsin flag were killed or wounded during the charge that overwhelmed Davis' brigade in the railroad cut. The 6th's colonel, Rufus Dawes, kept his command together, shouting, "Close up on that color."

"I was in a tight place . . . was disgusted with the idea of surrendering."

PRIVATE DAVID J. HILL

2d Mississippi Infantry, Davis' Brigade

Trapped in the railroad cut by the 6th Wisconsin, some 250 Mississippi men were forced to surrender. Private Hill from Ripley, Mississippi, escaped capture by feigning a wound, only to become a prisoner on July 3.

I . . . found to my dismay that I was in a tight place, saw no chance of escape, was disgusted with the idea of surrendering and in fact became very much demoralized. I saw a bloody, muddy blanket lying on the ground also two wounded men lying near me. I tumbled down by them and covered myself with that blanket. I then went to practicing all maneuvers and moaning that I thought would become a badly wounded and suffering man. . . . I got out as soon as I thought it safe to do so and the first man I met was a federal soldier wandering about as if dazed or lost and not knowing what to do. I saw that all one side of his lower jaw was torn off. I got him to a shade and fixed him down with his oil cloth, blanket and knapsack, then brought him a canteen of water and how pitiful to see him trying to drink by pushing the mouth of the canteen through the wound in his throat. I could do nothing more for him. He couldn't talk so I did not learn his name nor what command he was of.

In a sketch based on the fuzzy recollection of a participant, artist Alfred R. Waud portrayed the surrender of Archer's brigade in the railroad cut as being a stiffly formal affair, rather than the melee that it actually was. Recognizing that the account may have been in error, Waud warned of possible mistakes in a note to his publisher.

CORPORAL ORSON B. CURTIS

24th Michigan Infantry, Meredith's Brigade

An onslaught of Rebel reinforcements pushed the Iron Brigade back from McPherson's Ridge. Orson Curtis, a veteran who had been wounded at Fredericksburg, became the historian of the 24th Michigan and pieced together several of his comrades' accounts to recall the regiment's desperate fighting withdrawal.

The enemy having completely drawn two battle-lines in front and on the flanks of the First and Eleventh Corps, the onset of battle was again sounded. They approached in two splendid lines of battle, after forming in the woods beyond the open field. Their serpentine lengths of grey soon appeared, their right overlapping the Federal left by a quarter of a mile. . . .

As the enemy approached, just in the rear of their line rode a Colonel on a mule repeating "Give 'em —— boys," when a bullet knocked his cap off. Catching it in his hand, he continued to urge on their line.

From the nature of the ground but little injury was inflicted on the enemy at this time, as their advance was not checked, and on they came, yelling like demons. The Nineteenth Indiana fought valiantly, but overpowered by flanking numbers, with a disadvantage of position, they were forced back after severe loss and formed on a new line. This exposed the Twenty-fourth Michigan to a terrible cross fire, the men falling like grass before the scythe. . . .

The enemy . . . were held for some time, the work of death going on without ceasing. They were the Twenty-sixth North Carolina and expected to meet militia only, and have an easy victory. But their dead and wounded lay quite as numerous as our own among the trees. The Iron Brigade wearing a different head gear from the rest of our army (stiff, broad brimmed, tall, black hats), this unique feature made them recognized by their old antagonists who now were heard by our own

William B. Murphy, colorbearer of the 2d Mississippi, lost this battle flag (left) in hand-to-hand fighting with the men of the Federal Iron Brigade on July 1. A soldier of the 6th Wisconsin, Lieutenant Ashby Waller, captured Murphy and his flag.

Nine colorbearers of the 24th Michigan were shot down during the struggle for McPherson's Ridge. The regiment's flag, shown at right in a photograph taken after Gettysburg, bore 23 bullet holes and was so damaged that it was retired.

wounded to exclaim: "Here are those —— black-hat fellows again! This is no militia." They had met this Iron Brigade before, and well knew when they did so that business was meant.

The Second Line of Battle of the Twenty-fourth Michigan was speedily formed. . . . The ranks of the Twenty-fourth had again become thinned, a windrow of killed and wounded indicating the position of this line. Overwhelmed again, it was forced to take another new position beyond a small ravine.

On this Third Line of Battle its third color-bearer was killed, and Major Edwin B. Wight (acting as Lieutenant-Colonel) lost an eye. He was thrown completely down and supposed by the men to be killed, but recovering himself he was forced to leave the field. Scarcely a fourth of the regiment taken into action could now be rallied. . . .

The Eleventh Corps was going to pieces, forced back by superior odds. The valiant little First Corps, which had borne the brunt of the battle since early morning, had been forced back on its right. . . .

The Twenty-fourth regiment had now retired from the woods into the open field towards the Seminary.

A Fourth Line of Battle was next attempted. The last of the color-guard planted the flag around which to rally the men. He was shot in the breast and left on the field. The entire color-guard now being gone, Colonel Morrow took the flag to rally the remnant of his devoted band of Wayne County boys and men, when a private took the colors from his hands and was instantly killed by the Colonel's side. Lieutenant Humphreyville was killed on this line, and Colonel Morrow again seized the colors.

A Fifth Line of Battle was attempted where he planted the colors. On this new line, while waiving his sword over his head to rally the men, Captain O'Donnell was instantly killed, and Lieutenant Grace received two wounds, both of which were mortal. Gradually contesting every foot of ground, step by step, frequently almost surrounded, through and out of the woods and over the open field, what was now left of the Twenty-fourth had been forced back to the friendly rail fence barricade just west of the Seminary.

Its Sixth Line of Battle was attempted to be formed at this place. It fought for a time, during which Colonel Morrow, holding aloft the bullet-riddled flag, received a wound in his head and was forced to leave the field, first turning the command of the regiment over to Captain A. M. Edwards, the senior officer now present.

Captain Edwards took the flag and waiving it, the men who were left gallantly rallied to it as well as some of the rest of the Iron Brigade.

Sergeant Philander Wright of the 2d Wisconsin added brass ventilators to his tall felt army hat, the trademark headgear of the Iron Brigade. The round I Corps badge, red for the 1st Division, bears the regiment's number in brass. Sergeant Wright was wounded carrying the regimental colors.

This was the last stand made by the Union troops on that part of the field. . . .

Captain Edwards, still carrying the flag, led the way through the town to the Cemetery, followed by only twenty-six of the Twenty-fourth Michigan, in comparative good order. What were left of the Iron Brigade were soon after moved to Culp's Hill and a new line formed with the Twenty-fourth Michigan on the left. It reached from the top of the elevation to the foot of the hill facing the town. A sorrowful band, indeed, that night! Of the Twenty-fourth Michigan only ninety-nine men and three officers could be rallied to the flag, out of 496 who followed it into action that morning.

On the afternoon of July 1, Confederates of Colonel John Brockenbrough's Virginia brigade advance at a run along the Chambersburg Pike toward the Federal battle lines extending from the McPherson farm south along McPherson's Ridge (right).

SERGEANT EDWIN A. GEARHART

142d Pennsylvania Infantry, Biddle's Brigade

The men of Colonel Chapman Biddle's brigade, fighting to the left of the Iron Brigade on McPherson's Ridge, were outflanked by Pettigrew's Confederates and retreated toward Seminary Ridge, suffering heavy losses. Exhausted on the march to Gettysburg, Sergeant Gearhart had abandoned his rifle and intended to report sick, but the prospect of action seemed to revive him.

I went out with the left wing and had nothing to carry except my haversack and a pound of butter which I had bought and was in my tin cup. At last, right below a steep hill that we were climbing a shell came whistling over and bursted in the tree tops near an old house. I went into this house to see if I could buy some soft bread to use with my butter, which began to run away before the fight began. While in here another shell exploded near, which made things rattle. A young lady who was just in the act of cutting a pie for me and another soldier screamed and shoved the plate and pie off the table; the plate was broken and the pie mussed, but we gathered it up and hurriedly got out of there.

We soon came to the top of the hill when we turned to the right, and in a short distance came into the open and in full view of the field beyond the valley and upon the hill where we had the fight in the beginning of that 1st of July. Here the men jumped over the fence to the left and formed in battle line. I was told to stay there with the musicians until further orders. Walking down the road a few rods I came to where a sick man was lying in a fence corner on the left side of the road. A sudden impulse caused me to ask him for his gun and equipments. I remember it as plain as if it was today. I shouldered the gun after strapping the cartridge box . . . to my side jumped the fence, ran and overtook the regiment. The boys gave me a cheer and I felt real happy because I was in Pennsylvania. . . .

. . . In a short time a line of the enemy came out of the woods in front of us about one mile off; soon another and yet another.

They kept steadily advancing until we could see their officers stepping in front swinging their swords. Suddenly a cloud of smoke arose from their line and almost instantly the balls began to whistle about us and the men next to my right fell. The order rang along the line, fire! fire! and we all discharged our guns and commenced to load and fire at will, as they call it. I think we fired about five rounds. The enemy were not getting close and still they came. Someone yelled retreat. I forgot to say that when I saw those three lines come out and then looking to the left saw our cavalry being forced back and the enemy getting around on our left, my heart sank within me, our line single and stretched out so that it could hardly be said that we were standing shoulder to shoulder and I had also noticed coming up the hill that where a bend got in the line several gaps appeared to my view. Our line kept falling back slowly firing as it went, but the enemy giving us a heavy volley at pretty close range we broke. The colonel was now standing by the flag where it had been advanced by Col. Sickles, acting brigadier at the time, so I was told and as I ran past I heard the colonel shout "rally round the flag," his sword pointing to it. I turned and joined the cluster of men who stood around the flag and fired one shot, that was the last I saw of our colonel. The men were running in retreat without order. Coming to an old broken down rail fence we stopped but not many of us, as I soon learned. When the "rebs" appeared on the crest of the hill we fired on them; as soon as the report of our muskets were heard we knew that a very small part of our line was there. The "rebs" did not return our fire but came rushing down the hill yelling. We up and ran, getting down to the lowest part of the valley and looking up the slope in front of me I could see our men running, carrying rails and I began to feel sure the "rebs" wouldn't get me, but all at once our cannon began to fire canister at the "rebs" coming down the other side and their cannon was run up and began shooting in turn. I saw I was between my friends and my enemies and I knew neither would stop their desperate game of ball for anything that might chance to be between. I threw myself down amidst the high grass that covered this part. . . .

As the "rebs" came lower our fellows shot lower and although I could not see the balls that whistled close over me I could see the timothy heads around me falling from their stem as if by magic, the stalks standing still and their heads falling off apparently of themselves. . . .

Well the result of the first day was we were run back, the town taken away from us, chased out of our rail breast works, 1500 of us taken prisoner, of whom I was one. . . .

The man who captured me had three muskets on his shoulder and as many blue coated prisoners with him. He had passed by me a short distance when he glanced back and saw me sitting. He then bade me fall in. I got upon my feet with some difficulty on account of a wound upon the inner side of the knee of my right leg, a piece of shell having hit it in a glancing manner, tearing a three cornered piece out of the pantaloon leaving a blue bruised spot which was very sore. He took my gun and put it on his shoulder with the others. The cartridge box he took also, throwing it to one side on the ground. He asked me if I belonged to the army of the Potomac and wanted to know how many of the old army men had been in the fight, saying that he thought that we were all new men until the prisoners began to be taken.

CAPTAIN ABNER SMALL

16th Maine Infantry,
Paul's Brigade

Northwest of Gettysburg, Paul's Federals, low on ammunition and under attack from their front and right flank, were forced to extricate themselves and fall back toward town. The 16th Maine waged a suicidal rearguard action, suffering 232 casualties out of the 298 men in action.

Major General Abner Doubleday (third from right) sits surrounded by members of his staff. At Gettysburg on July 1, Doubleday commanded the Federal I Corps, and following the death of General John Reynolds, temporarily took charge of all Federal forces on the field.

We hurried on towards a low ridge a little west of the town. Along the ridge was a scattering of trees and houses, and lording it over them was a brick building, the Lutheran seminary, which gave the ridge a name. Our brigade went around to the western face of the building, and there we threw up a barricade of fence rails and anything else that was handy. The barricade took the shape of a crescent, bending to the west. Beyond it the ridge sloped away through trees into fields, and beyond the fields was another low rise of ground, topped with woods. There was fighting . . . beyond our right. I recall that as I looked up at the building behind us and saw some officers in the cupola taking a view, I noticed them pointing northerly. . . .

As we waited by the seminary, Captain Whitehouse came to talk with me. "Adjutant," he said, "I wish I felt as brave and cool as the colonel appears." "Why, Captain," I said, "he's as scared as any of us. Cheer up! 'Twill soon be over." He tried to cheer up, and made sad work of it; his face wore a look of foreboding, and his smile was a stiff mockery. While we were talking we heard the command to fall in; and he looked me full in the face and said:

"Good-bye, Adjutant. This is my last fight."

We moved around the northern end of the seminary, and passed in rear of a battery there, and slanted northeast. We crossed the Cashtown pike, which led to our left across the ridge, and a little beyond the pike we crossed an unfinished line of railroad, which ran through the ridge

The imposing main building of Gettysburg's Lutheran Theological Seminary was the scene of fighting during the withdrawal of the Federal I Corps on July 1. The structure would serve both sides as a field hospital and observatory.

in a sharp cut. Then we slanted northwest towards the ridge again and went across a field towards a grove. Along the edge of the grove were low heaps of stones. They had been hauled from the field and dumped there by some farmer, years back, and among them now were thick bushes. We clambered over the stone heaps and bushes, wheeled to the right, and went up through the trees to a rail fence. This brought us under fire, and some of our men were hit, and Captain Whitehouse was killed.

We went into line along the fence. Beyond it was another field, and from behind a fence at the farther side of the field a rebel line was firing. Corporal Yeaton of our color guard was shot dead. Captain Waldron, shouting to his men to keep cool and aim low, was struck; I saw him put up his hand as blood gushed from his neck. He clung to a tree, and stood there stubbornly, keeping his place and refusing to be taken to the surgeons. Colonel Tilden rode up to the line, his mount was shot, and horse and rider went down; but the colonel was on his feet in a moment, unshaken. Under his steady eye and voice our men poured a hot fire across the field. Other regiments were blazing away. The rebels took to the rear. Up went our colors and over the fence, and the regiment followed with a shout; but our line was recalled. As we came back over the field a rebel battery shelled us, and some of our men fell.

We returned to the grove, and presently we moved around to the right and took up a position by a stone wall near the crest of the ridge. We joined with Baxter's brigade there and beat off an attack. I remember the still trees in the heat, and the bullets whistling over us, and the stone wall bristling with muskets, and the line of our men, sweating and grimy, firing and loading and firing again, and here a man suddenly lying still, and there another rising all bloody and cursing and starting for the surgeon. Lieutenant Deering picked up a musket and fired without first removing the rammer, and the rammer went hurtling away with a crazy whizz that set the boys of his company to laughing. It was strange to hear laughter there, with dead men by. . . .

As the afternoon wore by, the rebel forces increased and ours didn't. . . . Our right flank was exposed.

I should say it was after four o'clock when our regiment moved yet farther along the ridge. My recollection is that we crossed the Mummasburg road. We saw a brigade of rebels coming against us, and we looked around for support, and saw none, and were falling back for a more favorable position, when an aide came from General Robinson with an order for us to advance and hold the ridge as far north as possible. A few moments later the general himself rode up to Colonel Tilden and repeated the order. The colonel protested that our regiment without support couldn't hold the ridge; we numbered fewer than two hundred, all told; as well set a corporal's guard to stop the rebel army; but the general insisted: "Hold it at any cost!"

"You know what that means," said Colonel Tilden, turning to us, and in the same breath he gave the commands that sent us hurrying back towards the Mummasburg road again. The stone wall came along on the left, and bent sharply ahead of us to face the road. (Or was it a fence by the road? It doesn't matter.) We made a dash for the corner, and planted our colors in the angle. We got there just as a flag and a line of battle showed up across the way; we heard distinctly the commands of a rebel officer directing his men to fire; and a volley crashed, and we saw some of our men fall. Our line blazed away in reply, and the rebel flag went down, and the officer pitched headlong in the stubble. In the field across the road were dead men and scattered equipments, wreckage of a rebel repulse earlier in the day; and now there were more. But the attacking line came on, and following behind it was another, and we knew that our little regiment could not withstand the onset. With anxious hope we looked again to the rear for support—and saw that the other regiments of our brigade, our division, were falling back rapidly towards the town. The rebels were sweeping in through the fields beyond our right. The ridge could be held no longer. We were sacrificed to steady the retreat.

How much time was then passing, I can't say; it was only a matter of minutes before the grey lines threatened to crush us. They came on, firing from behind the wall, from fences, from the road; they forced us, fighting, back along the ridge; and Captain Lowell fell, and some of our men. We got to the railroad cut, which offered a means of defense against the rebels following us, but just then we saw grey troops making in from the west, and they saw us. We were caught between two fires. It was the end. For a few last moments our little regiment defended angrily its hopeless challenge, but it was useless to fight longer. We looked at our colors, and our faces burned. We must not surrender those symbols of our pride and our faith. Our color bearers appealed to the colonel, and with his consent they tore the flags from the staves and ripped the silk into shreds; and our officers and men that were near took each a shred. I have one with a golden star.

Though the rebel lines were fast closing in, there was yet a chance for some of us to escape, and nothing now forbade our risking that desperate hazard. We that took the chance bolted across the Cashtown pike, and made our way, in a fever of anxiety, to a hill south of the town.

COLONEL GILBERT G. PREY

104th New York Infantry, Paul's Brigade

Confederate musketry took a heavy toll of the officers of Robinson's division as the Federals struggled to stem the enemy advance. Because of casualties, Colonel Gilbert Prey suddenly found himself elevated to the command of his brigade.

While the brigade was awaiting orders and the regiments were taking position I received an order from General Robinson in person to form on the right of the Thirteenth Massachusetts. I moved to form on the right, and so moved obliquely to the line of the Thirteenth, when there came from the crest of the ridge of a stentorian voice: "Colonel Prey,——— ——- you, where are you going? Form on the left." I glanced to the rear and saw at once that I was just in position so that by flanking to the left I would form on the left of the Thirteenth as nicely as if on brigade drill. Remembering that the guns were unloaded, and knowing that we would be engaged immediately, I gave the command to "March! Load at will!" The One hundred and fourth formed on the left of the Thirteenth. . . .

Not until this time did General Paul appear on the field, and while riding up in the rear of the One hundred and fourth was shot through the face, destroying one eye and coming out under the other, but not injuring it. My horse was hit at the same time, obliging me to dismount, which General Robinson said he very much regretted as he wanted all his regimental commanders mounted; yet, I remember seeing all of the regimental commanders unmounted during that fight.

The brigade was getting demoralized by having no brigade commander. I saw General Robinson near where he had given me his forcible command, and asked who was in command of the brigade, as General Paul had been taken from the field wounded. He said, "Where is Colonel Root?" "Don't know; not here." "Where is Colonel Leonard?" "Not with his regiment." "You are next in rank, take command of the brigade!"

Brigadier General Gabriel R. Paul (above) was shot in the head and blinded while riding in the rear of one of his regiments, the 104th New York. He survived and later served at an administrative post until the war's end. This blue silk embroidered state flag (left) of the 104th New York was made by the prestigious New York firm of Tiffany and Company. Colonel Gilbert Prey recalled his men retreating with their colors through Gettysburg, "running the gauntlet through a storm of bullets."

"I was too small and too young to be a soldier."

LIEUTENANT JOHN CABELL EARLY

Staff, Major General Jubal A. Early

John Cabell Early was only 15 years old when he accompanied his father, Captain Samuel H. Early, to join the staff of his uncle, Major General Jubal Early, in Pennsylvania. Resplendent in a new uniform of English cadet gray wool, the young soldier faced his first taste of combat as General Ewell's corps descended from the north to drive the Federal XI Corps back toward Gettysburg.

As we neared Gettysburg, we met General Early returning with his forces from York. Upon seeing me, the latter said to my father that I was so much smaller than he had expected that he was afraid I would not do, but at any rate, he wished my father to keep me out of the battle that was then impending. I was greatly crest-fallen, but determined, so I just kept out of General Early's way the rest of the time. We marched up the road which leads directly into the main street of Gettysburg. My father and I were then with Peck's brigade. When we got very near to Gettysburg there was a road that crossed at right angles the road we came by. . . .

Artillery firing then commenced on the part of the enemy, and our men were ordered to lie down in this road, which was a few feet below the general level of the adjacent fields, and so it perfectly protected our men against the enemy's balls. . . .

As I said before, artillery firing on us had commenced and all our foot soldiers were lying down, but the officers were on horseback on the bank back of the road, and my father and I with them. I proposed to my father that we also should lie down with the soldiers, but he laughed, and told me to keep my seat. The balls began to come thicker and closer and to be mixed with grape or canister. One ball seemed to come so close that I thought it would take my head off, so I bent my shoulders to the horse's neck, whereon my father teased me much, telling me that the ball was at least a mile off, also asking me how I thought I would like the life of a soldier. I replied, with much feeling, that I wouldn't be surprised if Uncle Jubal was right and I was too small and too young to be a soldier. . . .

We passed through a corn field and in riding through it, attending to my duties, it seemed to me that the grape and canister mowed down the corn-stalk over me and around me and under me in every direction, so it seemed a miracle that none of them struck me or my horse. I stopped a few minutes behind a large Dutch barn to blow, and while there I saw a dead officer lying with his pockets turned out. There were two papers lying on the ground close by him, one of them a furlough which was to have commenced two days before the battle and which was granted to allow him to go home and get married, and the other was a letter from his bride-to-be, expressing her happiness on the approaching event. The man was from New York, seemed to be about twenty-five years old and was a tall, well-made blonde. He had on a solid steel waistcoat, but this had not protected him, as his left arm had been torn from the socket, and he had bled to death. I saw another man, a German, this (Wednesday) afternoon, lying on the ground with the whole top of his skull taken off, and a mass of blood and brain on the ground. I did not attempt to move him, as there was no possibility of his recovery, but the citizens did, for I saw him on the following Friday afternoon several hundred yards from where he had fallen, and he was still alive.

In the fight for McPherson's Ridge, Major John T. Jones of the 26th North Carolina was struck by a shell fragment but stayed on the field to command his regiment after the loss of his two senior officers. Jones, the only field officer of Pettigrew's brigade to survive the charge of July 3, was killed leading his regiment at the Battle of the Wilderness on May 5, 1864.

PRIVATE WILLIAM M. CHEEK

26th North Carolina Infantry, Pettigrew's Brigade

In its advance against the Iron Brigade, the 26th North Carolina lost 588 of its 800 men. Private Cheek was nearby when the regiment's popular young colonel, Henry King Burgwyn, was mortally wounded. Burgwyn was the youngest regimental commander in the Army of Northern Virginia.

Our regiment had been formed in line of battle and advanced a considerable distance towards the Federal lines. Our colors were very prominent in the center. Time after time they were shot down by the hot fire of infantry and artillery, and in all they fell fifteen times, sometimes the staff being broken and sometimes a color-bearer being shot down.

The color-sergeant was killed quite early in the advance and then a private of F company took the flag. He was shot once, but rose and went on, saying, "Come on, boys!" and as the words left his lips was again shot down, when the flag was taken by Captain McCreary, who was killed a moment or two later. Then Colonel Burgwyn himself took the colors and as we were advancing over the brow of a little hill and he was a few feet in advance of the center of the regiment, he was shot as he partly turned to give an order, a bullet passing through his abdomen. He fell backwards, the regiment continuing its advance, Lieutenant-Colonel John R. Lane taking command and at the same time taking the flag from Colonel Burgwyn. In a moment, it seemed, he was shot, and then Captain W. S. Brewer, of my company, took the flag and carried it through the remainder of the advance, Major John Jones having then assumed command of the regiment. Our regiment was recalled and retired. I was knocked down by the explosion of a shell, which injured my eyesight somewhat, but soon rose, and as myself and some comrades went back I saw Colonel Burgwyn being carried off the field by two soldiers, named Ellington and Staton, who were using one of their blankets for that purpose.

Colonel Burgwyn asked me, whom he recognized as being a member of his command, to help carry him off the field, and I at once gave my aid. We carried him some distance towards the place where our line of battle had been formed, and as we were thus moving him a lieutenant of some South Carolina regiment came up and took hold of the blanket to help us. Colonel Burgwyn did not seem to suffer much, but asked the lieutenant to pour some water on his wound. He was put down upon the ground while the water was poured from canteens upon him. His coat was taken off and I stooped to take his watch, which was held around his neck by a silk cord. As I did so the South Carolina lieutenant seized the watch, broke the cord, put the watch in his pocket and started off with it. I demanded the watch, telling the officer that he should not thus take away the watch of my colonel, and that I would kill him as sure as powder would burn, with these words cocking my rifle and taking aim at him.

This North Carolina issue shell jacket and jean-cloth forage cap were worn at Gettysburg by Private Amzi L. Williamson of the 53d North Carolina. Williamson was wounded during the late afternoon attacks.

I made him come back and give up the watch, at the same time telling him he was nothing but a thief, and then ordering him to leave, which he did. In a few moments Colonel Burgwyn said to me that he would never forget me, and I shall never forget the look he gave me as he spoke these words. We then picked him up again and carried him very close to the place where we had been formed in line of battle. Captain Young, of General Pettigrew's staff, came up and expressed much sympathy with Colonel Burgwyn. The latter said that he was very grateful for the sympathy, and added, "The Lord's will be done. We have gained the greatest victory in the war. I have no regret at my approaching death. I fell in the defense of my country."

About that time a shell exploded very near us and took off the entire top of the hat of Captain Brewer, who had joined our party. I left and went to search for one of our litters, in order to place Colonel Burgwyn upon it, so as to carry him more comfortably and conveniently. I found the litter with some difficulty, and as the bearers and myself came up to the spot where Colonel Burgwyn was lying on the ground, we found that he was dying. I sat down and took his hand in my lap. He had very little to say, but I remember that his last words were that he was entirely satisfied with everything, and "The Lord's will be done." Thus he died, very quietly and resignedly.

ELIZABETH M. THORN

Resident of Gettysburg

Elizabeth's husband, Peter, was caretaker of the Evergreen Cemetery at the southern edge of Gettysburg. When he joined the Federal army, Elizabeth assumed his job, living with her parents and children in the cemetery gatehouse.

So at last they came to the Cemetery House and wanted a man to go along out with them (a young boy was there about thirteen years, and I thought he was too young, and my father was too old) I offered myself to go along. He refused at first, but I thought there was danger all around, and said I wasn't afraid, so he said "Come on."

We walked through flax, and then through a piece of oats, and then we stood in a wheat field. They all held against me coming through the field, but as he said I was all right, and it did not matter, why they gave three cheers and the band played a little piece, and then I walked a little past a tree to where I could see the two roads. I showed him the Harrisburg Road, the York Pike, and the Hunterstown Road. It was with one of General Howard's men that I went. Then he took me back home. He said, "They will commence very heaving firing now, walk on the other side of my horse." And so as soon as I jumped on our porch he went back again.

I wanted to go upstairs once more to see if our men gained, but when I came on the stairway a shell had cut in the window frame, then jumped a little, then went through the ceiling, so I would not go up any more. . . .

Soon one of General Howard's men came and ordered me to have supper for Gen. Howard. I complained I had no bread, for I had given it all away in the morning. But I said I could make cakes, and he said they were good enough for war times.

They did not come for so long, it was near twelve o'clock. . . .

After they had had some supper and I found they were going to leave I asked them if they thought I should leave the house in the night. Gen. Howard rubbed his forehead and said: "Leave the house? Leave the house?" Then he looked towards the others and said: "Comrades, I say stay." Then he said we should take our best things and pack them up and in two hours he would send two men to carry them to the cellar. . . . He said they would begin hard fighting about daybreak, near four o'clock, and then we should go to the cellar.

About two hours after they left the men came and took the things to the cellar. Gen. Howard said: "When I give you orders to leave the house, don't study about it, but go right away."

About four o'clock we went to the cellar. There were seventeen of us . . . in the cellar about two or three hours. The noise of the cannonading was terrible. At last the door flew open and some said: "This family is commanded by Gen. Howard to leave this house and get as far in ten minutes as possible. Take nothing up but the children and go." They said we should keep the pike, where the soldiers could see us, and that would save us. When we were a little way down the pike a shell bursted back of us, and none of us were killed, but we commenced to walk faster. We went down the pike one and one half miles when we began to feel weak and sick, we were so hungry, for we had eaten nothing that day before we were so scared when the battle commenced. So we went into a farm house to buy bread . . . but the bread was doughey and we could not eat it. Later we stopped at a farm house,—Musser's. We did not feel like going farther as it was full of soldiers and army wagons and provision wagons.

MAJOR THOMAS W. OSBORN

Chief of Artillery, XI Corps

A law student from Jefferson County, New York, Osborn volunteered in 1861 and swiftly rose to the command of the XI Corps' artillery. The late afternoon attack of Jubal Early's Confederates flanked Howard's XI Corps along the Harrisburg road, and as it fragmented, Osborn's batteries waged a valiant and costly rearguard action.

I again returned to Wilkeson's battery, where I met Wilkeson being carried to the rear by his men on a stretcher. One leg had been cut off at the knee by a cannon shot. He spoke to me and was cheerful and hopeful. I knew at a glance that the wound was fatal. There was no time for me to stop and, after talking with him, perhaps a quarter or half-minute, I left him. I never saw him again, as he died a few hours later. . . .

I soon hurried on to the front where I found the battery engaged in line with Barlow's division. The lines of battle were in the open field and very close together. The enemy's line overlapped ours to a considerable extent on both flanks. Lieutenant Bancroft was in command of Wilkeson's battery and doing good work. I knew that the two divisions must soon fall back or would be drawn back. I gave Bancroft what instructions were necessary and returned to get the other four batteries into satisfactory positions. A few moments after I left the line, General Barlow was seriously wounded and fell into the hands of the enemy.

Lieutenant Bayard Wilkeson, 19-year-old commander of Battery G, 4th U.S. Artillery, directs his guns in action on Barlow's Knoll on the Federal right. When struck by a shell that nearly severed his right leg, Wilkeson calmly amputated the damaged limb with his pocketknife, using his sash for a tourniquet. Evacuated to a nearby building, the young officer died several hours later.

CAPTAIN FREDERICK BARON VON FRITSCH

68th New York Infantry, von Gilsa's Brigade

With the XI Corps in disorganized retreat and the I Corps giving way on Seminary Ridge, orders were shouted for Federal units to fall back through the town of Gettysburg toward Cemetery Hill. The retreat became a rout; von Fritsch narrowly eluded capture.

Orders were shouted to fall back through Gettysburg on to Cemetery Hill, and it was high time to do so, as from all sides Confederate masses approached the town on the double quick. Brave General Barlow about this time received a shot and fell from his horse. I rode behind our men into the town and saw many captured by Grey-coats everywhere.

Passing a church on the outskirts, Surgeon Schultz, frightened to death, stopped me and asked if he would be taken prisoner, if caught. I said: "Put a white handkerchief on your arm, and attend to the wounded. There are lots of them in the streets."

This delayed me and some twenty Confederates came rushing on, halloing to me to surrender. One excited fellow got hold of Caesar's bridle with his left hand and was ready to plunge his bayonet into me with the right, screaming: "Surrender! get down, you damned Yank!"

Tidy houses line Gettysburg's Carlisle Street (above), a route used by the Federal XI Corps in its southerly retreat through town. At right, in a photograph taken from Seminary Ridge, the unfinished railroad cut (left) and the Chambersburg Pike (right) lead east toward Gettysburg, where the orderly retreat of the Federal I Corps grew chaotic as units became entangled in the city streets. Beyond the town loom Culp's and Cemetery Hills, the goal of the retreating Federals.

"*You* be damned," I answered, and cut off his hand with my Saxon sword. Then I started off, gave spurs to my horse, but to my horror found myself in a yard, surrounded by high fence rails. They shot at me from behind and demanded surrender.

"Marie!" I gasped, "save me!" And Caesar, with an enormous effort, jumped the fence and made off towards Cemetery Hill. Reaching the Arch, I dismounted and examined my horse; the poor fellow had been shot twice, but they were only slight flesh wounds. My left leg was wounded, and I felt the blood filling my right boot. My left shoulder strap had been shot away and the shoulder was badly scratched. One bullet had damaged the back of my saddle, partially protected by a rubber blanket, and when I tried to replace my sabre, I found the scabbard bent. I had hurt my right knee badly on the fence, and torn off one of my stirrups.

"Orders were shouted to fall back through Gettysburg on to Cemetery Hill."

MARY MCALLISTER

Resident of Gettysburg

Forty-one-year-old Mary McAllister lived with her sister and brother-in-law above their general store on Chambersburg Street in Gettysburg. As the Federal troops abandoned their positions north of town, the trickle of wounded became a demoralized flood.

They carried the wounded in there as fast as they could. We took the cushions off the seats and some of the officers came in and said, "Lay them in the aisles." Then we did all we could for the wounded men. After a while they carried in an awfully wounded one. He was a fine officer. They did not know who he was. A doctor said to me, "Go bring some wine or whiskey or some stimulant!" When I got outside I thought of Mr. Guyer near the church. "Well," I said, "Mr. Guyer, can you give me some wine?" He said, "The rebels will be in here if you begin to carry that out." "I must have it," I said. "Give me some." I put it under my apron and went over to the church with it. They poured some of it into the officer's mouth. I never knew who he was, but he died.

Well, I went to doing what they told me to do, wetting cloths and putting them on the wounds and helping. Every pew was full; some sitting, some lying, some leaning on others. They cut off legs and arms and threw them out of the windows. Every morning the dead were laid on the platform in a sheet or blanket and carried away.

. . . in the house was Lieutenant Dailey of the 2nd Wisconsin. "He was so mad when he found out what a trap they were in. He leaned out of the kitchen window and saw the bayonets of the rebels bristling in the alley and in the garden." I said, "There is no escape there." I opened the kitchen door and they were tearing the fence down with their bayonets. Dailey . . . says, "I am not going to be taken prisoner, Colonel!" And he says to me, "Where can I hide?" I said, "I don't know, but you can go upstairs." "No," he says, "but I will go up the chimney." "You will not," said the Colonel. "You must not endanger

Victorious Confederates extended their battle line into Gettysburg along the Hagerstown road (left, on the right) as retreating Federals withdrew south onto Cemetery Hill. Above, the handsome gatehouse of Evergreen Cemetery, its windows smashed by bullets, stands on the crest of Cemetery Hill. Federal artillery batteries nearby helped keep Confederate attackers at bay on the evening of July 1.

this family." So he came back. He was so mad he gritted his teeth. Then he says to me, "Take this sword, and keep it at all hazards. This is General Archer's sword." He surrendered it to me. "I will come back for it." I ran to the kitchen, got some wood and threw some sticks on top of it.

Col. Morrow [of the 24th Michigan] says to me, "Take my diary. I do not want them to get it." I did not know where to put it, so I opened my dress and put it in my dress. He said, "That's the place, they will not get it there!" Then all those wounded men crowded around and gave me their addresses. Then Lt. Dailey had another request. "Here is my pocketbook, I wish you would keep it." Afterward I did not remember what I did with it, but what I did was to pull the little red cupboard away and put it back of that. In the meantime Martha had gone upstairs and brought a coat of John's. She said, "Here, Colonel, put this coat on." But he would not take the coat she brought him. He would not stoop to disguise himself and he gave the others orders that they were to give their right names when they were taken prisoner. . . .

Then came a pounding on the door. Col. Morrow said, "You must open the door. They know we are in here and they will break it." By this time the Rebels came in and . . . demanded his sword. . . .

. . . the Rebels said, "Those that are not able to walk we will not take; we will parole them." But they said to these wounded men, "Now if you ever get to fight you know what we will do." But the wounded ones did not pay much attention to that. Then they took away as prisoners all that could walk.

The next thing then was to get these wounded fixed. Then the firing ceased for the evening. That was the time we went upstairs to get some of the wounded ones in bed and to get pillows to make the others as comfortable as we could. Five surgeons came in and one of them said, "Now if you had anything like a red flag, it would be a great protection to your house, because it would be considered a hospital, and they would have respect." Well, Martha thought of a red shawl she had. She got it and I got the broom and we hoisted the front window.

"There were the groaning and crying, the struggling and dying, crowded side by side. . . ."

The sign of William T. King's tailor shop, located near Gettysburg's town square, was pierced by bullets during the fighting on the first day. At the time, King was serving with Company B of the Adams County Cavalry, a local home guard unit; he left the shop in the care of his wife.

TILLIE PIERCE

Resident of Gettysburg

Fifteen-year-old Tillie Pierce was sent by her worried parents to a refuge to the south of town, the Jacob Weikert farm on the Taneytown road behind the Round Tops. Even there, on the afternoon of July 1, the wounded began to arrive.

Some of the wounded from the field of battle began to arrive where I was staying. They reported hard fighting, many wounded and killed, and were afraid our troops would be defeated and perhaps routed.

The first wounded soldier whom I met had his thumb tied up. This I thought was dreadful, and told him so. "Oh," said he, "this is nothing; you'll see worse than this before long." "Oh! I hope not," I innocently replied. Soon two officers carrying their arms in slings made their appearance, and I more fully began to realize that something terrible had taken place.

Now the wounded began to come in greater numbers. Some limping, some with their heads and arms in bandages, some crawling, others carried on stretchers or brought in ambulances. Suffering, cast down and dejected, it was a truly pitiable gathering. Before night the barn was filled with the shattered and dying heroes of this day's struggle.

That evening Beckie Weikert, the daughter at home, and I went out to the barn to see what was transpiring there. Nothing before in my experience had ever paralleled the sight we then and there beheld. There were the groaning and crying, the struggling and dying, crowded side by side, while attendants sought to aid and relieve them as best they could. We were so overcome by the sad and awful spectacle that we hastened back to the house weeping bitterly.

ANNA LOUISE GARLACH

Resident of Gettysburg

Young Anna Louise recorded the strange odyssey of a Federal officer who went into hiding near the Garlach barn on Washington Street while the town of Gettysburg swarmed with Rebels.

General Schimmelfennig was mounted and in retreat on Washington street. At that time there was an alley running from Washington street which ended at the barn of my father Henry Garlach, and connected with another alley north to Breckenridge street, but had then no outlet south. He turned down this alley and then found that his only outlet in either direction was toward the Confederates.

The Rebels were at his heels and when he reached our barn his horse was shot from under him. He jumped over the alley fence into our yard and ran toward Baltimore street, but the rebels were in possession of that street and he realized that he must be captured.

There was an old water course in our yard at the time, now converted into a sewer, and for 12 feet from the street it was covered with a wooden culvert and General Schimmelfennig hurriedly crawled out of sight under the culvert.

He remained there until after dark. It was night when my mother went out of the house following the path to the stable for the purpose of feeding our hogs. Along the pathway was the woodshed and against the shed and running some distance from it was several ranks of wood and in front of the wood two swill barrels. We had been using wood from the rank nearest the barrels and there was a space between the barrel and the next rank of wood big enough to hold a man. As mother went up to the barrel the General said, "Be quiet and do not say anything."

He had taken off the wood and built a shelter over his head to better hide himself.

It was remarkable that he had not been captured. The Rebels had torn down fences from Breckenridge street southward through the yards and there were Rebels on all sides of us and any movement of his in daytime might have been seen from a number of points.

On the second day mother made a pretense of going to the swill barrel to empty a bucket. In the bucket however was water and a piece of bread and instead of these going into the barrel they went to the General in hiding. Mother was so afraid that she had been seen and that the General would be found that she did not repeat this.

General Schimmelfennig was in hiding between the barrel and the rank of wood from the evening of the first day to the morning of July 4th. That last night everything grew so quiet and as soon as there was light we got up and mother hurried down and out, anxious to know what had become of the man.

He was already out of his hiding place before she reached him. When I first saw him he was moving across our yard toward the Benner property. He was walking stiff and cramped like. At the fence was a number of Union men and they proved to be some of his own men. They thought he had been killed and when they saw him they went wild with delight. I saw them crowd around him and some kissed his hand. They seemed beside themselves with joy.

Alexander Schimmelfennig served with the Prussian Army before immigrating to the United States. Appointed colonel of the 74th Pennsylvania in 1861, he rose to command a brigade in the XI Corps. After Gettysburg, Schimmelfennig requested a transfer to Union-occupied coastal South Carolina. Ill with malaria and tuberculosis, he died in September 1865.

ELIZABETH SALOME MYERS

Resident of Gettysburg

"Sallie" Myers worked as assistant to the principal of the Gettysburg public schools. At first stunned by the carnage, the 21-year-old soon pitched in to help the wounded who filled Gettysburg's churches, homes, and barns.

I went to the church, where men were lying [on] the pews and on the floors. I knelt by the first one inside the door and said: "What can I do for you?" He replied: "Nothing, I am going to die.". . .

To be thus met by the first one addressed was more than my nerves could stand and I went hastily out, sat down on the church steps and cried.

In a little while I re-entered the church hospital and spoke again to the dying man. He was Sergeant Alexander Stewart of the 149th Pennsylvania Infantry Regiment. He spoke of his home, his aged father and mother, of his wife, and of his younger and only brother, who had been severely wounded and was then at home, and asked me to take their addresses and send them his dying message. . . .

He lingered until Monday, July 6. He had been sinking gradually all evening. About 9 he had a spell of coughing until 10 o'clock, he suffered dreadfully. I held him in my arms until nearly 11 when his head sank on the pillow and he died with only a slight struggle. [He] was buried in the graveyard of the United Presbyterian Church, in which his father had been baptized 63 years before.

LIEUTENANT ADOLFO CAVADA

Staff, Major General Andrew A. Humphreys

Born in Cuba, Cavada was the son of a Spanish-born planter and his American wife. After his father's death, Cavada's mother returned to her native Philadelphia where Adolfo and his two brothers were educated. In 1861 Cavada joined the 23d Pennsylvania and was later detached to General Humphreys' staff.

A dispatch from Genl. Sickles arrived urging the greatest haste in pushing forward to Gettysburg. "Genl. Reynolds' Corps is fighting against great odds and is in danger. Genl. Reynolds is killed." One of our brigades was already on the road, everything pushing on in earnest. With some difficulty the Genl. and staff made their way through the mass of men struggling forward. Fatigue hunger and sickness are all forgotten when a battle became certain. . . . At dark we reached Marsh Run. Lt. Col. Hayden Inspector Genl. of the Corps met us at the stream with instructions to guide our column. After crossing the stream we diverged to the left along the bank of the creek and followed it for a short distance then took a short road to the right for half a mile. Our guide fearing that he had taken a wrong direction came to a halt. The night was very dark and the sky lowering, and the enemy supposed to be near at hand. Genl. Humphreys issued orders along the line to prevent all noise then dismounted and accompanied by Col. Hayden went cautiously up the road to the Black Horse Tavern, which was only a few hundred feet, and discovering a rebel picket close by understood the exact condition of things. At this time a Rebel Artillery Sergeant, who mistook our column for his own troops, was brought in and revealed the pleasing fact that we were almost within the rebel lines and that over thirty pieces of artillery crowned the very hill we were about to ascend and completely commanded the point we then stood on. Silently and quickly the regiments 'about faced' and noiselessly filed off over the road we came by.

MAJOR JOHN W. DANIEL

Staff, Major General Jubal A. Early

A native of Lynchburg, Virginia, Daniel came through Gettysburg without mishap, but a leg wound suffered in the Battle of the Wilderness in May 1864 crippled him for life. Daniel served 18 years in the Virginia legislature before being elected to the United States Senate in 1885. There he served three terms before complications from his old wound caused his death in 1910.

As the enemy's sharpshooters were posted so as to cover Baltimore Street, it was dangerous to cross it. The soldiers stacked arms, rested themselves on the door steps and side walks. I stood around the corner for a time to warn both footmen and horsemen from crossing the street, as I knew the sharpshooters on house tops or in alleys or windows had a bead on them. After being diverted for a moment I was suddenly startled by seeing Captain Sam Henry Early halt his horse in the middle of the street, I had not noticed his approach. Instinctively I ran out in the street and slapped him with my hand on his left leg as he sat on his horse looking up Baltimore Street. A bullet from a sharp shooter's rifle struck his leg just below my hand simultaneously, inflicting a wound which laid him up for a while. It is needless to say that he required no further warning, and congratulated himself that he was no more gravely injured.

CORPORAL SIDNEY J. RICHARDSON

21st Georgia Infantry, Doles' Brigade

The 23-year-old corporal wrote home describing his regiment's part in the battle, along with his misgivings about fighting on enemy soil. Richardson served until April 18, 1864, when he was killed at the Battle of Plymouth, North Carolina.

Maryland
Camp Near Hagerstown
July the 8th 1863

It is the first fight we every was in that we was not put in the hardest part of the battle. I let you know, I was glad when the yankees turned to run back, but one time I felt sad, one yankee regiment charge us, but we all fell down behind a fence, and received the charge first before they got to us, we fired a volley into them and then charged them as quick as we could, they turned to run and we continued the charge until they got away. I think they fight harder in their own Country then they do in Virginia, I had rather to fight them in Virginia then here, for we had to leave a great many of our wounded in the hands of the yankees.

Federal marksmen fire at the Rebels from buildings near the intersection of Baltimore Street and the Emmitsburg road south of Gettysburg. Throughout the battle, sharpshooters from both armies made a no man's land of the neighborhood of houses and workshops at the foot of Cemetery Hill.

hill among the rock
1
3
4
4
5

July 2
In Hell's Terrain

Shortly before midnight of July 1, 1863, Major General George Meade arrived on the battlefield at Gettysburg to face the greatest crisis of his 28-year military career. Meade had not expected to give battle at Gettysburg, and as Generals Winfield Scott Hancock and Oliver O. Howard briefed him on the situation, the army commander realized how precariously close the Union had come to disaster on the first day of fighting. Two of his seven corps—the First and Eleventh—had suffered crippling losses, and while the survivors held a formidable position on the high ground south of Gettysburg, Meade knew that unless the bulk of his army arrived by dawn, the Federals might not be able to stave off the inevitable Confederate assault.

Urged on by their apprehensive commander, the footsore Yankee soldiers trudged through choking clouds of dust all through the hours of darkness, northward to Gettysburg. Although hundreds gave out along the way, by sunrise of July 2 Meade was able to plug the exhausted troops of his Second, Third, Fifth, and Twelfth Corps into line. These new arrivals enabled Meade to occupy the wooded slopes of Culp's Hill, southeast of Gettysburg, and to extend his position southward from Cemetery Hill along the low crest of Cemetery Ridge. The Federal line now resembled a tight horseshoe with its strength facing north and northeast, where most of the Confederate troops were apparently concentrated. But the Union left, at the end of Cemetery Ridge, was exposed and thinly defended. Few of the weary Federals had strength enough to pitch their tents, and most dropped down where they stood in ranks, to snatch what sleep they could before facing the terrible ordeal of battle.

If the first day at Gettysburg had been a near calamity for the Union, it had proved to be a time of lost opportunities for Robert E. Lee's Army of Northern Virginia. Lee knew that if his troops were to defeat a numerically stronger enemy, the second day's fight would require strategic enterprise and tactical boldness. Audacity in the face of extreme pressure was a hallmark of Lee's generalship, and, rising from a fitful sleep an hour before dawn, he set about implementing a daring offensive

Shadowed by Big and Little Round Tops, a Confederate battle line advances into the hotly contested, rock-strewn valley of Plum Run.

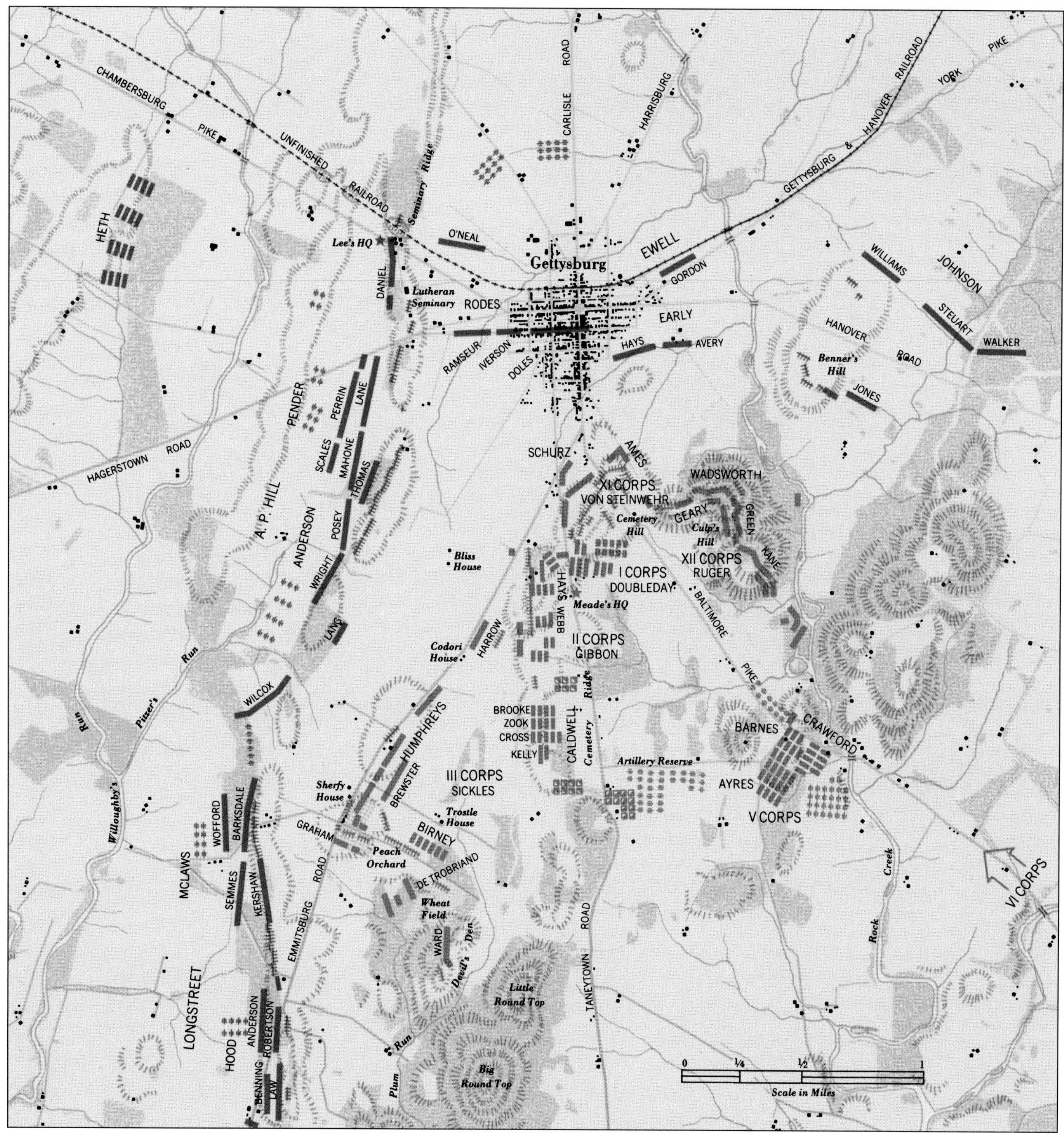

Meade's army held a position partially entrenched on the hills south of Gettysburg. Lee planned an echeloned attack on the thinly held Federal left.

plan reminiscent of his successful strategy at Second Manassas and Chancellorsville.

Two of General Longstreet's three divisions had arrived to bolster Hill's and Ewell's corps, and Lee intended to use these fresh troops to strike at the vulnerable Union left. As the morning wore on with little except an occasional skirmish between the opposing forces, Lee explained his strategy to his subordinate commanders.

From his position on Herr Ridge, west of Gettysburg, Longstreet would march the divisions of Generals John Bell Hood and Lafayette McLaws southward, using Seminary Ridge as a natural barrier to screen the movement from enemy observation. Once these troops were deployed west of the Emmitsburg road, Longstreet would initiate an advance *en echelon*—committing Hood's and McLaws' brigades in a sequential series of triphammer attacks from south to north. Once the last of Longstreet's men were under way, General Richard H. Anderson's division of Hill's corps would continue the en echelon attack, striking at the Union center on Cemetery Ridge. In order to divert Federal troops from the point of assault, Lee instructed General Ewell to launch an attack on the Union right.

Longstreet, however, was reluctant to attack without Major General George E. Pickett's division, which was still a day's march away. In fact, Longstreet favored a strategy that was markedly different from Lee's—no attack at all. Longstreet wanted to sideslip past Gettysburg, find more suitable ground to defend, and force Meade to launch an attack, as General Ambrose E. Burnside's troops had at Fredericksburg the previous year, with disastrous results. But Lee was determined to maintain the initiative, and as Longstreet began to maneuver his divisions into place, he did so with a reluctance that many officers felt verged on insubordination. It was nearly 4:00 in the afternoon before Longstreet was ready to begin his attack on the Federal left, and by then the situation to his front had changed dramatically. An entire Yankee corps had moved forward from Cemetery Ridge to the Emmitsburg road, and lay directly in Longstreet's path.

Like Lee, George Meade had also to contend with the actions of an opinionated subordinate. When Major General Daniel E. Sickles decided that his Third Corps was not deployed on favorable ground, he took the liberty of shifting his two divisions west to what he judged a better defensive position. The combative politician-turned-soldier established a new line running south along the Emmitsburg road, across a crest marked by a peach orchard, and angling southeastward on a ridge that terminated in a heap of jumbled granite boulders called Devil's Den. By the time Meade was fully aware of Sickles' action, it was too late to readjust the line. Longstreet had begun his attack, and the battle was joined.

Commencing with Hood's men on the Confederate right, each of Longstreet's brigades surged forward in sequence, the en echelon assaults smiting the Federals a series of sledgehammer blows. Screaming the Rebel yell, wave after wave of Confederate soldiers advanced into the smoke and flame of battle that rolled steadily northward from Devil's Den, across the corpse-strewn Wheat Field, to the Peach Orchard salient. Sickles' men fought desperately but began to give way, and the Southern juggernaut rolled on toward Cemetery Ridge.

As on the preceding day, the Confederates came up just short of victory on July 2. Through the decisive actions of junior officers, Federal soldiers secured the crucial elevation of Little Round Top—an impregnable anchor for Meade's left flank. A stalwart defense by General Hancock's Second Corps maintained the Union hold on Cemetery Ridge, and Ewell's belated assault on Culp's Hill was easily repulsed. As darkness fell a desperate Rebel charge on Cemetery Hill briefly pierced the defenses of the Union Eleventh Corps but recoiled before a Yankee counterattack.

The bloodiest of the three days of battle at Gettysburg ended in stalemate. If Robert E. Lee's army was to win a decisive engagement on Northern soil, victory would have to come on July 3.

TILLIE PIERCE

Resident of Gettysburg

The outlying refuge chosen by Tillie Pierce's parents—the farm of Jacob Weikert near the eastern slope of Little Round Top—would in fact become an extremely dangerous place as the armies converged on the rocky slopes of the Round Tops.

The day dawned bright and clear; the hot rays of the July sun soon fell upon the landscape. As quickly as possible I hurried out of the house, and saw more troops hurrying toward town. . . . I soon engaged in the occupation of the previous day; that of carrying water to the soldiers as they passed. . . .

During the early part of the forenoon my attention was called to numerous rough boxes which had been placed along the road just outside the garden fence. Ominous and dismal as was the sight presented, it nevertheless did not prevent some of the soldiers from passing jocular expressions. One of the men near by, being addressed with the remark that there was no telling how soon he would be put in one of them, replied:

"I will consider myself very lucky if I *get* one."

Federals of J. H. Hobart Ward's brigade grudgingly fall back from Devil's Den under pressure from Hood's Confederates. One of Ward's colonels, Augustus Van Horne Ellis, colonel of the 124th New York, was wounded atop his horse. When a member of his staff pleaded with him to dismount he answered, "The men must see us today."

"TOUT-LE-MONDE"

Unidentified Confederate Soldier, 17th Georgia Infantry, Benning's Brigade
On the afternoon of July 2, the 17th Georgia and fellow regiments of Brigadier General Henry L. Benning's brigade charged Captain James E. Smith's New York battery, posted above the jumbled boulders of the Devil's Den, and captured its four Parrott guns. On July 22 the Savannah Republican newspaper printed an obituary for Captain V. A. S. Parks of the 17th Georgia, who was killed in the attack. The eulogy included an account of the action by a soldier-correspondent who identified himself only as "Tout-le-Monde."

Letter from the Army—Hagerstown, July 7, 1863
. . .The enemy's skirmishers were in full view. The dead of the battle which had been fought the day before lay in many places over the ground, and also a large no. of the wounded of both armies were seen lying about the farm houses which we passed. These unmistakable signs of blood left us no longer in doubt of the path that was before us.

. . . As soon as everything was adjusted the advance was ordered. . . . As soon as we came in sight a furious blast of cannon broke from the tops of the hills and mountains around and the terrific cry and screams of shells began. Slowly the line moved in order fwd. . . . undismayed by the terrors that seemed to awake from the infernal regions. . . . Down the plunging shot came, bursting before and around and everywhere tearing up the ground in a terrific rain of death. Still the old brigade moved on in a solid and beautiful line the red star gemmed cross floating defiantly in the midst. As it approached, the guns, the rain of grape and canister began, mingling their sharp cries with the shrill whistle of the mad minnie balls which seemed to come in showers. . . .

The line reached the foot of the hill. . . .The 15th and 20th [Ga.] clambered over the rocks and pressed fwd. and the 17th and 2nd plunged through the raking fire that now, more terrific than before, swept the gorge like a furious torrent. The enemy, dismayed at such daring, began to break before the fire which was now hurled through his ranks. . . .The gunners fled from their guns, leaving the 3 splendid Parrott pieces which had been pouring death into the old brigade for one mile. The hill and its arty. [artillery] was ours.

PRIVATE JOHN R. WILKERSON

3d Arkansas Infantry, Robertson's Brigade
As part of Robertson's Texas Brigade, the 3d Arkansas advanced past Devil's Den and swung northward, into the rock-strewn 40-acre tract called Rose Woods. Shortly before sundown, Private Wilkerson was severely wounded by a bullet that shattered his left leg below the knee. Captured by the Federals, he was exchanged in February 1864 and returned home, permanently disabled.

As soon as we were seen by the "Yankees" they began to shell us. We double-quicked around and formed in line of battle on a long ridge facing Cemetery Heights and Little Round Top. Lay down to await orders the enemy soon got range of us. It looked like they could hit our line every time. . . . Longstreet . . . led us down the hill over two stone fences, where we met the "Yanks" in a wheat field, then in a skirt of timber at the foot of Little Round Top where there was a great many large rocks, then back in the wheat field. By evening our ranks were getting thin. It was fight all the time. Each side wanted the protection of those rocks, one in particular, that was a very large forked rock about four or five feet high.

I saw smoke coming from behind that one so I made around for it and to the right with my gun ready and cried "Hands up," when they dropped their guns and came out from behind the rock, six of them. They said young man where is your crowd and I told them I was, so I showed them the way to the rear and watched them to see that they went.

At another time I made the run for that rock but went on the wrong side, right on to the muzzle of the "Yanks" gun. He could easily put his gun in my face, he stuck the gun out and fired and never touched me, then threw his gun up and begged for me to spare his life. And I told him alright that I was not hurt, and at that instant a comrad came on the other side of the rock and would have shot him had I not kept him from it.

The 3d Arkansas Infantry carried this battle flag into action in the Rose Woods and Devil's Den.

Little Round Top

Three miles south of Gettysburg, the troops of Major General John B. Hood launched the Confederate attack—the brigades of Generals Evander M. Law and Jerome B. Robertson in the first wave, Henry L. Benning and George T. Anderson in the second. The left half of Robertson's line was savaged by the fire of Captain James E. Smith's 4th New York Battery, four guns of which were deployed on the crest above Devil's Den. One shell exploded near General Hood as he rode behind the line of battle; his left arm shattered, Hood was borne to the rear.

Robertson's 1st Texas and 3d Arkansas pushed on across a rocky, triangle-shaped field and into the woods of the Rose Farm to the north. There they were brought to a bloody standstill by the volleys of Brigadier General J. H. Hobart Ward's Federal brigade.

The hulking, hard-drinking General Ward anchored the left of the Third Corps line, and he was not about to yield his ground without a fight. As Smith's New York battery continued to rain shrapnel and canister on Robertson's Texans, one of Ward's units, the 124th New York, mounted a counterattack that pushed the Rebel forces back across the triangular field.

The commander of the 124th, Colonel Augustus Van Horne Ellis, stood in the stirrups of his white horse with upraised sword, urging on his men, when a Confederate bullet slammed into his forehead. Benning's Georgia brigade had entered the fray, and with Ellis' death, the battle began to turn in favor of the South. Devil's Den, and the guns of Smith's battery, were overrun by the advancing tide of gray-clad troops.

Hood's rightmost brigade, Evander Law's, extended beyond the Yankee left and was able to push unhampered toward the looming hills known as the Round Tops. Some of Law's regiments swung left, moving up the valley of Plum Run to strike at Devil's Den from the south. Other Confederate units, among them the 15th and 47th Alabama, crested the wooded height of Round Top and advanced toward the rocky crest of Little Round Top to the north.

During a reconnaissance, Meade's chief topographical engineer, Brigadier General Gouverneur Kemble Warren, had been shocked to find Little Round Top bare of Federal troops. If the Rebels gained the summit, their artillery would have a clear field of fire down the entire length of the Union line. Warren and his staff officers began rushing units of the Fifth Corps to the threatened point, and they managed to get Colonel Strong Vincent's brigade in place minutes before the Alabamians began scaling Little Round Top's southern flank.

Vincent's line staved off repeated assaults in a grim battle amid the boulder-strewn woods. Colonel William C. Oates led the 15th Alabama in a charge against the Yankee left but was checked and hurled back by the gritty defenders of the 20th Maine. Inspired by the valor of their colonel—former college professor Joshua Lawrence Chamberlain—the Maine men repulsed the Alabamians at the point of the bayonet. Chamberlain's desperate counterattack broke the Rebel line, scooped up dozens of prisoners, and sent Rebels scurrying for cover.

Meanwhile, Gouverneur Warren had hastened troops of Brigadier General Stephen H. Weed's brigade to the summit of Little Round Top, along with the Parrott guns of Lieutenant Charles E. Hazlett's Battery D, 5th U.S. Artillery. These reinforcements arrived in the very nick of time, just as the 4th and 5th Texas were about to overlap the right of Vincent's brigade. Led by Colonel Patrick H. O'Rorke, a young Irish-born West Pointer, the 140th New York plowed into the Texans and unleashed a deadly fire at point-blank range. O'Rorke, Vincent, Hazlett, and Weed were struck down with mortal wounds, but their decisive actions secured Little Round Top for the Union.

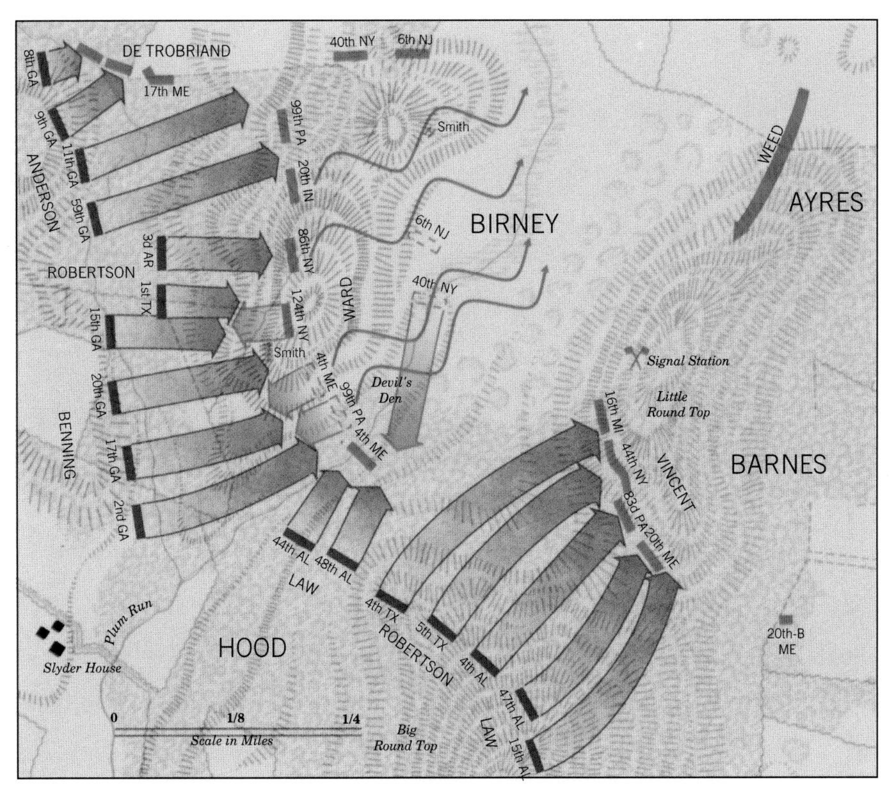

During the late afternoon of July 2, Alabamians and Texans of Law's and Robertson's brigades advanced into Plum Run Valley and crossed the slopes of Big Round Top. At the same time, the Georgia brigades of Benning and G. T. Anderson, along with two of Robertson's regiments, struck the Federal lines above the boulder-strewn hillside known as Devil's Den. In repeated attacks the Confederates forced back Ward's brigade, which held the exposed left flank of Sickles' III Corps. As the fight for Devil's Den raged, the Confederate push on Little Round Top was blocked by the timely arrival of Vincent's brigade, dispatched at the last minute to defend the summit.

LIEUTENANT PORTER FARLEY

140th New York Infantry, Weed's Brigade

A law student before the war, 22-year-old Porter Farley rode on July 2 with his colonel, Patrick O'Rorke, at the head of their 500-man regiment as it hurried up the steep hillside of Little Round Top. The remainder of the brigade, led by Brigadier General Stephen H. Weed, followed. When the 140th New York reached the hilltop, the regiments of Colonel Strong Vincent's brigade were already fighting for their lives, and about to be flanked by the Rebels.

We turned off the road to our left and rushed along the wooded, rocky, eastern slope of Little Round Top, ascending it while at the same time moving toward its southern extremity. It was just here that some of the guns of Hazlett's battery came rapidly up and plunged directly through our ranks, the horses being urged to frantic efforts by the whips of their drivers and the cannoniers assisting at the wheels, so great was the effort necessary to drag the guns and caissons up the ragged hillside.

As we reached the crest a never to be forgotten scene burst upon us. A great basin lay before us full of smoke and fire, and literally swarming with riderless horses and fighting, fleeing and pursuing men. The air was saturated with the sulphurous fumes of battle and was ringing with the shouts and groans of the combatants. The wild cries of charging lines, the rattle of musketry, the booming of artillery and the shrieks of the wounded were the orchestral accompaniments of a scene like very hell itself—as terrific as the warring of Milton's fiends in Pandemonium. . . . But fascinating as was this terrible scene we had no time to spend upon it. Bloody work was ready for us at our very feet.

Round Top, a conical hill several hundred feet in height, lay just to the south of us, and was separated from Little Round Top, on whose crest we were now moving, by a broad ravine leading down into the basin where the great fight was raging. Right up this ravine, which offered the easiest place of ascent, a rebel force, outflanking all our troops in the plain below, was advancing at the very moment when we reached the crest of the hill. Vincent's brigade of the First division of our corps, had come up through the woods on the left and were just getting into position, and the right of their line had opened fire in the hollow on our left when the head of our regiment came over the hill. As soon as we reached the crest bullets came flying in among us. . . . O'Rorke did not hesitate a moment. "Dismount," he said to me, for the ground before us was too rough to ride over. We sprung from our horses and gave them to the sergeant major. O'Rorke shouted, "Down this way, boys," and following him we rushed down the rocky slope with all the same moral effect upon the rebels, who saw us coming, as if our bayonets had been fixed and we ready to charge upon them. Coming abreast of Vincent's brigade, and taking advantage of such shelter as the huge rocks lying about there afforded, the men loaded and fired, and in less time than it takes to write it the onslaught of the rebels was fairly checked, and in a few minutes the woods in front of us were cleared except for the dead and wounded. Such of the

Warned that Little Round Top was a poor position for artillery, battery commander Charles E. Hazlett replied, "Never mind that, the sound of my guns will be encouraging to our troops and disheartening to the others."

rebels as had approached so near as to make escape almost impossible dropped their guns, threw up their hands, and upon a slight slackening of our fire rushed in upon us and gave themselves up as prisoners, while those not so near took advantage of the chance left them and retreated in disorder.

. . . But the sharpshooters were still doing their best against Hazlett's gunners, and it was while standing among them that Weed received a mortal wound. Believing that he was about to die he was in the very act of committing his last messages to his friend Hazlett, who stooped over him, when there came the whiz and thud of another bullet as it sunk into Hazlett's brain, and that brave artilleryman fell a corpse across the body of his dying friend.

"A great basin lay before us full of smoke and fire . . . swarming with riderless horses and fighting, fleeing and pursuing men."

COLONEL WILLIAM C. OATES

15th Alabama Infantry, Law's Brigade

An Abbeville, Alabama, lawyer and publisher, Oates led the 15th Alabama, part of Law's brigade, in a series of desperate attacks that nearly carried them to the summit of Little Round Top. To Oates' left was the 47th Alabama, commanded by 57-year-old Colonel Michael J. Bulger. Both colonels survived the war. Oates would be elected governor of Alabama and serve two terms in the U.S. Congress. In his memoirs he recounted his regiment's withdrawal from Little Round Top. "When the signal was given," he said, "we ran like a herd of wild cattle."

I saw no enemy until within forty or fifty steps of an irregular ledge of rocks—a splendid line of natural breastworks. . . . From behind this ledge, unexpectedly to us, because concealed, they poured into us the most destructive fire I ever saw. Our line halted, but did not break. . . . As men fell their comrades closed the gap, returning the fire most spiritedly. I could see through the smoke men of the Twentieth Maine in front of my right wing running from tree to tree. . . .

When the Fifteenth was driven back, Colonel Bulger was left sitting by a tree, sword in hand, shot through one lung and bleeding profusely. A captain in the Forty-fourth New York approached and demanded his sword. The old Colonel said, "What is your rank?" The reply was, "I am a captain." Bulger said, "Well, I am a lieutenant-colonel, and I will not surrender my sword except to an officer of equal rank." The captain then said, "Surrender your sword, or I will kill you." Colonel Bulger promptly replied, "You may kill and be d—d! I shall never surrender my sword to an officer of lower rank." The captain was so amused at the old Colonel's high notions of military etiquette that he went for his colonel, Rice, to whom the sword was gracefully surrendered.

Stone and log breastworks crown the crest of Little Round Top in this July 7, 1863, photograph. After the Confederate attacks ceased, Federal troops constructed the defenses as protection from sharpshooters.

"A handful of men can't drive those Yankees from that place, can't you get Major Coleman to call the boys off before all are killed?"

LIEUTENANT ROBERT T. COLES

4th Alabama Infantry, Law's Brigade

Among the Alabamians who pushed through the Slaughter Pen and clawed their way up the rugged slope of Little Round Top was Lieutenant Robert Coles. He survived the assault and lived to surrender at Appomattox in 1865.

During our third and last ineffectual effort to dislodge the enemy from his stronghold, there emerged from our scattered ranks a youth whom I well knew in our boyhood days, Rufus Franks. He walked erect and rapidly to the rear, still grasping his rifle, with no apparent evidence whatever of being the least wounded. A man hard hit invariably dropped his gun. As he brushed past me he remarked in a trembling voice, his face deathly pale, "Adjutant, a handful of men can't drive those Yankees from that place, can't you get Major Coleman to call the boys off before all are killed?" I knew he was a good soldier, yet his actions forced me to imagine "there goes a soldier whose heart is gone." I called in a rather pleading tone to him to come back. Without looking back or stopping and still with his gun at a trail, he replied, "I am wounded." Thinking he was only slightly wounded, I dismissed the incident, and in the confusion of battle would henceforth have been forgotten, had I not learned, as we lay in our rude "breastwork of rock" the next morning that he was shot in the bowels and died soon after he was taken to the hospital.

. . . John Young of I Company, who before entering the army was an editor, while scouting, had his rifle lying on a large rock with his right hand resting on the barrel. As he stood partially concealed behind the boulder a Union sharpshooter fired and knocked off his middle finger. He came down to the regiment and holding up his hand, manipulating his thumb and forefinger, remarked: "Well, boys, there is one consolation about this loss; I can, when this cruel war is over, set type as well as ever."

"I'm as dead a man as Julius Caesar."

LIEUTENANT PORTER FARLEY

140th New York Infantry, Weed's Brigade

Lieutenant Farley recalled the preparations for death made by his mortally wounded brigade commander, Brigadier General Stephen H. Weed.

The general was carried at once behind the shelter of a rock, and was soon taken in an ambulance to the farmhouse of Louis A. Bushman, which, as well as his barns and outhouses, had been taken possession of and was being used as our division hospital. Weed suffered intensely, but for some time after he was hurt was entirely conscious and able to communicate the messages which he had begun to give to Hazlett. This he did to Lieutenant William H. Crennell, quartermaster of our regiment. . . . Among other things, Weed asked that when he was dead the ring which he wore might be taken from his finger, and with the pocketbook containing his private letters, be carried to the young lady to whom he was engaged to be married. . . .

Weed's bravery even unto death, and his bluff, outspoken manner, were well exemplified by the clearness with which he made his dying requests, well knowing they were such, and by the emphasis with which he spoke, particularly in a reply . . . made to Crennell when he said to him, "General, I hope you are not so very badly hurt." Said Weed, "I'm as dead a man as Julius Caesar."

Brigadier General Stephen H. Weed was mortally wounded by a bullet that passed through his arm and into his chest. Shortly before, Weed had remarked to a friend, "I would rather die on this spot than see those rascals gain one inch of ground."

This massive target rifle, fitted with a telescopic sight, was found in Devil's Den after the battle.

TILLIE PIERCE

Resident of Gettysburg

Venturing from her refuge, Tillie Pierce volunteered to nurse the wounded who overflowed the Weikert farm near the Round Tops. There she encountered the mortally wounded General Weed. Tillie returned to her house in town on July 7, walking across a once familiar countryside now transformed into "a strange and blighted land."

"I wanted to do something for the poor soldiers if I only knew what."

One soldier, sitting near the doorway that led into a little room in the southeast corner of the basement, beckoned me to him. He was holding a lighted candle in his hand; and was watching over a wounded soldier who was lying upon the floor. He asked me if I would get him a piece of bread saying he was very hungry. I said certainly, ran away and soon returned. I gave him the bread and he seemed very thankful. He then asked me if I would hold the light and stay with the wounded man until he came back. I said I would gladly do so, and that I wanted to do something for the poor soldiers if I only knew what.

I then took the candle and sat down beside the wounded man. I talked to him and asked if he was injured badly. He answered: "Yes, pretty badly." I then asked him if he suffered much, to which he replied: "Yes, I do now, but I hope in the morning I will be better."

I told him if there was anything I could do for him I would be so glad to do it, if he would only tell me what. The poor man looked so earnestly into my face, saying: "Will you promise to come back in the morning to see me." I replied: "Yes, indeed." And he seemed so satisfied, and faintly smiled.

The man who had been watching him now returned, and thanked me for my kindness. I gave him the light and arose to leave. The poor wounded soldier's eyes followed me, and the last words he said to me were: "Now don't forget your promise." I replied: "No indeed," and expressing the hope that he would be better in the morning, bade him good night.

The sun was high in the heavens when I awoke the next day. . . . I hastened down to the little basement room and as I entered the soldier lay there dead. . . . As I stood gazing in sadness at the prostrate form, the attendant looked up to me and asked, "Do you know who this is?" I replied: "No, sir." He said: "This is the body of General Weed, a New York man."

SERGEANT VALERIUS C. GILES

4th Texas Infantry, Robertson's Brigade

Giles and his fellow Texans were ordered to attack across the slopes of Big Round Top near the Devil's Den and drive the Federals from their positions on nearby Little Round Top. Failing to capture the Federal position, Giles and his comrades were forced to take shelter among the boulders on the lower slopes of Big Round Top.

The side of the mountain was heavily timbered and covered with great boulders that had tumbled from the cliffs above years before. These afforded great protection to the men. Every tree, rock and stump that gave any protection from the rain of Minié balls that were poured down upon us from the crest above us, was soon appropriated. John Griffith and myself pre-empted a moss-covered old boulder about the size of a 500-pound cotton bale. By this time order and discipline were gone. Every fellow was his own general. Private soldiers gave commands as loud as the officers. Nobody paid any attention to either. To add to this confusion, our artillery on the hill to our rear was cutting its fuse too short. Their shells were bursting behind us, in the treetops, over our heads, and all around us.

Nothing demoralizes troops quicker than to be fired into by their friends. I saw it occur twice during the war. The first time we ran, but at Gettysburg we couldn't. This mistake was soon corrected and the shells burst high on the mountain or went over it.

Major Rogers, then in command of the Fifth Texas Regiment, mounted an old log near my boulder and began a Fourth of July speech. He was a little ahead of time, for that was about six thirty on the evening of July 2d. Of course nobody was paying any attention to the oration as he appealed to the men to "stand fast." He and Captain Cousins of the Fourth Alabama were the only two men I saw standing. The balance of us had settled down behind rocks, logs, and trees. While the speech was going on, John Haggerty, one of Hood's couriers, then acting for General Law, dashed up the side of the mountain, saluted the Major and said: "General Law presents his compliments, and says hold this place at all hazards." The Major checked up, glared down at Haggerty from his perch, and shouted: "Compliments, hell! Who wants any compliments in such a damned place as this? Go back and ask General Law if he expects me to hold the world in check with the Fifth Texas Regiment? . . .

From behind my boulder I saw a ragged line of battle strung out along the side of Cemetery Ridge and in front of Little Round Top. Night began settling around us, but the carnage went on. There seemed to be a viciousness in the very air we breathed. Things had gone wrong all the day, and now pandemonium came with the darkness. Alexander Dumas says the devil gets in a man seven times a day, and if the average is not over seven times, he is almost a saint.

At Gettysburg that night, it was about seven devils to each man. Officers were cross to the men, and the men were equally cross to the officers. It was the same way with our enemies. We could hear the Yankee officer on the crest of the ridge in front of us cursing the men by platoons, and the men telling him to go to a country not very far away from us just at that time. . . .

The advance lines of the two armies in many places were not more than fifty yards apart. Everything was on the shoot. No favors asked, and none offered. My gun was so dirty that the ramrod hung in the barrel, and I could neither get it down nor out. I slammed the rod against a rock a few times, and drove home ramrod, cartridge and all, laid the gun on a boulder, elevated the muzzle, ducked my head, holloaed "Look out!" and pulled the trigger. She roared like a young cannon and flew over my boulder, the barrel striking John Griffith a smart whack on the left ear. John roared too, and abused me like a pickpocket for my carelessness. It was no trouble to get another gun there. The mountain side was covered with them. . . .

Our spiritual advisers, chaplains of regiments, were in the rear, caring for the wounded and dying soldiers. With seven devils to each man, it was no place for a preacher, anyhow. A little red paint and a few eagle feathers were all that was necessary to make that crowd on both sides into the most veritable savages on earth. White-winged peace didn't roost at Little Round Top that night! There was not a man there that cared a snap for the golden rule, or that could have remembered one line of the Lord's Prayer. Both sides were whipped, and all were furious about it.

Dead Confederates sprawl among the rocks of the Slaughter Pen, the rocky, open area between Devil's Den and Little Round Top. Most were killed during attempts to storm Little Round Top.

The Peach Orchard and Wheat Field

As the fighting raged in the triangular field and Confederate troops began their advance on Little Round Top, the last of John B. Hood's brigades entered the fray. Brigadier General G. T. Anderson, a veteran of the Mexican War whose combative nature had earned him the nickname "Tige," led four Georgia regiments through a wood lot on the Rose Farm and toward a field of ripening wheat. Anderson's men were met with a crashing volley and screaming artillery shells that splintered the trees overhead. Within minutes Anderson's attack had fragmented along a stone wall at the southern edge of the Wheat Field.

Firing from the cover of the stone wall, the 17th Maine decimated G. T. Anderson's Georgians. Private John Haley noted that "we could see them tumbling around right lively." Haley's unit was part of the brigade commanded by Brigadier General Regis de Trobriand, a French aristocrat turned New York newspaper editor. When ammunition began to give out, de Trobriand exhorted his men to "hold them with the bayonet," and the line held.

But trouble was brewing on de Trobriand's right, where units of the Fifth Corps had been hastily positioned on a wooded knoll west of the Wheat Field. Lafayette McLaws' division had joined the great en echelon advance, and Brigadier General Joseph B. Kershaw's South Carolina brigade—one of the finest units in Lee's army—was sweeping across the Emmitsburg road. Federal artillery tore bloody gaps in Kershaw's line, but the South Carolinians pressed forward, linked up with Anderson's Georgians, and shoved the Federal defenders from the wooded knoll.

The Wheat Field changed hands six times during the battle that began in the late afternoon of July 2. Longstreet's attacking Confederate corps faced elements of three Federal corps.

Soon hundreds of blue-clad soldiers were falling back through the trampled wheat, the Rebels in hot pursuit. But victory was not to come so easily; Brigadier General John C. Caldwell's division of the Second Corps had moved up at Hancock's order to plug the widening gap. Two of Caldwell's four brigade commanders were fatally wounded, but the veteran troops—which included the famous Irish Brigade—forged ahead, and the Rebels gave way before them.

The corpse-strewn Wheat Field would

remain only briefly in Union hands, however. McLaws hurled two more of his brigades into what the field survivors would remember as a "whirlpool of death," and again the Yankees fell back. Caldwell appealed for help from the Fifth Corps, but the handful of units that came to his aid were overwhelmed in savage hand-to-hand combat. When Colonel Harrison Jeffords of the 4th Michigan saw a South Carolinian seize the regimental colors, he leaped at the Rebel with drawn sword but was run through the body by a bayonet. In the frenzied melee that followed, the Michiganders recovered their flag and hauled the bloodied banner and their dying commander to safety, Jeffords moaning, "Mother, mother, mother!"

At 6:30 p.m. McLaws launched his final blow against the Union Third Corps. Four regiments from Mississippi —1,600 strong—headed directly for the Peach Orchard salient. These soldiers were commanded by Brigadier General William A. Barksdale, a stocky former congressman noted for his fiery demeanor.

As General Barksdale rode among his men, waving his hat and yelling encouragement, the Mississippians stormed past the Sherfy farmhouse and barn, crossed the Emmitsburg road, and crashed through the Yankee line. The Federal infantry were hurled back through the bullet-splintered peach trees, and Yankee artillerymen frantically limbered up their guns and joined the chaotic withdrawal.

After clearing the Peach Orchard, some of Barksdale's units charged to the east in pursuit of Union batteries pulling back toward Cemetery Ridge. Others of Barksdale's men swung north, striking the left flank of Brigadier General Andrew A. Humphreys'

The attack by General Lafayette McLaws' division broke the apex of the salient held by the Federal III Corps, forcing the withdrawal of the Federal line.

division. At the same time Humphreys' front—along the Emmitsburg road—was being assailed by R. H. Anderson's division, the final hammer blow of the en echelon assault. Humphreys' line crumbled; his embattled units waged a fighting retreat to the north and east.

General Sickles, whose Third Corps had paid a heavy price for his ill-considered redeployment, was himself a casualty of the escalating debacle. A glancing blow from a Confederate round shot ripped across Sickles' right leg, nearly severing the limb at the knee. Demonstrating characteristic aplomb, the general calmly puffed on a cigar as he was carried to the rear.

SERGEANT JACOB B. FUNK

62d Pennsylvania Infantry, Sweitzer's Brigade

Color Sergeant Jacob Funk bore his regiment's state flag onto a rocky hill northeast of the Wheat Field. Then, outflanked to the south and under severe pressure from the Rebels to their front, the Pennsylvanians were forced to withdraw, suffering more than 40 percent casualties. Although wounded, Funk survived the action. He was discharged in December 1863 and reenlisted as a veteran volunteer. On May 24, 1864, at the Battle of Laurel Hill, Virginia, he was mortally wounded.

Just then I came up to where some Prisoners were that had been taken a short time before. The bullets were falling like hail & the Guard that had the Prisoners ran and left the Prisoners go when they immediately picked up Guns and began to shoot our men. I saw [one] pick up a Gun and looking round he spied me with the Colors of the Old Keystone state immediately he leveled his Gun and ordered me to surrender my Colors or he would shoot me but I thought that was rather a saucy demand & I could not see the point. . . . I took Leg Bail for security and increased the distance between him and me very fast I had to jump a stone fence and came very near loosing my ballance but I managed to get over. I then went straight ahead when directly I heard the report of a Gun just behind me. I just concluded that was for me, and sure enough the Ball struck my arm four or five inches from the shoulder passing under the Bone and coming out in the chest near the arm pit. I called out for some one to take the Colers one of the men ran out & took them & I then made tracks to get out of farther danger. . . . after leaving the Battle field I went about 2 miles and then got my wound dressed.

Supported by sheltering Federal infantry, Captain George B. Winslow's Battery D, 1st New York Light Artillery, trades fire with Kershaw's advancing South Carolina brigade. When the Confederates closed in, Winslow withdrew his guns despite heavy losses of men and horses, proudly reporting, "all of my pieces could not have been brought off had my men been less brave."

"We were in the open, without a thing better than a wheat straw to catch a Minnie bullet. . . . Of course, our men began to tumble."

LIEUTENANT CHARLES A. FULLER

61st New York Infantry, Cross' Brigade

In 1861 Fuller was living in Cleveland, Ohio, studying law in a private firm. When news of Fort Sumter reached him he determined to enlist and set out for his home in Sherburne, New York, walking the last 50 miles when his transportation proved unreliable. At Gettysburg, Fuller's regiment stepped off into the Wheat Field in the face of Anderson's attacking Confederates. The wounds Fuller suffered in the attack cost him a leg and the use of his left arm.

We were in this wheat field and the grain stood almost breast high. The Rebs had their slight protection, but we were in the open, without a thing better than a wheat straw to catch a Minnie bullet that weighed an ounce. Of course, our men began to tumble. They lay where they fell, or, if able, started for the rear. Near to me I saw a man named Daily go down, shot through the neck. I made a movement to get his gun, but at that moment I was struck in the shoulder. It did not hurt and the blow simply caused me to step back. I found that I could not work my arm, but supposed that hurt was a flesh wound that had temporarily paralyzed it, and that it was not serious enough to justify my leaving the fighting line. So, I remained and did what I could in directing the firing. Sometime after this, I felt a blow on the left leg, and it gave way, so that I knew the bone was broken. This stroke did not hurt, and I did not fall, but turned around and made a number of hops to the rear, when my foot caught in the tangled grain and I went down full length. While lying here entirely helpless, and hearing those vicious bullets singing over my head, I suffered from fear. . . .

In a short time I heard a line of battle advancing from the rear. As the men came in sight I sang out, "Don't step on me, boys!" Those in range of me stepped over and rushed forward and fought the enemy in advance of the line we occupied. It was not many minutes after these troops passed me that the rattle of musketry was again heard from that wheat field. It was kept up for a good while, and then it died down. . . .

After a while I was aware that a skirmish line was coming from the front, and soon discovered that the skirmishers were not clothed in blue. The officer in command was mounted and rode by within a few feet of me. . . . This fighting was not severe and a short time after these gentlemen in gray moved back in the same manner they had advanced, greatly to my relief. I did not fancy remaining their guest for any length of time.

As the Rebs went back, a nice looking young fellow, small of stature, with bright black eyes, whose face was smutted up with powder and smoke, came along where I lay. My sword was on the ground beside me. He picked it up, and said, "Give me that scabbard!" I said "Johnny, you will have to excuse me, as my arm is broken and I can't unbuckle my belt." He made no comment, but went off with my sword.

Private James H. Williford of the 10th Georgia Infantry, part of General Paul J. Semmes' brigade, lost his hat fighting in the Peach Orchard. Williford survived the battle, but his hat was recovered as a trophy by a Federal officer.

Colonel Paul J. Revere (left) of the 20th Massachusetts, grandson of the Revolutionary War patriot, was mortally wounded during the second day's fighting. Lieutenant Colonel Charles Pierson inherited Revere's field glasses, which were later smashed by the shell fragment that wounded Pierson at Spotsylvania Court House.

"Their Chaplain, or Priest, performed some religious ceremony of a few minutes duration, while the men stood, undisturbed by bursting shells. . . ."

Absolution on Wheat Field 2d July 1863

CORPORAL HENRY MEYER

148th Pennsylvania Infantry, Cross' Brigade

Meyer watched the men of Colonel Patrick Kelly's famed Irish Brigade prepare for action before they moved, along with Meyer and the Pennsylvanians, toward the Wheat Field to stem the Confederate breakthrough. Corporal Meyer would survive Gettysburg to be discharged for poor health in 1864.

We had read in the papers of McClellan's soldiers, in the series of battles on the Peninsula, lying down along side of batteries and going to sleep while the roar of battle went on; this seemed incredible, but such a possibility was verified that day at Gettysburg. While lying in the hot sun in line of battle, some of the boys slept, though shells and solid shot came crashing into our midst.

. . . The Irish Brigade, which belonged to the Division, was first assembled in solid mass and their Chaplain, or Priest, performed some religious ceremony of a few minutes duration, while the men stood, undisturbed by bursting shells, with bowed heads in reverent silence. Then the whole Division was marched off at a "double quick" across fields and through patches of woods in the direction of the conflict. . . . We were the first troops to cross the field, and the yellow grain was still standing. I noticed how the ears of wheat flew in the air all over the field as they were cut off by the enemy's bullets. . . .

Men in battle will act very differently; some become greatly excited, others remain perfectly cool. One of the boys in my rear was sitting flat on the ground and discharging his piece in the air at an angle of forty-five degrees, as fast as he could load. "Why do you shoot in the air?" I asked. "To scare 'em," he replied.

He was a pious young man, and the true reason why he did not shoot at the enemy direct, was because of his conscientious scruples on the subject. What struck me as being peculiar was that some of the boys swore energetically, who never before were heard to utter an oath.

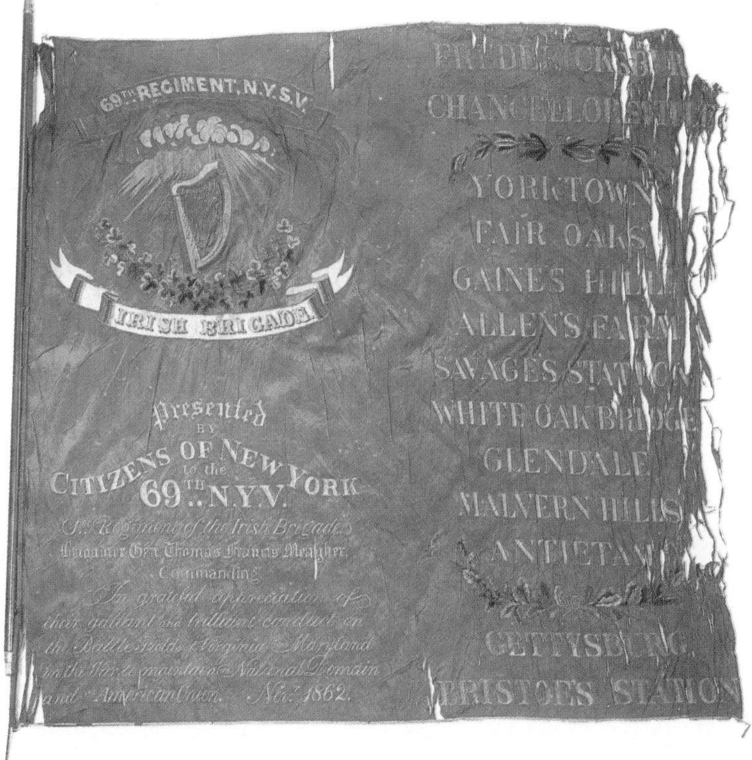

The once emerald green regimental flag of the 69th New York, the premier regiment of the Irish Brigade, was carried into action across the Wheat Field where the Irishmen drove back part of Kershaw's line.

Brigade chaplain Father William Corby grants a general absolution to the kneeling men of New York's Irish Brigade in this sketch by soldier-artist Charles Reed. Corby added a stern injunction to his blessing: "The Catholic Church," he stated, "refuses Christian burial to the soldier who turns his back upon the foe."

MAJOR GEORGE B. GERALD

18th Mississippi Infantry, Barksdale's Brigade

When William Barksdale's Mississippi brigade charged into the Peach Orchard, Major Gerald led a party of men to clear Federal marksmen from the barn of the nearby Sherfy farm. Gerald survived a wound at Cedar Creek in 1864 and settled in Waco, Texas, five years later. There he held the office of county judge and postmaster, and edited a local newspaper. In 1897 he killed the editor of a rival newspaper and his brother in a gunfight in Waco. He died in 1914 and his cremated remains were scattered in the Gulf of Mexico.

The order was given to "strip for the fight." The men carried their scanty change of clothing wrapped in their blankets and thrown over their shoulders; each regiment piled these in a heap and each left a man with the baggage. The field officers dismounted from their horses, the reason for this being that an order had been issued some time before that no officer below the rank of brigadier or acting brigadier-general should ride into battle, because of the fact that the government had a great deal of difficulty in replacing the horses killed. I gave my horse and watch as well as some other belongings to my servant. After these orders had been complied with the order was given "Dress to the colors and forward to the foe!"

After moving through the woods a short distance, we came to a fence

around a field of grain; the battle was progressing. Before us lay open fields dotted with houses and right in our front were some farm houses with a grove of trees to the left, and the enemy drawn up in a double line of battle some five or six hundred yards distance and supported by artillery. We steadily advanced, driving the enemy before us until we reached the houses with the trees on the left, the trees proved to be a peach orchard. On the end of the orchard was a barn in which a part of the enemy had taken refuge. . . . I with most of the regiment was directly in front of the barn. . . . I called to the men that the barn must be captured and to follow me and I would open the door. They followed me with a rush and I forced the door open, and within less than two minutes we had killed, wounded or captured every man in the barn. The barn was filled with smoke so dense that it was very nearly impossible to distinguish a man's body in it, such a continuous fire had the enemy within kept up. We left the barn and the brigade moved through the orchard towards the heights, still driving the enemy before them. General Barksdale encouraged the men by shouting, "Forward men, forward," which was the only command that I ever heard him give after a battle commenced. By this time we were under the heavy fire of two lines of battle and their artillery and our losses had been very heavy, and recognizing the impossibility of breaking these fresh lines of battle, we fell back to the orchard, where we spent the night.

Captain James Thompson's Pennsylvania and Captain Nelson Ames' New York batteries, supported by a regiment of prone infantrymen, bombard oncoming Confederates from their post near the Peach Orchard. The position anchored a salient in the III Corps lines that was broken by Confederate general Barksdale's assault. Artist Edwin Forbes keyed the building on the left as number three—a canning factory.

CAPTAIN EDWARD R. BOWEN

114th Pennsylvania Infantry, Graham's Brigade

Near the Sherfy farm buildings, the exotically garbed soldiers of the 114th Pennsylvania, "Collis' Zouaves," met Barksdale's yelling Mississippians head on. But the Zouaves gave way with the rest of the Federal line and the Peach Orchard salient fell to the Confederates. Bowen rose to the rank of major before being mustered out of the service in 1865.

Capt. Fix afterwards stated that when we left the Emmittsburg Road, which was covered with our dead and wounded, and where he was laying, a battery of the enemy came thundering along it, and that when the officer commanding it saw our dead and wounded on the road, he halted his battery to avoid running over them and his men carefully lifted the dead to one side and carried the wounded into the cellar of a house, supplied them with water, and said they would return and take care of them when they had caught the rest of us. This they had no opportunity to do, for they themselves were driven back and the house containing our wounded remained within our lines and our men received the care and attention of our own surgeons.

LIEUTENANT FRANCIS E. MORAN

73d New York Infantry, Brewster's Brigade

Another Zouave regiment, the 73d New York, or Second Fire Zouaves, also traded fire with Barksdale's Confederates. The 73d was preparing to fall back when a Pennsylvania artillery officer implored Lieutenant Moran to save his cannon from imminent capture.

I called to the men of my company and those nearest me to follow the mounted officer and drag away the imperiled guns. We had scarcely started when this officer was shot and some of the men helped him from his horse. A minute later a shell burst near this group, a fragment wounded me in the ankle, and what felt like burning powder entered my left eye. . . . A comrade seeing me helpless assisted me a little, but being wounded badly in the leg himself, we, with several others, were left behind as our line now in considerable disorder retired across the Emmettsburg road. . . .

At last the enemy came hot and hard upon us. As the center of the Thirteenth Mississippi passed over me, the men firing and shrieking like Indians, a volley from our side tore through the ranks and scores of the Confederates fell. I had never in my experience seen such havoc from a single volley, and its effect was instantly manifested; the line of battle came to a halt without command, and it took the utmost exertions of the officers to prevent a panic.

As I was assisted to the rear the field from the Emmettsburg road to the woods south of Sherfy's was strewn with killed and wounded Confederates, mixed with a number of our own men. Many of the wounded, friend and foe, had sought refuge in Sherfy's barn, which was riddled with shot and shell like a sieve from its base to the roof. . . . As my guards assisted me past the barn I could hear the groans of the poor fellows inside, many of whom were terribly wounded. . . .

Just after passing the barn I met General Longstreet riding, unattended, to the front. A shell from our side struck a pile of rails between us and sent them whirling through the air like so many straws. The General seeing me wounded, politely bowed and passed on without remark. He was looking attentively toward Round Top.

CAPTAIN JOHN BIGELOW

9th Massachusetts Light Artillery, Artillery Reserve

When the Federal infantry was driven from their positions near the Peach Orchard, the last Yankee guns to withdraw were the six bronze Napoleons of Captain John Bigelow's battery. With most of their horses down, Bigelow's gunners were forced to conduct a harrowing withdrawal toward the Trostle farmhouse yard. Bigelow later recalled that his guns fired 92 rounds of canister before being overrun.

Colonel McGilvery rode up, at this time, told me that . . . "I was alone on the field, without supports of any kind; limber up and get out." I replied that, "if I attempted to do so, the sharpshooters, on my left front, would shoot us all down." I must "retire by prolonge and firing," in order "to keep them off." He assented and rode away. . . .

Glancing towards the Peach Orchard on my right, I saw that the Confederates (Barksdale's Brigade) had come through and were forming a line 200 yards distant, extending back, parallel with the Emmetsburg Road, as far as I could see, and I must therefore move almost parallel with and in front of their line, in order to reach the exit of the stone wall at Trostle's house 400 yards away. No friendly supports of any kind, were in sight; but Johnnie Rebs in great numbers. Bullets were coming into our midst from many directions and a Confederate battery added to our difficulties. Still, prolonges were fixed and we withdrew—the left section keeping Kershaw's skirmishers back with canister, and the other two sections bowling solid shot towards Barksdale's men. We moved slowly, the recoil of the guns retiring them, while the prolonges enabled us to keep the alignment; but the loss in men and horses was severe. When we reached the angle of the stone wall at Trostle's house, a swell of ground, 50 yards on our right front, covered us from Barksdale's approaching line and we began to limber up, hoping to get out and back to our lines before they closed in on us;

With many of his battery's horses killed or disabled, Captain Charles A. Phillips and the men of his 5th Massachusetts Battery tow a gun through the Trostle farmyard. Behind them on the Trostle farm lane, the 9th Massachusetts Battery covered their retreat, firing canister to keep Kershaw's sharpshooters at bay while pounding Barksdale's line with solid shot.

Dead artillery horses litter the Trostle house yard, shot down when Captain John Bigelow's 9th Massachusetts Battery was overrun by the charging 21st Mississippi.

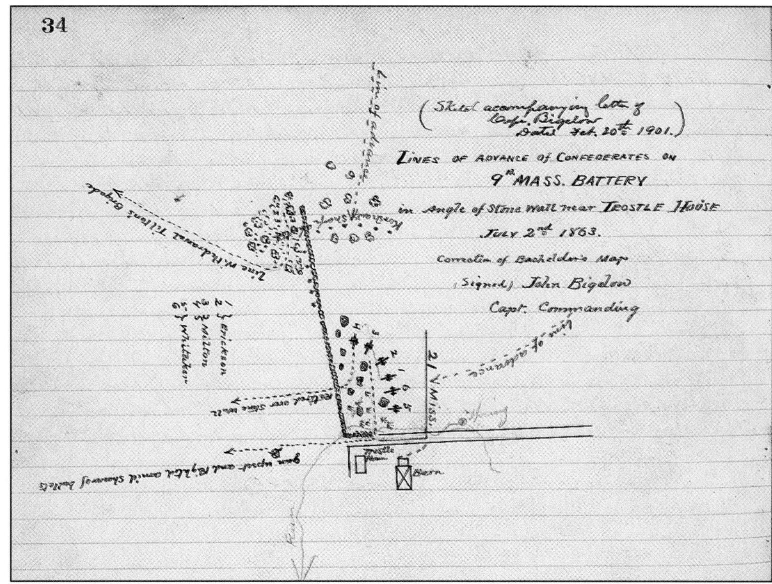

Captain John Bigelow sketched this map after the war to record the position of his guns in the Trostle farmyard. The chart, drawn with south at the top, marks the advance of the Confederate units that captured four of Bigelow's guns.

but McGilvery, again rode up, told me that back of me for nearly 1,500 yards, between Round Top and the left of the 2nd Corps, the lines were open; there were no reserves, and said, I must hold my position at all hazards. . . . orders were given to unlimber, take the ammunition from the chests, place it near the guns for rapid firing and load the guns to the muzzle. They were hardly executed before the enemy appeared breast high above the swell of ground 50 yards in front . . . and firing, on both sides, began. . . .

Just before they closed in, the left section, Lieut. Milton, could not be used, owing to some stone boulders, and was ordered to the rear. One piece went through the gateway of the stone wall, was upset, righted amid a shower of bullets and, Lieut. Milton assisting, was dragged to the rear, the other piece was driven directly over the stone wall. . . .

I rode to the stone wall, hoping to stop some of Milton's cannoneers and have them make a better opening, through which I might rush one or more of the remaining four guns, which were still firing. I sat on my horse calling the men, when my bugler, on my right, drew his horse back on his haunches, as he saw six sharpshooters on our left taking

deliberate aim at us. I stopped two, and my horse two more of their bullets. My orderly was near by, and, dismounting he raised me from the ground.

I then saw the Confederates swarming in on our right flank, some standing on the limber chests and firing at the gunners, who were still serving their pieces; the horses were all down; overhead the air was alive with missiles from batteries, which the enemy had now placed on the Emmetsburg Road. . . . I then gave orders for the small remnant of the four gun detachments to fall back.

Bleeding profusely from a lung wound, Lieutenant Christopher Erickson of Bigelow's battery shouts directions to one of his gun crews. "The enemy crowded to the very muzzles of Lieutenant Erickson's and Whitaker's sections," recalled Captain Bigelow, "but were blown away by the canister." Moments later Erickson fell dead from a head wound.

LIEUTENANT ADOLFO CAVADA

Staff, Brigadier General Andrew A. Humphreys

Lieutenant Cavada watched the collapse of the Federal salient at the Peach Orchard. Of particular interest to him was the 114th Pennsylvania, a Zouave regiment commanded by his elder brother, Frederic. When the salient gave way, Frederic was captured by the Confederates. Both brothers survived the war and later gave their lives in the cause of Cuban independence. Disease claimed Adolfo, and Frederic was executed by Spanish authorities.

The enemy's fire slackened then came the rebel cheer sounding like a continuous yelp, nearer and nearer it came. The "red legs" (zouaves) jumped to their feet, volley upon volley rained into them and the fire was bravely returned, but the enemy's column were upon them before they could fall back. All was confusion on that side. Our batteries kept up a rapid fire. . . .

The breeze blowing from the southward carried the heavy sulfurous smoke in clouds along the ground at times concealing everything from my view. Our skirmishers now began a lively popping, the first drops of the thundershower that was to break upon us. An aide from Genl. Birney rode up to Genl. Humphreys with the report that heavy masses of the enemy were gathering in our front and to prepare for an attack. . . .

A copious shower of shell and canister from the enemy was followed up by a diabolical cheer and yell and "here they come" rang along our line. At this moment my horse was shot in the leg and pranced around frantically. Our batteries opened, our troops rose to their feet, the crash of artillery and the tearing rattle of our musketry was staggering and added to the noise on our side. The advancing roar and cheer of the enemy's masses, coming on like devils incarnate. But our fire had not checked them and our line showed signs of breaking. The battery enfilading us redoubled its fire, portions of Birney's command were moving to the rear broken and disordered. Our left regiments took the contagion and fled, leaving a wide gap through which the enemy poured in upon us. In vain did staff officers draw their swords to check the flying soldiers and endeavor to inspire them with confidence.

For a moment the rout was complete. Finding myself precisely at the point where the enemy pierced us, I endeavored to make towards our right Brigade which by Genl. Humphreys orders had changed front in order to meet the enemy's charge, but my horse could scarcely stand and moved so slowly that I was enveloped by our retreating soldiers born down the hill. On reaching the hollow I tried together with several other officers, to stop our men, and partially succeeded. Three rebel battle flags at the head of the column were now within a few yards of me. Squads of our men dropping behind rocks and fallen trees kept up a spirited fire and just as I saw the head of the column of rebels hesitate . . . my poor Brickbat received his death wound and fell, holding me down to the ground by the weight of his body on my leg. After struggling a few seconds I disengaged myself from my horse and taking my brandy flask and pistol off the saddle stumbled on as fast as my weary legs could carry me.

Sergeant Henry H. Stone of the 11th Massachusetts Infantry, of Carr's brigade, was wounded in the left arm in the fighting along the Emmitsburg road. He declined to send his "lucky jacket" home as a memento of Gettysburg. Wearing the same garment, Stone survived a wound at Spotsylvania and imprisonment in Andersonville.

Cemetery Ridge and Cemetery Hill

As devastating as Longstreet's assault had been to the Federal Third Corps, the Confederates, too, had suffered heavy losses. Moreover, many Confederate units had become hopelessly intermingled as they pressed their advance eastward, through the woods that flanked Plum Run. Brigades had fragmented and lost all cohesion. With little more than an hour of daylight remaining, Lee's Army of Northern Virginia had yet to gain the crucial heart of the Yankee position—Cemetery Ridge.

Although Meade had provided little in the way of supervision, most of his subordinates had ably risen to the challenge. Little Round Top had been secured, and the charge of the Fifth Corps' Pennsylvania Reserve division had shored up the Union's southern flank. The lead elements of John Sedgwick's hard-marching Sixth Corps were beginning to arrive, bolstering the massed artillery that thundered away on the lower reaches of Cemetery Ridge. As the heaviest combat shifted northward to the Union center, where R. H. Anderson's division was punching out with the left arm of the Rebels' en echelon assault, Meade gave Hancock command of Third Corps' survivors in addition to his own Second Corps.

Flushed with the excitement of battle, General Hancock galloped along his embattled line, personally throwing units into the vortex of combat wherever crisis beckoned. Passing one small contingent that lay in reserve, Hancock shouted, "What regiment is this?"—"The First Minnesota," Colonel William Colvill replied. Pointing at the red battle flags that marked the oncoming line of a Confederate brigade, Hancock barked out the order, "Advance, Colonel, and take those colors!"

The Minnesotans charged forward with leveled bayonets and hurled the vanguard of Brigadier General Cadmus M. Wilcox's Alabama brigade back across the shallow swale of Plum Run. The attack cost the 1st Minnesota 215 of their 262 men, but Wilcox's advance was checked.

Farther along the line of Cemetery Ridge, Hancock ordered a similar counterattack to be carried out by Colonel George L. Willard's brigade. This was the first great bloodletting for Willard's men; they had been captured en masse at Harpers Ferry soon after their enlistment and had only recently been exchanged. The men of Willard's brigade had much to prove to their comrades in the Union Second Corps, and to themselves.

Colonel Willard led his cheering troops against the remnants of Barksdale's Mississippi brigade and drove the Rebels across Plum Run and into the open fields beyond. There Willard's advance foundered in the face of artillery salvoes that belched forth from massed batteries in the Peach Orchard; one shell tore off half of Willard's head, and the Yankees recoiled. But Barksdale had been toppled from his horse with fatal wounds to his chest and leg, and his courageous troops could do no more.

In a final effort to pierce the Federal defenses of Cemetery Ridge, R. H. Anderson's leftmost brigades pushed toward a stone wall that lay several hundred yards east of the Emmitsburg road. Brigadier General Ambrose R. Wright's Georgians gained a momentary foothold at the wall, near a little copse of trees, but they got no support, and Wright was forced to withdraw. The Confederate juggernaut had run out of steam.

A day of decidedly mixed results for Confederate hopes concluded with a series of attacks on the northern end of the Union line. Because of mixed signals, misunderstanding, and Lee's uncertainty regarding Federal strength in the Culp's Hill sector, Richard Ewell's Second Corps had failed to provide the diversionary assault planned to coincide with Longstreet's great offensive. When Ewell finally did launch an attack on Culp's Hill, it was made piecemeal and was easily repulsed by the Union Twelfth Corps, hunkered down behind formidable log breastworks.

The last great clash on July 2 came just after sunset, when Brigadier General Harry Tompson Hays' "Louisiana Tiger" brigade briefly overran some Yankee guns and fought partway up the slope of Cemetery Hill—perhaps the most heavily defended position at Gettysburg. The Federals rallied, a fresh brigade was sent rushing in from Second Corps, and the firing subsided.

The groans of thousands of wounded soldiers, punctuated by an occasional musket shot, echoed over the blood-soaked fields when General Meade called a late-night council of war to determine the Federal strategy for the following day. As exhausted, sweat soaked, and powder stained as their men, Meade's senior officers made the decision to stick it out—to hold the line against whatever Lee held in store on the third day of battle at Gettysburg.

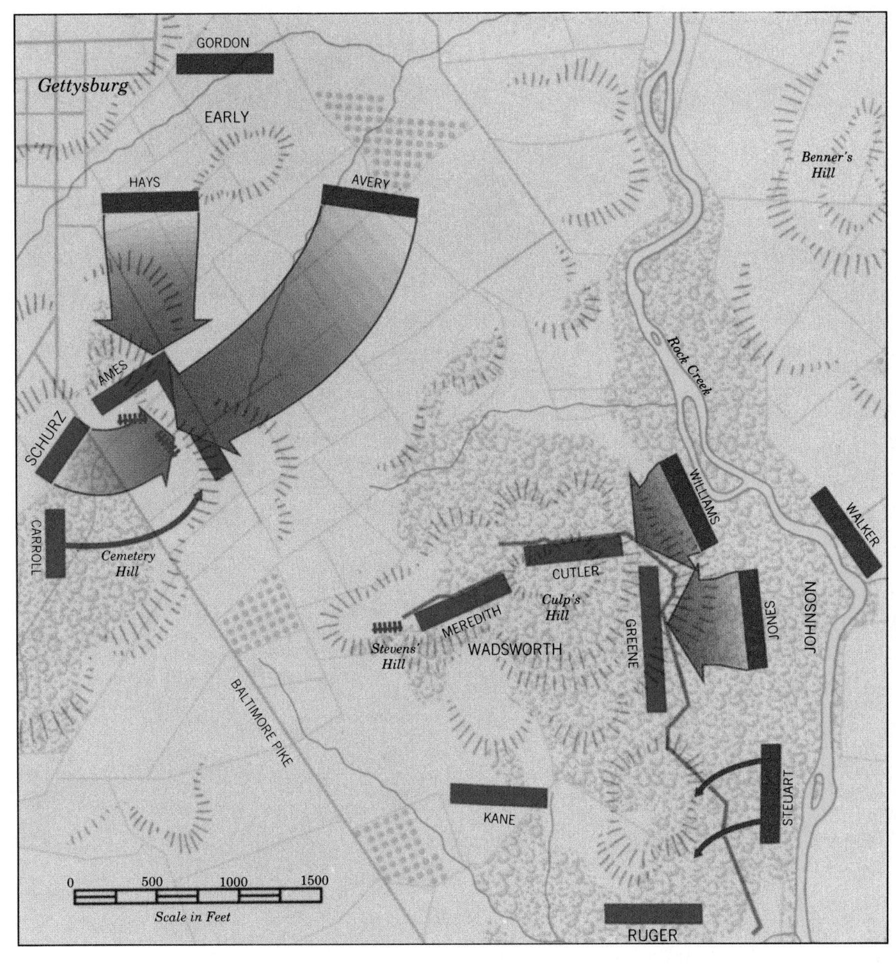

At twilight on July 2, Major General Richard Ewell finally launched his attack on the Federal right. Major General Edward Johnson's division assaulted Culp's Hill; the brigades of George H. Steuart, John M. Jones, and J. M. Williams clawed their way up the tree-covered slopes, only to be driven back by entrenched Federals of George S. Greene's brigade. At 8:00 p.m. Jubal Early's Confederates—the brigades of Harry Hays and Isaac E. Avery—charged onto the crest of Cemetery Hill into the Federal batteries. The Rebels, disorganized by darkness and heavy casualties, were driven from the hilltop by a counterattack by the brigade of Samuel S. Carroll and elements of Major General Carl Schurz's division.

LIEUTENANT CHARLES E. TROUTMAN

12th New Jersey Infantry, Smyth's Brigade

In the last major Confederate attack on July 2, the 12th New Jersey lost their ground on the Bliss farm but later staged a raid to silence Rebel sharpshooters there. Troutman and his fellow New Jerseymen again fell back under punishing fire. The 12th lost 42 men but brought out 99 Rebel prisoners.

Towards evening a body of North Carolina sharpshooters had ensconsed themselves in a house and barn about midway between the lines of the opposing armies, and were rendering it unsafe to work the batteries on our right and left front. A battalion of the regiment to which I was attached was ordered to dislodge them so down the slope we went. . . .

A captain of one of the companies running beside the writer was struck just above the right eye, and the noise of the bullet sounded exactly as that made by throwing a nail into a boot. It was zip, zip all the way across the meadows. Over the fence we went and through the barn yard knee deep in manure, and we were in the stable, but not an enemy was to be seen.

A constant shuffling above told us, however that the foe was still in possession, and so were we. It was certain death to charge up the ladder leading through the three-by-five hole to the loft above, but at last a venturesome youth, whose curiosity exceeded his fear, climbed up the ladder until his eyes were above the level of the upper floor. The sight he got satisfied him, for with a shout he loosened his hold and came down among us, accompanied by three Confederates, who, in making a dash at him, had fallen through. I do not know how or why it happened, but this fortunate capture seemed to be the signal for the surrender of the whole force above, and after throwing down their arms and accouterments they descended into the stable. After gathering them together

they were shown the general direction to the rear and away they went in huddled groups, with guards over the field strewn with our dead and wounded. A detail of ten or fifteen men was then ordered to charge the house as we were convinced that there was a body of sharpshooters there. We ran through the budding beauties of the garden through lilacs, rose bushes and raspberry bushes, the berries of which the size of a mans thumb, were temptingly hanging. But there was more serious

business on hand. A rattling, splitting sound and the picket fence went down and the remnant of us dashed into the kitchen door where twelve men were captured. Then we sat to a toothsome repast that had been prepared by the hungry North Carolinans whom we had interrupted. After capturing one more man who was discovered in an old fashion cupboard, we heard the sound of the recall and ran back over the meadow under a live archway of shells, regaining our lines.

Bodies swollen by the hot July sun, Federal dead of the III Corps lie in a trampled field near the Peach Orchard. Many of the bodies lack shoes, which were scavenged by Confederate soldiers who had occupied the ground on July 2.

"Tell my father I died with my face to the enemy."

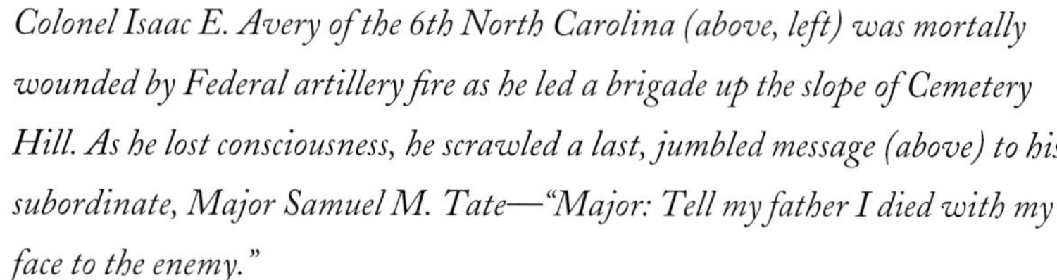

Colonel Isaac E. Avery of the 6th North Carolina (above, left) was mortally wounded by Federal artillery fire as he led a brigade up the slope of Cemetery Hill. As he lost consciousness, he scrawled a last, jumbled message (above) to his subordinate, Major Samuel M. Tate—"Major: Tell my father I died with my face to the enemy."

The six Napoleon guns of Battery D, 5th Maine Light Artillery, pour canister into the flank of Jubal Early's Confederates on Cemetery Hill.

Entrenched guns
Gettysburg on left
Stevens battery

LIEUTENANT EDWARD N. WHITTIER

5th Maine Light Artillery, I Corps
In the fading light of July 2, from a knoll facing the eastern slope of Cemetery Hill, the 5th Maine Battery's six Napoleons poured over a ton of searing metal into the left flank of Avery's North Carolina brigade as it pressed forward in a gallant but costly advance up the hill. Lieutenant Whittier recalled the event in his official report.

SERGEANT OSCAR D. LADLEY

75th Ohio Infantry, Ames' Brigade
A dry-goods clerk from Yellow Springs, Ohio, 23-year-old Oscar Ladley enlisted just a week after the firing on Fort Sumter. He fought in the Shenandoah Valley and in the Second Manassas campaign and late on July 2 found himself under withering fire on Cemetery Hill. Ladley sought a Regular Army post after the war; he died of pneumonia while on duty in Farmington, New Mexico, in 1880.

We made out the lines of the enemy at a distance of 1,000 yards, forming near the house and farm of William Culp. . . . as quickly as the enemy appeared, even while his lines were forming, the battery opened with case shot, each one bursting as if on measured ground, at the right time and in the right place in front of the advancing lines. . . .

The enemy swept past the left flank of the 5th Maine Battery with such rapidity that the right half battery could not be brought to bear upon their lines hastening to gain a new position and re-form on ground from which they could more successfully charge the crest of the hill. . . . The trails of the guns of the left battery were swung sharp and hard to the right, the right half battery was limbered to the rear, and in the darkness hurried into position on the left of the guns remaining in the works, and in a moment the whole battery at close range was pouring a most destructive, demoralizing, enfilading fire of double canister into a confused mass of the enemy struggling in the uncertain shadows of the crest of East Cemetery Hill.

July 5 Battle Field, Gettysburg Pa
They came on us about dark yelling like demons with fixed bayonets. We opened on them when they were about 500 yards off but still they came their officers & colors in advance. We lay behind a stone wall and received them with our bayonets. I was standing behind the wall when they came over. A Rebel officer made at me with a revolver with his colors by his side. I had no pistol nothing but my sword. Just as I was getting ready to strike him one of our boys run him through the body so saved me. There was a good man killed in that way. They had driven back the dutch Brig on our right and had got behind us, and rebels & Yankees were mixed up generally. But we finally drove them back. I never saw such fighting in my life. It was a regular hand to hand fight. Our Brig (Ohio) had sworn never to turn so they stood but it was a dear stand to some of them. I have 6 men left the Regt. has 60 the Brig. has 300 out of 1500.

SARAH M. BROADHEAD

Resident of Gettysburg

In Gettysburg, Sarah Broadhead and her husband, Joseph, huddled in their neighbor's cellar listening to the thunder of artillery on the nearby battlefield. Confederate soldiers occupied the town, and sharpshooters kept up a constant fire against Federal marksmen holding the houses in the southern end of town. Rifle fire from both sides made Gettysburg's yards and streets places of deadly peril.

The cannonading commenced about 10 o'clock, and we went to the cellar and remained a little while until it ceased. When the noise subsided, we came to the light again, and tried to get something to eat. My husband went to the garden and picked a mess of beans, though stray firing was going on all the time, and bullets from sharpshooters or others whizzed about his head in a way I would not have liked. He persevered until he picked all, for he declared the Rebels should not have one. I baked a pan of shortcake and boiled a piece of ham, the last we had in the house, and some neighbors coming in, joined us, and we had the first quiet meal since the contest began. I enjoyed it very much. It seemed so nice after so much confusion to have a little quiet once more. We had not felt like eating before, being worried by danger and excitement. The quiet did not last long. About 4 o'clock P.M. the storm burst again with terrific violence. It seemed as though heaven and earth were being rolled together. For better security we went to the house of a neighbor and occupied the cellar, by far the most comfortable part of the house. Whilst there a shell struck the house, but mercifully did not burst, but remained embedded in the wall, one half protruding. About 6 o'clock the cannonading lessened, and we, thinking the fighting for the day was over, came out. Then the noise of the musketry was loud and constant, and made us feel quite as bad as the cannonading, though it seemed to me less terrible. Very soon the artillery joined in the din . . . and we again retreated to our friend's underground apartment, and remained until the battle ceased, about 10 o'clock at night. . . . We expect to be compelled to leave town tomorrow, as the Rebels say it will most likely be shelled. I cannot sleep, and as I sit down to write, to while away the time, my husband sleeps as soundly as though nothing was wrong. I wish I could rest so easily, but it is out of the question for me either to eat or sleep under such terrible excitement and such painful suspense. We know not what the morrow will bring forth, and cannot even tell the issue of to-day.

WILLIAM H. BAYLY

Resident of Gettysburg

Thirteen-year-old Billy Bayly and his parents lived on a farm three miles west of Gettysburg, and on July 1, the teenager and his mother had nearly been trapped by the fighting while visiting an uncle in town. On July 2, the youngster got a look at the battle raging to the south of town from a safe distance.

I had stood during the day looking from a point of vantage over the battlefield, but the movements of the forces fighting there could not be distinguished, partly because of the distance, but more particularly, perhaps, because of the clouds of smoke that hung over the whole field. A flash of flame and the angry crack of guns a few seconds afterwards indicated where the opposing forces were engaged. But that was all the eye could distinguish save here and there a wagon train or reinforcements of artillery moving into position.

Just before nightfall . . . I had the sensation of a lifetime. . . . There was a thunder of guns, a shrieking, whistling, moaning . . . of shells before they burst, sometimes like rockets in the air. . . . No results of the conflicts would be noted; no shifting of scenes or movement of actors in the great struggle could be observed. It was simply noise, flash, and roar, the roar of a continuous thunderstorm and the sharp angry crashes of the thunderbolt.

. . . The firing ceased. . . . All was . . . [as] uncanny in its silence as the noise had been satanic in its volume.

July 3
The Great Rebel Charge

The fighting on July 2 had been chaotic, bloody, and inconclusive. Several times that day General George G. Meade's Army of the Potomac had come perilously close to disaster. But each time subordinate officers had risen to the occasion, met the crisis, and staved off defeat.

Confederate commander Robert E. Lee had been repeatedly frustrated in his efforts to break through the formidable Federal line that ran from Culp's and Cemetery Hills in the north, southward down the low spine of Cemetery Ridge to the boulder-covered crest of Little Round Top.

Determined to maintain the offensive on July 3 and force the battle to a decisive conclusion, Lee conceived a simultaneous two-pronged assault on Meade's position. On the far Confederate left, Ewell's corps would try again to seize the wooded height of Culp's Hill, while Longstreet—whose corps had been reinforced by the arrival of Pickett's division—would strike at the Union center on Cemetery Ridge. Lee knew that Culp's Hill was heavily defended and that the Federal defenders were dug in behind substantial breastworks. But even if Ewell was unsuccessful, his assault might cause Meade to shift troops and thereby weaken other portions of his line. Lee knew that the troops holding Cemetery Ridge had suffered heavy losses in the previous day's fighting; if Meade stretched that portion of his line too thin, Longstreet stood a good chance of tearing the Army of the Potomac asunder.

Shortly after dawn Lee's plan began to go awry when the muffled roar of musketry and artillery alerted the Confederate commander that Ewell's attack on Culp's Hill was already underway. As it happened, elements of the Federal Twelfth Corps had initiated the clash by attempting to wrest control of rifle pits that had earlier fallen to Major General Edward Johnson's division. Johnson had little choice but to fight back, and the battle for Culp's Hill rapidly escalated into a series of valiant but futile Confederate assaults on the entrenched Yankee positions.

By afternoon the fighting on Culp's Hill had died out in stalemate. If the Army of Northern Virginia was to achieve victory at

Early on July 3 (opposite), Federal reserves hurry northward along the Baltimore Pike with Cemetery Ridge in the background.

Gettysburg, it would have to come at the Union center on Cemetery Ridge.

Despite the collapse of his plan for simultaneous assaults, Lee never wavered in his resolve to break the Federal line on Cemetery Ridge. He placed that heavy responsibility in the hands of James Longstreet, his "old war horse." Longstreet had grave doubts and repeatedly expressed his concern that a head-on charge against the enemy center was to risk unacceptable losses with little chance for success. Lee overruled his subordinate, and the reluctant Longstreet spent the morning hours deploying the divisions of Generals Johnston Pettigrew, Issac R. Trimble, and George Pickett for the daunting task.

At 1:00 p.m. some 170 Confederate cannon launched a massive bombardment in an attempt to soften up the Union positions on Cemetery Ridge and pave a way for the onslaught. General Hancock, whose Federal Second Corps defended the point of attack, ordered his own guns to return fire, and for two hours the greatest artillery barrage in the history of North America raged across the open fields between the Southern position on Seminary Ridge and the smoke-shrouded slope of Cemetery Ridge, where Yankee soldiers hugged the earth as the ground trembled and reeled beneath them.

Although the Confederate barrage savaged the Federal artillery, exploding caissons and limber chests, cutting down horses in their traces, and dismounting guns, much of the Rebel fire passed over the waiting Yankee infantry. In a dramatic gesture, Hancock rode slowly along the line of his Second Corps, inspiring the men with his sang-froid as they awaited the charge.

At 3:00 p.m. the artillery fire began to slacken, and the three Confederate divisions—about 12,500 men in all—started forward from their staging area on Seminary Ridge. Pettigrew's North Carolinians and Pickett's Virginians were in the lead; Trimble's division would follow in support of Pettigrew's men on the left wing of the advance. Pickett's division was formed in two lines: the brigades of Generals Richard B. Garnett and James L. Kemper in the first wave, that of General Lewis A. Armistead in the second.

Deployed in lines of battle, the Confederates marched with parade-ground order over the mile-wide expanse that separated them from Hancock's defenders. The Federal artillery tore great gaps in the Rebel lines, but the survivors closed up and pressed on. As the first brigades clambered over the rail fences that lined the Emmitsburg road, enemy musketry began to scythe through their ranks, and shotgunlike blasts of canister mowed down scores of onrushing soldiers.

Now their formations broke up into desperate clusters of men who sprinted toward the low stone wall and copse of trees that marked their objective. General Kemper was severely wounded, Pettigrew was unhorsed and shot in the hand, and Garnett disappeared amid the carnage.

With the leading brigades torn and broken, Armistead led his men toward a projecting angle of the stone wall, jabbing his hat on the tip of his sword and holding it aloft as a beacon on which to guide. Armistead shoved his way through the jostling crowd, shouting, "Come on boys! Give them the cold steel! Who will follow me?" and the screaming mob of gray-clad troops surged forward to the wall.

With some 200 followers Armistead crossed the wall and leaped among the carnage-strewn wreckage of Lieutenant Alonzo H. Cushing's battery. Cushing had fallen with a third and fatal wound, and Sergeant Frederick Fuger loosed a last deadly salvo of canister before the surviving gunners bolted for the rear. Brigadier General Alexander S. Webb's Philadelphia brigade wavered and began to break, and for a few moments it seemed that the Federal center would indeed be split asunder.

Spurring his horse down the Second Corps line, Hancock hurled reserves toward the looming gap and urged the troops on his left flank—Brigadier General George J. Stannard's Vermont brigade—to swing out toward the Emmitsburg road and enfilade the Rebel lines. A bullet slammed into Hancock's upper right thigh, but despite the serious wound, the general refused to be borne from the field until he saw the Confederate assault recoiling in defeat.

As Federal reinforcements charged into the melee at the Angle, Hancock's prewar comrade Lewis Armistead fell mortally wounded beside one of Cushing's abandoned guns. With their leader down, the Confederates became woefully disorganized. Soon every Rebel who crossed the wall was killed or captured. The attack that would live in history as Pickett's Charge had failed utterly.

As the survivors of the failed assault stumbled back across the fields to Seminary Ridge, Robert E. Lee rode among them muttering, "It is all my fault . . . It is all my fault." Confederate officers succeeded in re-forming their shattered units, but Lee's soldiers could do no more. The last great Confederate invasion of the North had spent its force, and nothing remained but to retire back across the Potomac River into Virginia. At a cost of more than 50,000 casualties on both sides, Lee's cause had reached its highest tide, and the ebbing of Confederate hopes had begun.

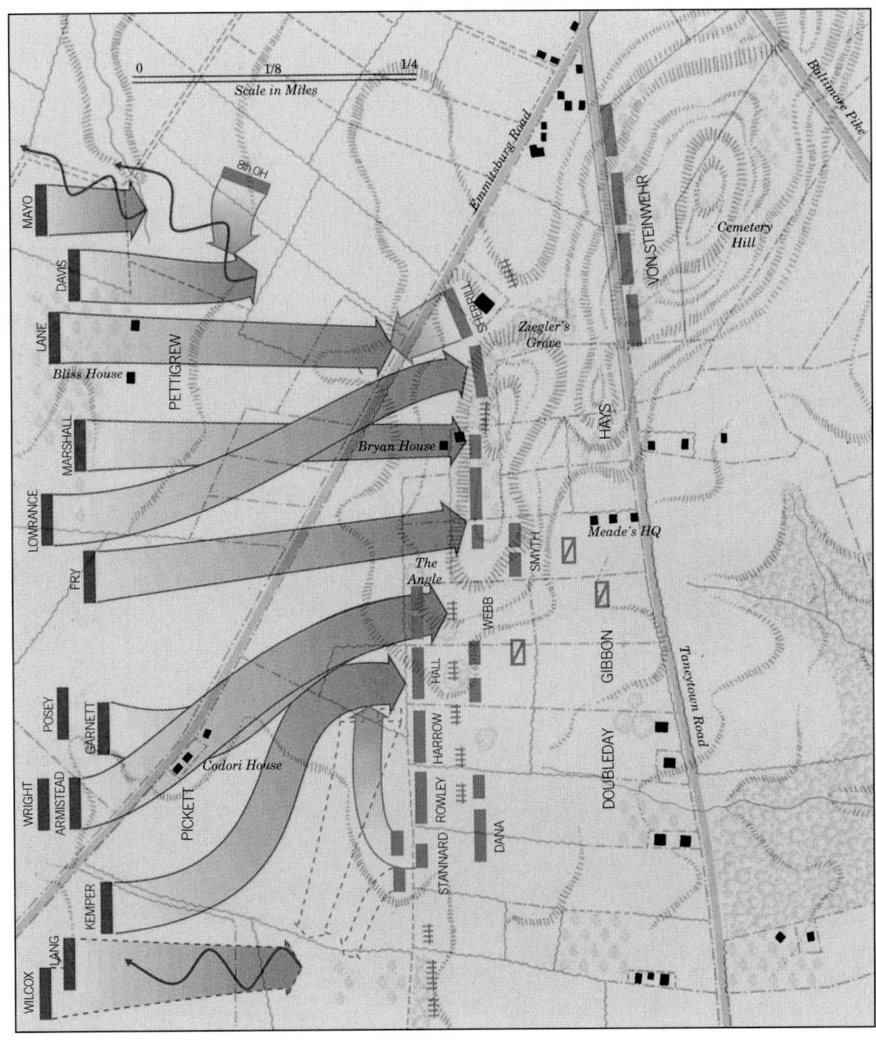

On the afternoon of July 3, the Confederate divisions of Pickett and Pettigrew, along with additional elements, attacked Federal II Corps positions on Cemetery Ridge in what would be called Pickett's Charge. The brigades of Kemper, Garnett, and Armistead advanced obliquely to their left to close up with Pettigrew's troops, exposing their right flanks to enemy fire. Pettigrew's brigades, meanwhile, were mauled by Federal batteries on Cemetery Hill. The Confederate flanks contracted and were overlapped by Union forces. Suffering fearful losses, Pettigrew's men charged at the Federal line defended by General Alexander Hays' division and were brought to a halt. Pickett's survivors attacked the Angle, a jog in a stone wall, where they were stopped by fire from General John Gibbon's division. With that repulse, the Confederates began streaming to their rear.

"The men voluntarily rose up and stood in line with uncovered heads and hats held aloft. . . ."

PRIVATE DAVID R. HOWARD

1st Maryland Battalion, Steuart's Brigade

Wounded at Gettysburg and captured, Howard was exchanged and wounded again at the Weldon Railroad on August 19, 1864, losing his right leg. In Johnson's attack up Culp's Hill early on July 3, Howard wrote that the 1st Maryland was in dire straits, as "the Federals opened on us from front, left flank and rear."

CAPTAIN HENRY T. OWEN

18th Virginia Infantry, Garnett's Brigade

Owen, a 31-year-old railroad agent, mustered into the Confederate army as captain of Company C, 18th Virginia, in 1861. On the morning of July 3, he recalled the massing of Pickett's division for the grand assault.

On Friday morning, July 3, Pickett's Division left its bivouac at dawn of day and moving around to the right reached the position assigned it in the ravine behind Cemetery Ridge soon after 6 o'clock. Long dark lines of infantry were massed along the bottoms, concealed from the enemy's view, and orders were given "to lie down and keep still to avoid attracting the attention of the enemy." About 8 o'clock Generals Lee, Longstreet and Pickett, in company, rode slowly along up and down in front of the long lines of prostrate infantry, viewing them closely and critically as they rode along. They were not greeted with the usual cheers, as orders had preceded them forbidding this, but the men voluntarily rose up and stood in line with uncovered heads and hats held aloft while their chieftains rode by.

We pressed on until near their breastworks, when, turning my head to the right, I saw a sight which was fearful to behold. It appeared to me as if the whole of my company was being swept away. . . . Not wishing to surrender, I turned to go back, not expecting to reach my command alive, but determined to fight as long as I could. Catching my gun by the muzzle, I attempted to get a cartridge out of my box to reload, but before I could do so I felt a burning, stinging sensation in my thigh, and as if all the blood in my body was rushing to one spot. Finding I was falling on my face, I gave myself a sudden twist which brought me to a sitting position, facing the Federals, with my broken leg doubled up over the other. Taking it up tenderly, I put it in its natural position; then tied my handkerchief above the wound, took the bayonet off my gun and made a tourniquet with it; then took my knapsack off and put it under my head for a pillow. Having made myself comfortable, I turned my attention to finding out who were lying around me and how they were wounded.

The firing was kept up after our men had gone back out of reach. It is a hard thing to say, but I am convinced the Federals deliberately shot at us while we lay there helpless on the field. Sergt. Thomas of my company, received two additional wounds; Nash of Co. C, was struck; a soldier at my left was shot and after writhing in agony for a few minutes, turned over and died. I was also struck in the hip, the ball striking a camp knife in my pocket breaking it up and cutting me in three places, but only deep enough to draw a little blood. You could tell by the sound when a ball struck a soldier, or went into the ground. It was a horrible position to be in; every moment I expected would be my last, so I straightened myself out folded my arms over my breast and waited for my time to come, having but one desire that I might die without a struggle, so that those who found me (members of my family, as I then thought,) would see that I died contented, in the consciousness of duty faithfully performed.

I don't know how long I laid there. . . . it could not have been more than an hour after the charge, when several of the Federals came out from their works, and beckoned for our men to come into their lines. Believing it was my duty to get out of danger if I could, I pulled myself towards them by placing my hands behind me as far as I could reach, and then pulling my body up to them. After going in this manner for a few yards, two Federals ran out and caught me under the arms, raising me just high enough from the ground to let my feet drag, and in this manner ran back with me into their lines, my broken leg swaying from side to side every step they took. . . .

Several other Federals then came up, and told me to take off my cartridge box, haversack, etc., as I would have no further use for them. My haversack looked very full, and I have no doubt they expected a feast, but they were sadly disappointed. The contents were one towel, tooth brush, comb, package of Confederate coffee, a piece of meat about the size of two fingers wrapped up in an old stocking, and a can of lard.

Many Confederate Marylanders wore some version of this silver pin—the heraldic cross from the state flag.

Moving from rock to rock, the soldiers of Major General Edward Johnson's Confederate division press their attack up the forested slopes of Culp's Hill on the morning of July 3. For more than three hours the Confederates launched a series of unsuccessful attacks against the log breastworks of the entrenched XII Corps. A Federal countercharge on Johnson's flank forced the withdrawal of the Rebels.

"The air might be said to be agitated by the wings of death."

CAPTAIN JOHN E. DOOLEY

1st Virginia Infantry, Kemper's Brigade

While the Rebel infantry filed into position, massed artillery unleashed the greatest bombardment of the war. The Union batteries roared out in response. Dooley describes the beginning of a barrage so thunderous that a fellow soldier remembered: "Men could be seen, especially among the artillery, bleeding at both ears from concussion."

PRIVATE JOHN H. MOORE

7th Tennessee Infantry, Archer's Brigade

John Moore survived the decimation of James Archer's brigade on July 1, and two days later, with the remnants of his regiment, lined up for the great charge. When the bombardment began, Moore was shocked to see that several seemingly abandoned houses between the lines were still occupied by terrified civilians.

A little further we take temporary position in the hollow of a field. Before us is a rising slope which hides the Yankee position from view. To the right of our front some quarter of a mile is a brick house near which one of our batteries now and then opens on the enemy who are generally ready to respond to the harsh greeting. Around us are some trees with very small green apples; and while we are resting here we amuse ourselves by pelting each other with green apples. So frivolous men can be even in the hour of death. . . .

Again, orders come for us to lie down in line of battle; that all the cannon on our side will open at a given signal, will continue for an hour and upon their ceasing we are to charge straight ahead over the open field and sweep from our path any thing in the shape of a Yankee that attempts to oppose our progress. This order is transmitted from Regt. to Regt., from Brigade to Brigade, and we rest a long time awaiting the signal.

At last it sounds away to the right and the echoes have scarcely rebounded from the rocks of the mountain when the earth, mountains and sky seem to open and darken the air with smoke and death dealing missiles. Never will I forget those scenes and sounds. The earth seems unsteady beneath this furious cannonading, and the air might be said to be agitated by the wings of death. Over 400 guns nearly every minute being discharged!

No imagination can adequately conceive of the magnitude of this artillery duel. It surpassed the . . . ordinary thunderstorm. As if to heighten the scene of terror and dismay, out from the devoted farm houses rushed old men, women and children. It was unaccountable that they had been neglected by the contending armies, but that they had remained at all after the fighting of the two days previous was still more singular. This is clear fact. I was a witness to the frenzied flight of some of them and Captain Harris, commander of the sharpshooters of Heth's Division, told me that he was forced to order some of the occupants to fly for shelter, and in one house a little stranger was shortly to make his appearance, to be baptized in a storm of shot and shell, the like of which had never before been witnessed on this continent.

Jennie Wade's bread dough trough (story at right)

Mary Virginia "Jennie" Wade (right) was 18 when she sat for this portrait in 1861 with her sister, Georgia (left), and neighbor Maria Comfort. The only civilian killed during the battle, she was in her sister's kitchen bent over her wooden dough trough making biscuits for Union soldiers when a bullet struck her in the back. Found in her apron pocket was a photograph of her fiancé, Johnston "Jack" Hastings Skelly, Jr. (above), a corporal in the 87th Pennsylvania, who had been mortally wounded trying to escape capture some two weeks earlier. Their graves are in Evergreen Cemetery, 100 paces apart.

Above, gunners of an unidentified Federal battery retire a damaged artillery piece to the reserve lines near Cemetery Hill during the Confederate bombardment of July 3. Although some of the batteries in the Union center suffered heavily, the Confederate fire caused little damage to most of the entrenched Federal guns.

An exploding Confederate shell damaged the muzzle of this 12-pounder Napoleon howitzer (left), of Battery B, 1st Rhode Island Artillery, and killed two members of its crew. When the survivors attempted to reload the piece, the shot stuck fast in the dented muzzle and could not be extracted.

LIEUTENANT FRANCIS W. DAWSON

Staff, Major General James Longstreet

The veterans of Longstreet's corps were well aware that the assault on the Federal center was a desperate gamble. Lieutenant Dawson overheard an exchange between two of Pickett's brigade commanders, Generals Lewis A. Armistead and Richard B. Garnett.

Prayers were offered up in front of Armistead's brigade and Garnett's brigade, before the advance began. Garnett remarked to Armistead: "This is a desperate thing to attempt." Brave old Armistead replied: "It is; but the issue is with the Almighty, and we must leave it in his hands." Just then a hare which had been lying in the bushes, sprang up and leaped rapidly to the rear. A gaunt Virginian, with an earnestness that struck a sympathetic chord in many a breast, yelled out: "Run old heah; if I were an old heah I would run too."

Captain Craig Wharton Wadsworth served on the staff of Major General John F. Reynolds, commander of the Federal I Corps, and later on the staff of General Meade. A highly regarded officer, Wadsworth was the son of Brigadier General James S. Wadsworth, commander of the 1st Division, I Corps, and one of America's wealthiest people.

MAJOR THOMAS W. OSBORN

Chief of Artillery, XI Corps

On the receiving end of the Rebel barrage, Brigadier General John Gibbon recalled, "The air was all murderous iron." In fact, many of the Confederate guns were overshooting the front lines and wreaking havoc in the rear, where Major Osborn played out a test of nerve with a fellow officer.

Captain Wadsworth, a son of General Wadsworth, was an aide on the staff of General Meade. . . .

While the artillery fire was still at its highest, he came to me with some directions and to make some inquiries for headquarters. I was at the moment on a nice horse thoroughly accustomed to me. His horse was the same. We halted close together in the midst of the batteries, the horses headed in opposite directions and our faces near together. Neither horse flinched. The forelegs of each horse were in line with the hind legs of the other, and we stood broadside to the enemy's fire. While we were talking, a percussion shell struck the ground directly under the horses and exploded. The momentum of the shell carried the fragments along so that neither horse was struck nor did either horse move. When the shell exploded, I was in complete control of my nerves and did not move a muscle of my body or my face. Neither did Wadsworth, but I dropped my eyes to the ground where the shell exploded, and Wadsworth did not. I never quite forgave myself for looking down to the ground when that shell exploded under us. I do not believe that there was a man in the entire army, save Captain Wadsworth, who could have a ten pound shell explode under him without looking where it struck.

"There, Orderly; hold it! If I can't get you killed in ten minutes, by God, I'll post you right up among the batteries!"

The loss of three successive leaders on July 1 propelled Colonel Richard Coulter of the 11th Pennsylvania to the command of his brigade. Coulter was wounded on July 3 but returned to lead his troops.

CAPTAIN ABNER SMALL

16th Maine Infantry, Paul's Brigade

On the morning of July 3, Small marched with his depleted regiment to a position near Meade's headquarters behind Cemetery Ridge. As the Confederate bombardment reached a crescendo, he encountered Colonel Richard Coulter, who had replaced the wounded Brigadier General Gabriel R. Paul as brigade commander.

We stayed an hour in our new position, exposed not only to shelling from both east and west, but also to the galling fire of rebel skirmishers.

Colonel Coulter, tearing up and down the line to work off his impatience, all of a sudden drew rein and shouted: "Where in hell is my flag? Where do you suppose that cowardly son of a bitch has skedaddled to? Adjutant, you hunt him up and bring him to the front!"

Away I went, hunting for the missing flag and man and finding them nowhere; and returned in time to see the colonel snake the offender out from behind a stone wall, where he had lain down with the flag folded up to avoid attracting attention. Colonel Coulter shook out the folds, put the staff in the hands of the trembling man, and double quicked him to the front. A shell exploded close by, killing a horse, and sending a blinding shower of gravel and dirt broadcast. The colonel, snatching up the flag again, planted the end of the staff where the shell had burst, and shouted:

"There, Orderly; hold it! If I can't get you killed in ten minutes, by God, I'll post you right up among the batteries!" Turning to ride away, he grinned broadly and yelled to me: "The poor devil couldn't be safer; two shells don't often hit the same place. If he obeys, he'll be all right and I'll know where my headquarters are."

Recklessly he dashed down the line. In a few minutes he returned, with one arm dangling. I recall the expression of his pain-distorted face when I, in my anxiety, asked him if he would not dismount; it was almost one of reproof.

"No, no," he said; "not now. Who in hell would suppose a sharpshooter would hit a crazy-bone at that distance?"

SERGEANT DAVID E. JOHNSTON

7th Virginia Infantry, Kemper's Brigade

Sergeant Johnston became a casualty before the infantry was ordered to advance. Left behind in a hospital, he was held captive. Exchanged in November, he was captured again at Sayler's Creek in 1865. After the war he returned to the new state of West Virginia and a long career as a lawyer, judge, and congressman.

I began to breathe a little more freely and raised my head off the ground and looked around, whereupon Lieut. Brown said to me, "you had better put your head down or you may get it knocked off." I replied, "well, Lieut., a man had as about as well die that way as to suffocate for want of air." I had barely spoken these words when a terrific explosion occurred, which for a moment deprived me of my breath and of sensibility, but it was momentary, for in a moment or so I found myself lying off from my former position and grasping for breath. Around me were brains, blood and skull bones; my first thought was that my Colonel's head had been blown off, but this was dispelled the next moment by his asking me if I was badly hurt, to which I replied I thought I was and called for that which a wounded soldier always first wants, a drink of water. The Col. sprang up and called to some one to bring water. By this time I had turned about and discovered that the heads of the two men who lay on my left side had been blown off just over the ears, and that the shell had exploded almost directly over me, a little below my left shoulder blade, breaking sever[al] of my ribs loose from my backbone, bruising severely my left lung and cutting my grey jacket almost into shreds and filling it with grains of powder.

Sergeant Thomas Elisha Marks transferred from the artillery to the 53d North Carolina Infantry in the winter of 1862. Marks was killed in action when his regiment, part of Brigadier General Junius Daniel's brigade, attacked Culp's Hill in the late morning of July 3, not long before the artillery bombardment that preceded Pickett's Charge.

CAPTAIN JOHN T. JAMES

11th Virginia Infantry, Kemper's Brigade

John Thomas James, newly commissioned a captain on July 3, endured the artillery duel between the opposing armies from the advanced position of a skirmish line. He observed that not all the casualties occurring around him were caused by the shelling—the weather also took its toll.

We waited patiently and wished, though dreaded, for the signal to commence the action, and probably for the order that would seal our fate. At last my company was thrown out as skirmishers . . . and soon afterwards the skirmishers of the other regiments were placed in a line with mine and marched some distance to the front and ordered to lie down and await until the artillery had ceased firing. Soon the signal gun fired, and then from the throats of

The companies of a Confederate regiment wheel into line on Seminary Ridge in preparation for the charge of July 3. Orders were given to "advance slowly, with arms at will. No cheering, no firing, no breaking from the common to quick step." The artist, Federal artilleryman Charles Reed, extended the skyline in the upper left corner.

over two hundred cannon such a storm of shot and shells were sent forth as no battle-field in America ever witnessed before. The Federals were not taken by surprise, for in a few seconds their solid shot were tearing up the ground around us, and their shells busting in our very faces. I have heard and witnessed heavy cannonading, but never in my life had I seen or heard anything to equal this. Some enthusiasts back in the Commissary Department may speak of it as grand and sublime, but unless grandeur and sublimity consist in whatever is terrible and horrible, it was wanting in both of these qualities. Whilst this artillery duel was in progress we were lying in a field with a very heavy growth of grass, so thick, in fact, it was impossible for any wind to get through it, and this, with the intense heat of the sun, produced several cases of sunstroke among our men.

CAPTAIN EDWARD R. BOWEN

114th Pennsylvania Infantry, Graham's Brigade

To the south along the Federal line, the men of Birney's battered division of the III Corps were ordered into reserve positions. Among them, Bowen and his mates in the 114th Pennsylvania watched as the long, drably clad lines of Rebel infantry moved forward into the storm of redoubled Federal artillery fire.

At a double quick we moved to the position assigned to us in the second line. . . . Here we waited the coming assault of Pickett's brave men. For a brief space there was an ominous pause of the artillery fire of both sides, General Hunt, chief of artillery of the Army of the Potomac, having ordered it to cease on our side in order that the guns might have an opportunity to cool and the ammunition be economized for the assault he knew was about to be made. The enemy, supposing from our artillery ceasing to fire that they had silenced our batteries, caused their firing to cease also. The silence was, however, of but short duration. The enemy rapidly crossed the intervening space. Our batteries, loaded with grape and cannister, were trained upon them at point-blank range and opened again upon them with deadly effect. Still they closed up the gaps and pressed on. Our men reserved their fire and allowed them to come so far as in their judgment was far enough and then blazed upon them such a withering musketry fire as literally mowed them down.

On July 5, after the withdrawal of the Confederates, special artist Edwin Forbes sketched the ground covered by Pickett's Charge from a position on Seminary Ridge. The artist added the attacking Confederate battle lines and keyed such features as (2) the copse of trees, (3) Ziegler's Grove, and (7) the point where General Lewis Armistead was killed. At the bottom, Forbes included quick sketches of a horse's head and a dead soldier.

The gaunt face of Brigadier General James L. Kemper displays the ravages of his nearly fatal wound in this photograph taken shortly after he was exchanged in September 1863. As he neared the stone wall on July 3, Kemper was shot from his horse by a bullet that struck the inside of his left thigh and passed upward to lodge near the base of his spine.

CAPTAIN JOHN T. JAMES

11th Virginia Infantry, Kemper's Brigade

At Pickett's command of "Charge the enemy and remember old Virginia!" the Rebel brigades began to advance. The men of Captain James' company, as skirmishers, were in front of the main line. James emerged from the charge unhurt and soldiered on to be captured at Dinwiddie Court House a few days before Lee's surrender at Appomattox.

After about an hour's work the artillery ceased firing and allowed the infantry to pass them. Slowly but steadily we marched forward, the line of battle suffering terribly; but we skirmishers being in front and extended across the field they shot over us, seeming to prefer the larger mass. I may remark here that this thing saved our company from the fearful loss that befell those in the regular line. By some mischance the line of battle, instead of following us, obliqued to the left, and by the time they came on a line with us we were on their right instead of being immediately in front, but as soon as I noticed this I tried to get my men to go with me to the brigade; but the noise was so great and the line of skirmishers so long I could not get them to hear me. I followed out with those near me, trusting the rest would follow as soon as they noticed the mistake. At every step some poor fellow would fall, and as his pitiful cry would come to my ear I almost imagined it the wail of some loved one he had left at home. The ground was covered with the dead, but not all ours, for the Federals had been driven over the same ground the day before. As the brigade reached nearer the enemy's position the death rate increased.

MAJOR JOHN M. TURNER

7th North Carolina Infantry, Lane's Brigade

Lane's North Carolinians, advancing in support of Pettigrew, were flanked by a Federal regiment when troops on their left gave way and were subjected to a fearsome cross fire. Major Turner's battle ended shortly after he negotiated the fences along the Emmitsburg road. He recovered from his wounds in a Federal prison, was exchanged in September 1864, and returned to fight at Petersburg.

This road known as the Emmettsburg Pike, had a post and rail fence on either side; the first, I ordered the men to rush against and push down, which they did, but having to run up out of the road they did not succeed in a like attempt on the second, and seeing that we were losing time, I climbed over on the right and my men were following me rapidly. I had advanced ten yards or more towards the works when I was shot down; the men who had gotten over returned to and laid down in the Pike, as did the entire regiment. The wound received proved to be a contusion on the instep of my foot, laming me and giving me great pain; in a little while I made my way back and over the fence to the left where Capt. Harris, the next officer in rank to myself, was. I had scarcely turned over the command when I was shot through the waist, the ball striking the spinal column, instantly paralyzing the parts below.

Brigadier General James Johnston Pettigrew took command of Heth's division after Heth was wounded on July 1. Although Pettigrew suffered a nasty wound in the hand leading his division in Pickett's Charge, he was among the last to leave the field. On July 13 Pettigrew was shot fighting a rear-guard action at Falling Waters and died four days later.

Federal reserves rush forward to stop the Confederate breakthrough at the Angle in this painting by Edwin Forbes.

CAPTAIN HENRY T. OWEN

18th Virginia Infantry, Garnett's Brigade

In order to close up with Pettigrew, the brigades of Kemper, Armistead, and Garnett advanced obliquely left, exposing their right flank to enemy fire. One of Owen's comrades recalled, "The last I saw of General Garnett he was astride his big black charger waving his hat and cheering the men on." Garnett's body was never recovered.

We were now four hundred yards . . . from Cemetery Hill, when away off to the right, nearly half a mile, there appeared in the open field a line of men at right angles with our own, a long, dark mass, dressed in blue, and coming down at a "double quick" upon the unprotected right flank of Pickett's men, with their muskets "upon the right shoulder shift," their battle flags dancing and fluttering in the breeze created by their own rapid motion, and their burnished bayonets glistening above their heads like forest twigs covered with sheets of sparkling ice when shaken by a blast. Garnett galloped along the line saying: "Faster, men! faster!" and the front line broke forward into a double quick, when Garnett called out: "Steady, men! steady! Don't double quick. Save your wind and your ammunition for the final charge!" and then went down among the dead, and his clarion voice was no more heard above the roar of battle.

PRIVATE RALPH O. STURTEVANT

13th Vermont Infantry, Stannard's Brigade

Stannard's Vermont brigade had moved up 100 yards from Meade's main line to occupy a small knoll. As Pickett's Confederates started up Cemetery Ridge, Stannard wheeled several regiments north and opened an enfilading fire. Private Sturtevant mustered out shortly after the battle and in 1911 wrote a history of his regiment.

Down the line of the 13th regiment comes the order from company to company "Steady boys, hold your position, don't fire until the word is given, keep cool, lie low till order is given to fire, make ready, take good aim, fire low." Then like an electric flash came down the line the order from Colonel Randall quickly repeated by every officer in the line "Fire," up rose the Green Mountain Boys, 3,000 strong as if by magic with forms erect took deliberate aim and with a simultaneous flash and roar fired into the compact ranks of the desperate foe and again and again in quick succession until a dozen or more volleys had been discharged with deadly effect. We saw at every volley the grey uniforms fall quick and fast and the front line hesitated, moved slowly and melted away.

Colonel Francis Randall's 13th Vermont opened a deadly flanking fire upon Kemper's advancing Confederates. "Not until the dead covered the ground so as to make progress almost impossible," recalled one of his soldiers, did the Confederates signal surrender. At the risk of his life, Randall stepped in front of his own line to stop the firing.

The soldiers of Company I of the 11th Vermont presented this sword (left) to their leader, Lieutenant William H. Hamilton, in February 1863. Hamilton was mortally wounded fighting with Stannard's brigade on July 3.

"We laid him upon the ground, and opened his clothing where he . . . was hurt."

LIEUTENANT GEORGE G. BENEDICT

12th Vermont Infantry, Stannard's Brigade

Major General Winfield Scott Hancock, commander of the Federal II Corps, was gravely wounded as he urged on Stannard's flank attack. Lieutenant Benedict, acting as aide to General Stannard, moved quickly to assist the stricken corps commander.

When General Winfield Scott Hancock rode down the lines of his II Corps, exposed to enemy fire, an officer urged him to dismount. "There are times," Hancock responded, "when a corps commander's life does not count."

Hooker and I with a common impulse sprang toward him, and caught him as he toppled from his horse into our outstretched arms. General Stannard bent over him as we laid him upon the ground, and opened his clothing where he . . . was hurt, a ragged hole, an inch or more in diameter, from which the blood was pouring profusely, was disclosed in the upper part and on the side of his thigh. He was naturally in some alarm for his life. . . .

"Don't let me bleed to death," he said, "Get something around it quick." Stannard had whipped out his handkerchief, and as I helped to pass it around General Hancock's legs I saw that the blood, being of dark color and not coming in jets, could not be from an artery, and I said to him: "This is not arterial blood, General; you will not bleed to death." From my use of the surgical term he took me for a surgeon, and replied, with a sigh of relief: "That's good; thank you for that Doctor." We tightened the ligature by twisting it with the barrel of a pistol, and soon stopped the flow of blood.

CAPTAIN ANDREW COWAN

1st New York Light Artillery, VI Corps

Born in Scotland in 1841, Andrew Cowan settled in Auburn, New York, as a youth. He left Madison College to enlist in the army. On July 3 his battery rolled forward to relieve the shattered guns of the 1st Rhode Island Battery and open fire at point-blank range as the Confederates crossed the stone wall just south of the copse of trees.

A body of the enemy who had taken shelter in my front behind an elevation covered with bushes, some 200 or 300 yards short of the wall, rushed forward. I had ordered our guns loaded with double canister, and also that they be pulled back by hand the moment we got a chance to fire. Lieut. Johnson had been badly wounded and borne from the field; Lieut. Atkins had been sun-struck, and now Lieut. Wright, who was at my side receiving my order, was shot thru the lungs. Most of the enemy stopped behind the wall, but a number of them came on led by a young officer, waving his sword and shouting, "Take the gun," at the instant we fired our double charge of canister (220 chunks of lead from each of the five guns). We buried that officer with honor.

Sergeant William E. Uhlster, marked "a," and the men of his gun crew stand at their posts around their 10-pounder Parrott rifle, one of Cowan's New York battery present at Gettysburg. Six months later at Cedar Creek, Uhlster was wounded and Corporal Henry Tucker, labled "B," was killed.

SERGEANT DENNIS B. EASLEY

14th Virginia Infantry, Armistead's Brigade

As Pickett's shattered brigades reached the stone wall that marked the Federal front, they halted and opened fire on their tormentors. General Armistead, his hat on his upraised sword tip, led the men near him over the wall and into an abandoned battery. Easley was captured and later exchanged in February 1865, only to fall once more into Federal hands at the Battle of Five Forks in April.

I brought down my bayonet, but soon saw that every man had his arms above his head; so I crowded through them with no other idea than to locate my company. By the time I was through them I struck the stone fence in a battery of brass pieces. I mounted the fence and got one glance up and down the line, while General Armistead mounted it just to my left, with only a brass cannon between us.

I forgot my company and stepped off the fence with him. We went up to the second line of artillery, and just before reaching those guns a squad of from twenty-five to fifty Yankees around a stand of colors to our left fired a volley back at Armistead and he fell forward, his sword and hat almost striking a gun.

Armistead's Confederates exchange fire over the stone wall with General Alexander S. Webb's Philadelphia brigade (left). Alfred Waud's drawing was printed as an engraving in the August 8, 1863, edition of Harper's Weekly.

Brigadier General Lewis Armistead (right) was mortally wounded leading his troops into the Federal lines on July 3. When his men stalled in the teeth of the enemy fire, he leaped onto the wall shouting, "Come on, boys! Give them the cold steel! Who will follow me?"

PRIVATE ANTHONY MCDERMOTT

69th Pennsylvania Infantry, Webb's Brigade

As the surviving Confederates lunged over the stone wall near the copse of trees, the soldiers of the 69th Pennsylvania, an Irish regiment raised in Philadelphia, stood fast around their green flag as other Federal units gave way around them. Private McDermott and his fellow Irishmen defended themselves with bayonet and clubbed rifle.

Kemper's men, some of them used their musket butts as clubs as well as some of our own men. . . . Corpl. Bradley of Co. "D" who was quite a savage sort of fellow, wielded his piece, striking right and left, and was killed . . . by having his skull crushed by a musket in the hands of a rebel, and Private Donnelly of some Co. used his piece as a club, and when called upon to surrender replied tauntingly, "I surrender," at the same time striking his would-be captor to the ground. . . .

We poured our fire upon him (the enemy) until Armistead received his mortal wound; he swerved from the way in which he winced, as though he was struck in the stomach, after wincing or bending like a person with a cramp, he pressed his hand to his stomach, his sword and hat (a slouch) fell to the ground. He made two or three staggering steps, reached out his hands trying to grasp at the muzzle of what was then the 1st piece of Cushing's battery, and fell. . . .

His men (Armistead's) threw down their arms, most of them ran back to the stone wall and lay down behind it.

Abram Bryan's house, used as a headquarters by Brigadier General Alexander Hays, was situated on the crest of Cemetery Ridge in the Federal lines. Bryan, a free black man, abandoned his home with his wife and two sons in June when news of the Confederate invasion reached Pennsylvania.

CAPTAIN ISAAC HALL

97th New York Infantry, Baxter's Brigade

At around 1:00 p.m. Baxter's brigade moved into reserve behind General Alexander Hays' division of the II Corps. As Longstreet's Confederates pressed home their attack, the brigade, including the 97th New York, was rushed forward to bolster the front line.

Just in advance of the 97th, a soldier wounded by a sharpshooter, falling out to the front from the files of his regiment, dropped upon the ground. His comrade came to his assistance, and as the 97th approached, bending over him, was struck by a bullet on the back of his head, and with his brains oozing from his forehead, fell across his companion and the column passed on; but the crack of that man's skull was long retained in memory by the beholder.

As the division took position in front of the guns of Hayes's command, on the slope southwest of the town, an indescribable scene of confusion and disorder presented itself. The havoc upon the field in our front was appalling; the dead lay at intervals one upon another, torn and mangled; and were strewn over the field in every conceivable condition. From among the slain arose the wounded, who struggled to reach our line; some in their vain endeavor, fell to rise no more; others who could not rise cried for help and for water.

General Hayes, mounted and with a large Confederate flag trailed in the dust, rode in front of his line, which made the fields echo again with shouts.

"From among the slain arose the wounded, who struggled to reach our line. . . ."

The battle flags of the 28th North Carolina, James Lane's brigade (above, right), and the 11th Mississippi, Joseph Davis' brigade (above, left), were both carried to the stone wall that marked the height of the Rebel advance on July 3. The Federal II Corps captured 33 Confederate colors.

LIEUTENANT WILLIAM PEEL

11th Mississippi Infantry, Davis' Brigade

To the left of Pickett's Virginians, the men of Pettigrew's and Trimble's commands rushed toward an angle in the stone wall. In a diary entry written in prison after his capture, Lieutenant Peel recorded the bravery of colorbearer George Kidd. The author died in prison in February 1865.

Four brave men had already fallen under the colors of our Reg't, & now the fifth bore them aloft, & rushed boldly forward, to embrace, if need be, the fate of the other four. The flag staff was now cut in two midway the flag, but without one moment's pause, the never-flinching Irishman, his flag now dangling in graceless confusion, from one corner, still pushed fearlessly, upon the stone fence.

SERGEANT JAMES P. SULLIVAN

6th Wisconsin Infantry, Meredith's Brigade

Wounded in the leg during his brigade's epic fight on July 1, Sergeant "Mickey" Sullivan hitched a ride with a passing cavalryman to a field hospital located in the courthouse in Gettysburg, which later fell into Confederate hands. From the cupola, Sullivan watched the climactic Rebel charge on July 3.

I got one of the band boys to help me, and hanging onto the railing of the stairs I climbed to the cupola and looking over towards the right of the town I saw what appeared like a whole rebel army in a chunk start for our lines with their infernal squealing yell. It seemed as if everything stood still inside of me for a second or two, and then I began to pray. Now I never was and am not yet, noted for the frequency and fervency of my prayers, but that time I prayed from the bottom of my heart that they would catch h--l, and they did. It seemed as if the fire from our lines doubled and doubled again, and I could see long streaks of light through the rebel columns, but they went forward. I was afraid they would capture our guns, but all of a sudden they seemed to melt away as our infantry opened on them, and then we could hear the Northern cheer. We knew that the rebs were scooped, and the old Army of the Potomac was victorious. There were ten or fifteen of us in the observatory, and they were wild with joy, some cried, others shook hands, and all joined in best cheer we could get up. I forgot all about my wound, and was very forcibly reminded of it when I went to shout as I had to sit down to keep from falling. The other wounded down below joined in the cheer, and a rebel officer came in and wanted to know what was the matter, and when told that Lee was cleaned, he growled out if we d----d Yankees were able to cheer we were able to go to Richmond. But our fellows felt good anyway, and the reb went out and we saw no more of him.

CAPTAIN ANDREW COWAN

1st New York Light Artillery, VI Corps

In the aftermath of the charge, Captain Cowan encountered the sad figure of Samuel Wilkeson, a correspondent for the New York Times. Wilkeson's eldest son, Lieutenant Bayard Wilkeson, had been mortally wounded directing his battery on July 1, and the father hoped to locate his body.

While we were stripping the harness from the dead horses and hastening to get the battery in good shape before we could even look after the wounded, I was stripped to my shirt, bareheaded and black with the grime and sweat of the struggle, and busy directing the work, when I heard this citizen asking the name of the battery. He was told that it was Cowan's, and I was pointed out, when he came forward, saying, "Captain, we met at Lee's Mills before Yorktown, where your sentry arrested me when I stumbled into your battery in the darkness, having become lost on the battlefield, and you took care of me." I remembered the incident, and how I had detained the man until after daylight, until I was convinced that he was not a spy, as had been suspected. He now told me that his son, a Lieutenant in a battery, had been mortally wounded in the first day's battle, on the right, and that he was pursuing his duty as a correspondent with a heavy heart. We stood there, with the dead and the wounded covering the ground before our eyes, and the blazing sun beating upon them mercilessly.

Samuel Wilkeson, reporter for the New York Times, arrived on the battlefield at Gettysburg on July 3. His report of the fighting, written beside the body of his slain son, contained the lament, "O, you dead, who at Gettysburg have baptized with your blood the second birth of Freedom in America, how you are to be envied!"

Dead artillery horses lie in their harness next to a damaged caisson near the grove of trees that marked the point of direction for Pickett's attacking brigades. Confederate artillery fire inflicted heavy casualties of men and animals among the batteries supporting General Gibbon's Federal division.

"Some fool prisoner hollered out, 'Three cheers for Jeff Davis.' "

Under the watchful eye of Federal guards, a long line of Confederate prisoners—soldiers of General Longstreet's corps taken after their grand assault—begin their long march to northern prison camps on the late afternoon of July 3. More than 792 unwounded Confederate prisoners were captured from the divisions of Generals Pickett, Pettigrew, and Trimble.

COLONEL JOHN A. FITE

7th Tennessee Infantry, Archer's Brigade

A 31-year-old lawyer from Carthage, Tennessee, Fite led his men across the fences bordering the Emmitsburg road on July 3, and found himself pinned down by Federal musketry in front of the stone wall. He was captured, along with Colonel Newton J. George of the 1st Tennessee, and led to the rear. Held prisoner until the war's end, Fite became a judge, legislator, and state adjutant general; he died in 1925.

I had a little flask of whiskey. I pulled it off and I said, "George lets take a drink to the health of them boys down yonder." George said, "I never do drink to the health, but I'll take a drink with you on that." Our guard broke and run, said "Come on they'll kill you." We took a drink and then went on back just behind an old barn and stopped there a little while, they then started us back to the rear. There was an officer in charge of us then. I had on a watch and it had a masonic cross on the little strap that I had it tied on with. The officer that had charge of us saw it and said that he was a Mason and he'd like to have that as a souvenir to remember me by. I told him he could take it by force but he couldn't get it otherwise that I'd forgotten all about the thing.

He carried us back down the hill and put us in a little field, it was the 3rd day of July and hottest day I think I ever saw. They had three or four thousand of our people there in that little field. We were nearly starved to death for water. Late in the evening they ordered a line of Yankees, and marched us back 100 yards to the creek. Yankee soldiers were there, cavalry, washing their old sore back horses in the creek and every other sort of filth that ever I saw at a place, but we had to drink it or nothing. They then put us back in the field. While I was sitting on a little stump, the fellows were sitting around and standing around everywhere, old General Kilpatrick in command of the Yankee cavalry, rode up close to the fence, and hollered out, "Attention Prisoners. If you behave yourselves and don't try to get away, I will treat you as prisoners of war, but if you attempt to escape, I'll order my cavalry to charge right and left, and hew you down." Some fool prisoner hollered out, "Three cheers for Jeff Davis." and you never heard such a yell on earth. The old General rode off.

LIEUTENANT ROBERT T. COLES

4th Alabama Infantry, Law's Brigade

As Longstreet's attack reached its height, Brigadier General Elon J. Farnsworth led his Federal cavalrymen in a suicidal attack on Confederate positions opposite the Federal far left. From behind stone walls and the edge of thick woods, Confederate infantrymen of Hood's division, including Lieutenant Coles, easily turned back one of the boldest but most foolhardy cavalry charges of the war.

Just as we were about to emerge from the timber into the open field we saw a squadron of Union cavalry bearing down upon us at a gallop. It came in smashing style from direction of Captain Reilly's battery, which occupied the same position on the extreme right flank we found it in when we arrived from New Guilford the evening before. The men, on account of the long hot and rapid march of the previous day and the strenuous time we encountered after reaching the battlefield, were unusually nervous, and our limbs stiffened and sore from over exertion. As soon as our foe was found to be cavalry we were to contend with, the excitement was materially allayed, for nothing afforded the regiment more delight than to have a scrap with them whenever a chance presented itself.

One little fellow of C Company, a new recruit, was particularly rattled, with pallid cheeks and trembling limbs, he advanced with the rest of us, determined to stand by his colors let the consequence be what they may; an illustration of many cases which occurred under similar circumstances of "triumph of mind over matter."

When Lieutenant Vaughn of his company called out in a loud voice, "cavalry, boys, cavalry; this is no fight, only a frolic; give it to 'em." The little fellow exclaimed, "Well, I will be dog-goned if we aint got the best Lieutenant in this whole army."

. . . In the confusion Sam Whitworth of F Company, not seeing me in his front, threw his rifle around to his right as the Vermonters came down in gallant style from that direction, and struck me on the left side of my head with the barrel of his piece and fired. I was only shocked for an instant but brave old Sam never tired afterwards with apoligies for his carelessness, when discussing "Gettysburg" around our camp fires.

When Sam fired the Union troopers leading the charge were not ten paces from us, and our whole line scattered along the edge of the timber were pouring a deadly fire into their ranks. A young trooper's beau-

tiful sorrel mare fell shot in the breast only a few paces from our line. The trooper came down with her, standing erect on his feet, astride of her. Instead of surrendering he quickly threw up his carbine and discharged it directly in our faces, but fortunately no harm was done. Then, throwing down his gun, jumped from over his horse and ran. A puff of dust flew out of the blouse which never covered a braver heart, as the bullet penetrated between the shoulders, and he fell, meeting the same fate as his horse.

Pocked by bullets, their limbs cut by shell fragments, trees on the densely forested slopes of Culp's Hill bear the marks of intense fighting. Within a year of the battle many trees on the hillside were either dead or dying from the damage suffered over three days of battle. The "dead soldier" in the center of the image is actually a photographer's assistant posed artistically for scale.

PRIVATE GEORGE C. PILE

37th Virginia Infantry, Steuart's Brigade

Private Pile distinguished himself at Cedar Mountain in 1862 by capturing a brigadier general, Henry Prince. At Gettysburg, following the abortive Rebel attacks on Culp's Hill on the morning of the third, Pile helped carry the regiment's wounded orderly sergeant to a field hospital. As he returned to Culp's Hill he found an opportunity to feed his men. In 1864 he survived a wound at Cedar Creek, Virginia.

I saw a house and went in. It had just been vacated and I found some buckwheat flour, lard and a hot stove. Here I fried hot cakes till my haversack was full. . . .

It was then I thought of my own command and that may be they too were engaged in fierce combat with the foe. I hurried down to where I had left them in the morning. The men were gone. They had been driven from the position they held and I found them at Rock Creek sheltered behind rocks, trees or anything that would protect them. In my hurry to get to my men that haversack full of buckwheat cakes was troublesome for it flopped against me like one of these old saddle bags against a rickety horse, but I held on to it for I knew the cakes would be needed. When I began to hand them out to the boys I had to walk along the top of the breastworks.

"Look out, there," the boys shouted, "the Yankees are shooting at everyone that shows himself."

"They will not shoot while I'm feeding you fellows," I told them and kept on. I saw General Stewart and went over and offered him one; he was glad to get it but advised me to get behind something or I would get shot. I had about finished giving out the cakes and going over to give the last one I picked up a gun, then it was the bullets flew thick and I took cover as soon as possible.

SERGEANT LAWRENCE WILSON

7th Ohio Infantry, Candy's Brigade

Wilson and the other men of the Federal XII Corps holding the summit and slopes of Culp's Hill found the night of July 3 full of alarms. Nervous pickets, startled by Confederate wounded and stragglers attempting surrender, sparked general fusillades of rifle fire and, in the case of the 7th Ohio, a brave Rebel tried to carry out a one-man raid.

On the night of July 3, about midnight, when the battle having ended and the stillness was only broken by the moans of the wounded yet uncared for in our front, and when the men in the trenches, exhausted from days of marching and fighting, were sound asleep, a Confederate Sergeant made his way stealthily up to our works, and seeing our regimental flag, with staff, leaning against the logs, he reached up, and being much lower, as he stood on the slope of the hill on the outside, could not reach over the head log, so grasped the staff through the firing space underneath and began to work it up so that it would topple over and fall into his arms.

This movement awakened our color Sergeant, who sprang up in a dazed, drowsy condition and shot and killed this handsome, reckless, and gallant soldier in gray before he was fairly aware of it and much to the sorrow and regret of his comrades when the facts became known. This shooting alarmed and aroused our line of battle, and supposing another attack was on, firing broke out afresh, but at daylight we could only find this lonely Sergeant as the cause and the only victim of the outbreak.

SERGEANT C. H. BLANCHARD

111th Pennsylvania Infantry, Cobham's Brigade

The slopes of Culp's Hill were littered with prostrate Confederates, and soon after the Rebel withdrawal the process of burying the dead began. One of Blanchard's fellow sergeants, Sherman R. Norris, wrote that he had been a "'Pall bearer' to the largest funeral I ever attended," noting that over 200 dead Rebels were interred in a trench in front of the 111th Pennsylvania.

The weather was hot, the battle raged all day and into the night on the first and second with thousands of dead men and horses, lying in the scorching sun—try and imagine what it would be like—in addition to the Pioneers, details were made from each regiment. Citizens were pressed into service to bury the dead. I got permission from Colonel Cobham and strolled around over the portion of the ground where we were engaged. I saw some strange pathetic sights. I saw a confederate soldier that a ramrod had passed through his body and pinned him to a tree, but the incident most vividly stamped upon my mind, was where I saw 108 confederates put into a trench, Whiskey had been issued to the Brigade Pioneers, as the stench was almost unbearable. There was a big red headed chap from the 29th Pa. regiment went by the name of Reddy. The last one put in the trench was an orderly sergeant. Reddy came dragging him by the legs and threw him in and said, "there, damn you, call the roll and see if they are all there."

In a drawing by Alfred Waud that he labeled "last Rebel shot," a Confederate gun posted near the Peach Orchard duels with Federal batteries on the smoke-shrouded crest of Little Round Top. After the repulse of Longstreet's attack on the afternoon of July 3, Confederate gunners kept up a steady fire to prevent a Federal counterattack.

hills on the left of our position from the rebel artillery
A-R-Waud

SERGEANT ISAAC N. DURBORAW

1st Pennsylvania Reserves, McCandless' Brigade

Sergeant Durboraw's Company K of the 1st Reserves was organized in the town and neighborhood of Gettysburg, and many of the men were fighting within sight of their homes. Durboraw, concerned for his family's safety, left his post near the Round Tops to visit his parents' house in rebel-occupied Gettysburg. As he relates, the journey was harrowing. Durboraw was mustered out of the service in the summer of 1864.

Many of the company whose homes were in Gettysburg or the immediate vicinity, quietly slipped away, and believing that our work, for a while at least, was ended, I also went, saying to the boys when I started, "Boys if you go home, don't fail to get back to-morrow morning." I am proud of the conduct of company K, at, as well as after the battle of Gettysburg, and why should I not be? These brave fellow[s] could easily imagine the dangerous surroundings of loved ones, during the terrible conflict, in their homes within the bounds of the battle-field, yet, not a man left the ranks or fled from duty, and while most of them got home after the battle, by a peculiar device, only one failed to return.

But to my story; I passed northward just in the rear of the line of battle, and through the Citizens cemetery, thence up Baltimore street to the Court-house on the corner of Middle street, which was a dangerous performance, as the whole route was exposed to rebel sharp-shooters, making it necessary to cross all streets and alleys at a bound. Having reached the point indicated, I found the residence of my father, on west Middle street one square from the Court-house, so completely covered by rebel sharp-shooters, that it was an impossible measure to go there.

I observed things closely, and saw a certain officer who was apparently not aquainted with the dangerous surroundings, turn the corner where I was standing, and walk deliberately down the middle of the street, without being molested, but, Alas! the poor fellow when he got below Washington street, was taken prisoner. So I took advantage of what I had seen, and walked down the street, with misgivings I confess, for doubtless many rifles were aimed at me, with a rebel finger on each trigger, ready to send as many messengers of death, if I should turn either to the right or to the left. It was an awful moment, but I determined to carry out my plan, which was to spring into a flower garden on the east side of the house, when I would reach that point, for I would then be in a safe place.

On! on, to hesitate would be fatal; and how terrible it would be to die so near to the loved ones; still on I went, not hurriedly, for the enemy must not even think that I have a purpose in view; Oh! If only the yard gate were open! Ah, it is open! A spring, and I am through it, and behind the cover of the house; I am safe, but what a shower of minnie balls strike the pavement over which I came, and how they tear through the palings of the fence on both sides of the open gate, terrible messengers they are, but harmless now as far [as] they concerned me.

None of the family were visible, so I entered the unlocked door of a back kitchen, which was empty, then into the main building I went and all through it from main floor to attic, and found no one; disappointed I turned to the cellar and was met on the stair-way by a sister, who failed to recognize me in the semi-darkness, who said, "Here! what do you want?" On the spur of the moment I said, "Can you supply me with just a bite to eat?" With this she retired below and I followed to the foot of the stairs, and took a seat near the lower step, and this is what I then saw: father and mother, four sisters and a brother, two or three improvised beds, an almost consumed tallow dip on the end of a barrel in a far off corner, and each person being a perfect image of dejection and despondency.

Sister Lucy whispered something to mother, who then entered an adjoining pantry, doubtless to get the "bite to eat," while a younger

sister approached me inquiring, "I wonder how much longer we will have to remain in this cellar?" I merely answered, "Not long," but I discovered that they were entirely ignorant of the state [of] affairs without. She looked at me closely, and then followed mother into the pantry.

Presently, mother approached me, bearing a huge piece of bread in her hand, and peering very closely into my face, then as if in glad surprise, she ejaculated, "Oh, you bad fellow, I know you now! Here's your supper."

Captain Henry M. Minnigh (officer at left) stands proudly in front of Company K of the 1st Pennsylvania Reserves. Sergeant Isaac N. Durboraw (front rank, far right), along with several of his fellow Gettysburg natives, received tacit permission from the captain to visit their homes in the Rebel-occupied town on the night of July 3.

Aftermath in Blood

As a lowering sky heralded the approach of rain, the exhausted armies confronted each other across the carnage-strewn field of Gettysburg. It was the Fourth of July, but few soldiers were in a mood for celebration. While the Army of the Potomac had obstinately held its ground against repeated Confederate onslaughts, Meade's forces had sustained some 23,000 casualties, and many Yankees feared that another Rebel assault was inevitable.

In fact Lee's Army of Northern Virginia was in no condition to renew the conflict. The Southern forces had lost in excess of 20,000 men—some place the figure as high as 28,000—and with nearly 40 percent of his command out of action, Lee had little choice but to abandon his invasion of the North and withdraw across the Potomac into Virginia.

By late afternoon the rain was falling, and Lee began the delicate task of extricating his troops from their positions north and west of the Federal defenses. The slowest-moving element of his force started first—a 17-mile-long wagon train carrying supplies and ambulances filled with groaning wounded. Brigadier General John D. Imboden's cavalry was detailed to escort the wagons toward the Potomac. Lee instructed General Jubal Early to keep his division in place until July 5, when he would bring up the rear of the retreating army.

As the dispirited Confederate soldiers donned their packs and blanket rolls and started southward, they passed through horrific scenes of slaughter. "The sights and sounds that assailed us were simply indescribable," recalled Virginia artillery lieutenant Robert Stiles, "corpses swollen to twice their original size, some of them actually burst asunder with the pressure of foul gases and vapors."

When Federal skirmishers moved tentatively forward to scout the vacated enemy positions, they too passed over the battlefield's human wreckage, gagging as they began to bury the decomposing dead. Sergeant Thomas Meyer of the 148th Pennsylvania noted that the stench "would come

Used as General Meade's headquarters and later as a hospital, the Leister farmhouse on Cemetery Ridge stands amid shattered stone walls and dead horses that show the effects of the Confederate bombardment on July 3.

up in waves and when at its worst the breath would stop in the throat; the lungs could not take it in, and a sense of suffocation would be experienced. We would cover our faces with our hands and turn the back toward the breeze and retch and gasp for breath."

With the realization of Union victory, the handful of reporters accompanying Meade's army scrambled to spread the news to the Northern public. On July 4 correspondent Samuel Wilkeson, who had arrived at Gettysburg midway in the battle, filed a detailed account for the *New York Times* that credited the stalwart Federals with "breaking the pride and power of the rebel invasion." But Wilkeson's elation evaporated when he learned that his 19-year-old son, Bayard, had been fatally wounded on the first day of the engagement.

"My pen is heavy," Wilkeson wrote. "O, you dead, who at Gettysburg have baptized with your blood the second birth of Freedom in America, how you are to be envied! I rise from a grave whose wet clay I have passionately kissed, and I look up and see Christ spanning the battle-field with his feet, and reaching fraternal and loving up to heaven. His right hand opens the gates of Paradise, —with his left he sweetly beckons to these mutilated, bloody, swollen forms to ascend."

Once it became clear that the fighting was over, Gettysburg's civilians began to emerge from cellars and hiding places to survey the damage that had been inflicted upon their community. Many townsfolk pitched in to help bury the dead, while those caught looting personal belongings from the fallen or making off with saddles and weapons were forced to do the grisly work at gunpoint. Mrs. Elizabeth M. Thorn, the wife of Evergreen Cemetery's superintendent, helped to bury 105 soldiers, despite the fact that she was in her sixth month of pregnancy. By the time she had finished, her clothing was saturated with blood.

Besides the corpses of more than 5,000 men and 3,000 horses and mules, the landscape was littered with the detritus of battle. "Trees were scarred and shattered," wrote Pennsylvania college professor Michael Jacobs, "thousands of minie balls, of solid shot and shells, lay scattered over the ground, and cast-off coats, knapsacks, blankets, cartouch-boxes, canteens, scabbards, and other accoutrements in vast numbers, were everywhere to be met with."

Virtually every house and barn in Gettysburg had been turned into an improvised hospital, where haggard surgeons struggled to save the mangled wounded. Carpets and floors were awash in gore, walls were spattered with blood, and piles of amputated limbs were heaped outside the open windows. Because of the sheer number of wounded, many sufferers had to wait days before receiving attention. A worker for the U.S. Sanitary Commission, a private relief organization, found Gettysburg's courthouse overflowing with casualties, "lying on the bare floor, covered with blood, and dirt, and vermin, entirely naked having perhaps only a newspaper to protect their festering wounds from the flies!"

Shaken by the carnage, and knowing that the Army of the Potomac had been strained nearly to the breaking point by forced marches and unprecedented casualties, Meade was slow to take up the pursuit of Lee's retreating columns. "Push forward," Army Chief of Staff Henry W. Halleck wired from Washington, "and fight Lee before he can cross the Potomac." But it was July 5 before the first of Meade's forces—Sedgwick's relatively unbloodied Sixth Corps—got underway, and two days later before the other corps began to follow in Lee's wake.

Riding south into Maryland, the Union cavalry clashed repeatedly with Jeb Stuart's Confederate horsemen, who skillfully fended off the Yankee troopers. Although days of downpours had turned roads into quagmires and slowed the Federal infantry to a tortuous crawl, the rain had also swelled the Potomac to such an extent that Lee's army was delayed on the Maryland side of the river. While engineers struggled to span the torrent with pontoons, the Confederate soldiers erected a line of massive earthworks covering the approaches to the bridgeheads.

By July 12 General Meade's army was in position facing the Rebel lines. But the sight of heavily entrenched opponents gave Meade pause and filled his soldiers with foreboding. The Army of the Potomac had learned what it was like to storm fortified positions at the Battle of Fredericksburg, and no one was eager for a repetition of that one-sided slaughter. When Meade called a counsel of war, most of his corps commanders advised against an attack, and the general decided to wait. Meanwhile, Lee was finally able to start his troops across the precarious pontoon bridges, and although 1,500 men of General Heth's division were cut off and captured above the crossing at Falling Waters, by July 14 the Army of Northern Virginia was once again on Southern soil.

No men in Lee's army felt the failure of their campaign more keenly than the Marylanders, who had all too briefly cherished the hope that the invasion of the North would forever free their native state from Federal occupation. Yet, as Major W. W. Goldsborough of the Confederacy noted, the spirit of the Southern soldiers was far from broken. "And still these men were cheerful to a degree that could hardly have been expected under the trying circumstances," Goldsborough wrote, "and they felt the loss of comrades left behind torn and bleeding on that bloody field at Gettysburg more than they did their own sufferings."

The high tide of the Confederacy had crested at Gettysburg, but the escape of Lee's army ensured that the terrible war would continue until a Federal commander brought that redoubtable force to bay. The Battle of Gettysburg did not prove decisive, but the experiences of those terrible three days, seared into the soul of every survivor, bear witness to the self-sacrifice of men who cherished idealistic beliefs above life itself.

Fifty years after the battle, with the country reunited and the torn landscape healed, Joshua Lawrence Chamberlain traveled to Gettysburg to revisit the scene of his epic fight as commander of the 20th Maine on Little Round Top. Just months before his death, Chamberlain wrote of the enduring message of that hallowed terrain:

"I went—it is not long ago—to stand again upon that crest whose one day's crown of fire has passed into the blazoned coronet of fame. . . . I sat there alone, on the storied crest, till the sun went down as it did before over the misty hills, and the darkness crept up the slopes, till from all earthly sight I was buried as with those before. But oh, what radiant companionship rose around, what steadfast ranks of power, what bearing of heroic souls. Oh, the glory that beamed through those nights and days. . . . The proud young valor that rose above the mortal, and then at last was mortal after all."

GETTYSBURG CASUALTIES

FEDERAL

Killed	3,070
Wounded	14,497
Captured and missing	5,434
Total	23,001

CONFEDERATE

Killed	2,592
Wounded	12,706
Captured and missing	5,150
Total	20,448

CORPORAL THOMAS D. MARBAKER

11th New Jersey Infantry, Carr's Brigade

On July 4 the guns fell silent and the two exhausted armies cautiously eyed each other across the corpse-strewn fields. Corporal Marbaker, like thousands of his fellow soldiers, was stunned by the scenes of carnage wrought by three days of fighting.

Upon the open fields, like sheaves bound by the reaper, in crevices of the rocks, behind fences, trees and buildings; in thickets, where they had crept for safety only to die in agony; by stream or wall or hedge, wherever the battle had raged or their weakening steps could carry them, lay the dead. Some with faces bloated and blackened beyond recognition, lay with glassy eyes staring up at the blazing summer sun; others, with faces downward and clenched hands filled with grass or earth, which told of the agony of their last moments.

Here a headless trunk, there a severed limb; in all the grotesque positions that unbearable pain and intense suffering contorts the human form, they lay. Upon the faces of some death had frozen a smile; some showed the shadow of fear, while upon others was indelibly set the grim stamp of determination.

All around was the wreck the battle-storm leaves in its wake—broken caissons, dismounted guns, small arms bent and twisted by the storm or dropped and scattered by disabled hands; dead and bloated horses, torn and ragged equipments, and all the sorrowful wreck that the waves of battle leave at their ebb; and over all, hugging the earth like a fog, poisoning every breath, the pestilential stench of decaying humanity.

The body of a young Confederate soldier lies in a sharpshooter's nest in the Devil's Den. Another photograph of the site has revealed that the soldier actually died elsewhere and suggests that the photographer, probably Timothy O'Sullivan, had the body moved about 40 yards for dramatic effect.

CAPTAIN JOHN E. DOOLEY

1st Virginia Infantry, Kemper's Brigade

In the Rebel charge of July 3, Dooley was shot through both thighs near the Federal batteries and fell into Union hands. He endured several days in an open field hospital before being taken to Fort McHenry in Baltimore for recuperation.

Morning dawns at last. Though raining still the chill of the small hours before day break no longer makes me shiver, and soon the carriers come around with their vessels of coffee, and this does much towards comforting the inner part of man. An officer (Yankee) is enquiring if any one here is acquainted with John Scammel. I tell him that he belongs to my company. "Here then," he said, "are some little things I took from his pocket; he died a few minutes ago just a few yards off." These little effects consist of a five dollar Confederate bill stained with his blood, and a paper showing the date, etc. of his enrollment. Poor fellow, he might have lived if proper care had been shown him. . . .

Here is a poor wounded Confederate who is walking up and down, wandering anywhere his cracked brain directs him. Just on top of his head and penetrating to his brain is a large opening made by a shell in which I might insert my hand. He walks about as if nothing was the matter with him, and pays no attention to any advice given him.

About two yards from me . . . is a Virginia Lieut., 24th Va. His leg is torn and mangled fearfully. . . . There he reclines with his back against a stump and his wounded stump of a leg dragging heavily on the ground, clumsily bound up and portions of the flesh exposed and bedraggled in the mud. I have watched this officer pretty closely and although I have seen much pain and agony in his expression, I haven't heard a single word of complaint or impatient exclamation break from his lips. Only once I heard him ask of some negro camp attendant in a tone of piteous expostulation to make a little fire near him, for the night was cold and the rain was chilling him to the very marrow of his bones. No fires were made however, for whether it was against orders or the result of neglect, we suffered a great deal from rain and the chilling night air. My poor friend appeared to suffer so much that after a selfish contest with my better impulses I sent him over my oil-cloth, that being doubled up and placed under his amputated member it might free him from much pain and distress. This gave him much relief and he appeared quite grateful; and now we were both equal in regard to exposure to the weather, for neither of us had any covering except our clothes.

In a rare hospital photograph, 1st Lieutenant Sanford Branch of the 8th Georgia Infantry (on cot at right) recuperates after being left for dead on the field by his own men. Captured and treated by the Federals, he was later exchanged in 1864.

SERGEANT GEORGE A. BOWEN

12th New Jersey Infantry, Smyth's Brigade

Federal burial parties attempted to identify and properly inter their own dead, but as a visitor to Gettysburg observed, "the Rebel dead, almost without exception, are buried promiscuously in single graves of trenches, where they lie unwept and unhonored." Sergeant Bowen helped bury Confederates in front of the II Corps lines.

On Sunday morning all were ordered out to bury the dead and help get the wounded off. We found few living as they had laid out there since Friday afternoon in the broiling sun, and in the rain of Saturday day and night. Many are dead that could have been saved if we had been allowed by the enemy to have cared for them. The ground here is very hard, full of rocks and stones, the digging is very laborious work, the dead are many, the time is short, so they got but very shallow graves, in fact the most of them were buried in trenches, dug not over 18 inches deep, and as near where they fell as was possible, so as not to have to carry them far, this in many instances was not necessary as I saw 60 buried in one trench, not one of which was carried 25 feet. Saw one man who had died with his arm in such position that it stuck up when put in the hole, a man took his shovel struck it a blow breaking his arm so that it fell, this was done to save having so much dirt to throw. I remonstrated with him, he said the man was dead, and would make no difference to him. The graves were filled by throwing the earth right on the body, no coffins, not even wrapped up in anything.

Confederate dead lie in a shallow grave near the Rose farm as a burial detail labors in the background in this Timothy O'Sullivan photograph.

A wooden plank bearing a Union soldier's name, unit, and date of death served as a temporary grave marker.

"The best blood of old Carolina has been shed and that freely in this battle."

PRIVATE ALEXANDER MCNEILL

2d South Carolina Infantry, Kershaw's Brigade

With a lull in the fighting and the Army of Northern Virginia retreating toward the Potomac, most soldiers, including Private McNeill, got their first chance to write letters to loved ones at home with news of the momentous battle. McNeill's regiment lost 27 dead and 125 wounded, some mortally, out of the 412 men who marched into battle.

Bivouac Near Hagerstown, Md.
July 7, 1863
My Dear Wife

I am thankfull to an ever kind and mercifull God that I have again been spared and that I have passed through the severest battle of the war unhurt. I am at a loss to know how any of us are left even to tell the tale for all of our boys freely acknowledge this to have been the most terrible fire to which they ever were exposed. But while a part of us are still unhurt, yet I regret to record the loss of many a gallant brother in arms. The best blood of old Carolina has been shed and that freely in this battle. . . .

. . . Our brave boys were all killed near the same spot. We buried them as well as we could in the same grave on the battlefield and placed a head board at each ones head with his name, Company and Reg't. We did the best we could with them under the circumstances and our brave boys now sleep in a cold and silent grave upon the enemy's soil. Our wounded left behind I doubt not will be well treated and such of them as recover will be returned to their friends and relatives.

. . . In my opinion we have made nothing yet by this campaign. We came here with the best army the Confederacy ever carried into the field but thousands of our brave boys are left upon the enemys soil and in my opinion our Army will never be made up of such material again. . . . The enemy will no doubt claim a great victory and say the backbone of the rebellion is again about to be crushed and broken. I never was so completely worn down in all my life as now. I will hope that we may get a few days rest and allowed to recruit up and recover from our broken down condition.

Tinie, I doubt whether I will have an opportunity to send this letter off soon or not, but hope that a chance may present itself for I know you are filled with anxiety to hear from us. The news of this terrible battle has, no doubt, already reached you and our entire Confederacy is full of anxiety to hear from their friends in the army. I must ask your pardon for this poor letter. I am so sleepy and worn down that I cannot collect an idea, although my theme should afford matter enough for pages. We are now at a halt but do not know how long we will remain here.

In haste I am as ever
Your loving Husband
Alex McNeill

Confederate Peter S. Hyde, his regiment unidentified, had this blue-and-white plaid shirt made for him in camp from an "old Dutchman's" bedspread purloined from a Pennsylvania home.

These brogans were recovered from a soldier's body during the process of removing the dead from temporary graves to military cemeteries.

The only clue to a dead Union soldier's identity, this ambrotype found on his body ignited a campaign to determine who he was. Thousands of copies were circulated, and in November a woman whose soldier-husband was missing recognized it as one she had sent him. He was Sergeant Amos Humiston of the 154th New York.

ANNA MORRIS HOLSTEIN

Nurse, II Corps Hospital

Anna Holstein was working in a hospital at Potomac Creek, Virginia, when word arrived of the battle at Gettysburg. A veteran nurse who helped care for the wounded of Antietam and Chancellorsville, she traveled with her husband, William, to join the staff of the II Corps hospital at Gettysburg.

I recall a burial where three were at one time taken to the little spot we called a cemetery. . . . the stretcher-bearers came tramping wearily, bearing three bodies of those who had given their lives for freedom; as the last reached the place, the men dropped with a rough, jolting motion the army couch whereon he rested. The impatient effort to be rid of their burden was probably the means of saving a precious life; for the man—dead, as they supposed—raising his head, called in a clear voice: "Boys, what are you doing?" The response as prompt: "We came to bury you, Whitey." His calm reply was "I don't see it, boys, give me a drink of water, and carry me back." And then glancing into the open grave: "I won't be buried by this raw recruit!" The raw recruit was a lieutenant of his own regiment. Not many stand so near the "dark valley" that they look into their own graves, and live. The "boys" did carry him back; and with the greatest care, his life was saved.

Upon receiving news of the carnage, hundreds of humanitarians flocked to the battlefield from eastern cities including Harrisburg and Philadelphia to tend the wounded. Among them were agents of the U.S. Christian Commission, seen here caring for men believed to be from the II Corps. Scores of civilian volunteers assisted military doctors and nurses in the field hospitals.

BUSHROD W. JAMES

Volunteer Doctor, U.S. Christian Commission

Dr. James of Philadelphia, who served in hospitals at Antietam, traveled to Gettysburg under the auspices of the U.S. Christian Commission. James and his party brought medical supplies, which they shipped by wagon from a rail stop near Harrisburg to the battlefield.

Here I found a corps of ladies, several of whom were of my clientele in Philadelphia, who had come down to the battlefield to do what good they could for the poor afflicted soldiers. Samaritan-like, they had given up their own comfort for a time in order to help the wounded and dying. They announced my arrival to the surgeon in charge, telling him that I was a surgeon, and he immediately placed me in charge of a row of hospital tents, the occupants of which had all undergone the severe operation of amputation at the hip-joint or along the femur. I made a careful examination of the general condition of the cases, instructed the nurses and the hospital stewards what should be done in case of hemorrhage occurring, which in the larger vessels in that region of the body would cause rapid death in the event of the ligature giving way, and instructed them as to other emergencies, and then I proceeded to the chief surgeon and asked if there were any additional duties that I could perform. My services were gladly accepted, and for several days, in conjunction with these responsible cases in the tents, which were my special care, I spent my available time at the operating tables, which were situated in the woods on the crest of the slope which receded to White Creek; the hospital tents were run in rows along avenues on the level area to the north. Every surgeon in the hospital was kept busy nearly a week amputating limbs, probing for and removing bullets, or sewing, bandaging and dressing the wounds of those who were too badly mangled and shattered to be aided in any more hopeful manner. Every hour the improvised operating tables were full, and many of the poor fellows had to be operated upon while lying upon the damp ground. We could not help it.

The kepi belonging to Captain Elliot C. Pierce, Federal ambulance officer, bears a I Corps staff badge combining the red, white, and blue colors of the corps' three divisions.

EMILY BLISS SOUDER

Volunteer Nurse, U.S. Christian Commission

Emily Souder, a Philadelphia resident, arrived in Gettysburg on the night of July 14 and for the next two weeks did volunteer duty in the hospitals of the II Corps and V Corps. In 1864 she published "Leaves from the Battlefield of Gettysburg," a collection of letters written to her husband, Edmund.

Gettysburg, July 15, 1863

My Dear —,

I must give you an account of our first day's experience in camp; a day of horror, I might almost say and yet a day of blessing. We arrived here last night, after a ride of excessive discomfort, from Hanover Junction. . . . While we were waiting, as the ambulances passed on their way to the depot, we handed the poor soldiers a drink from the doorstep and when the boxes were safely housed, we got into an ambulance and rode to the hospital tents of the Second Corps. We were driven by a pleasant fellow from Vermont, who told us many interesting things about the battle-ground, which we crossed. We saw the rifle-pits, the dead horses, the shattered windows and the stone walls, all scattered and many soldiers' graves. But who shall describe the horrible atmosphere which meets us almost continually? Chloride of lime has been freely used in the broad streets of the town and to-day the hospital was much improved by the same means; but it is needful to close the eyes on sights of horror and to shut the ears against sounds of anguish and to extinguish, as far as possible, the sense of smelling.

We dispensed buckets of milk punch and quantities of corn-starch, nicely prepared with condensed milk and brandy, besides sundry cups of tea, and unwonted luxury and broth made of beef jelly condensed, with many other services and a little chat occasionally with some poor fellow. I found a great many Maine boys; many from Wisconsin and Minnesota; scarcely one who had not lost an arm or a leg. I felt as if I could hardly wait upon the rebels; but the first call almost upon my sympathies, was to see a young Mississippian, and all day long we found the Union soldiers side by side with the rebels. Death is very busy with these poor fellows on both sides. It seems hard for no kind voice to speak a word of cheer to the parting spirit and yet there are many laborers in the vineyard; but the work is great. There are perpetual calls for "something for a wounded soldier who can't eat anything hard,"—"milk punch," "a cup of tea," or "a cup of coffee with milk." Two or three desperately wounded men begged for ice, with an earnestness of agonized entreaty which could brook no denial. I promised, if possible, to obtain it; but found that the surgeon had absolutely forbidden that the ice should be touched, as the lives of many men depended upon their having it.

Amputations for the wounded were performed as soon as possible to prevent the spread of infection. As this photograph indicates, such operations often took place on a makeshift table in the open air. Army bands played by detachments through the night to drown out the cries of the wounded and those undergoing surgery.

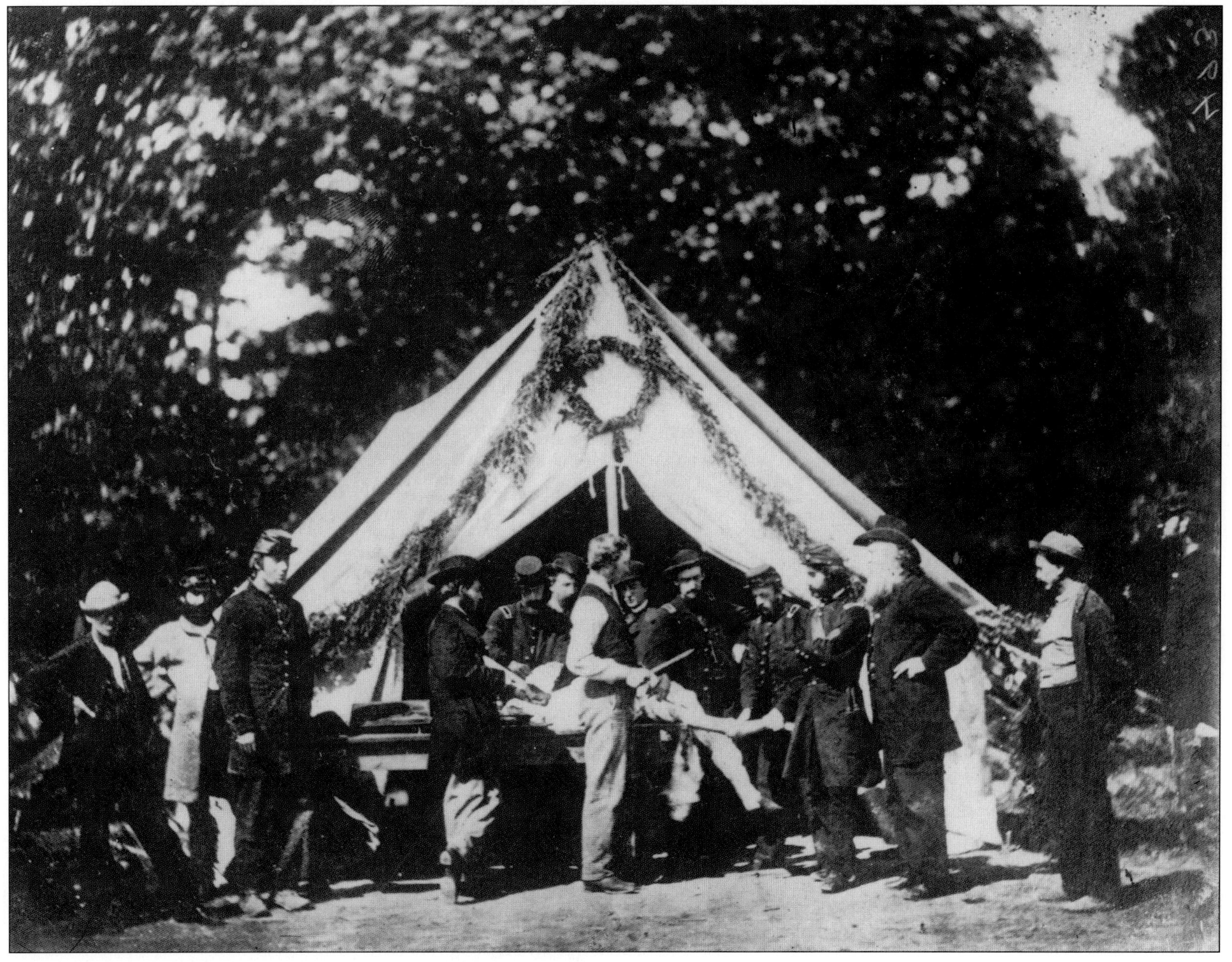

CORNELIA HANCOCK

Volunteer Nurse

Twenty-three-year-old Cornelia Hancock left home in Hancock Bridge, New Jersey, to volunteer as a nurse. Over the objection of Dorothea Dix, the superintendent of women nurses, who found her too young and attractive for such rough work among soldiers, Hancock took her place in the overcrowded field hospitals. After the war she opened a school for freedmen in South Carolina.

Every barn, church, and building of any size in Gettysburg had been converted into a temporary hospital. We went the same evening to one of the churches, where I saw for the first time what war meant. Hundreds of desperately wounded men were stretched out on boards laid across the high-backed pews as closely as they could be packed together. The boards were covered with straw. Thus elevated, these poor sufferers' faces, white and drawn with pain, were almost on a level with my own. I seemed to stand breast-high in a sea of anguish.

The townspeople of Gettysburg were in devoted attendance, and there were many from other villages and towns. The wounds of all had been dressed at least once, and some systematic care was already established. Too inexperienced to nurse, I went from one pallet to another with pencil, paper, and stamps in hand, and spent the rest of that night in writing letters from the soldiers to their families and friends. To many mothers, sisters, and wives I penned the last message of those who were soon to become the "beloved dead."

A tin cup issued by the U.S. Sanitary Commission likely served a double purpose. Not only was it used to serve broth and milk punch; a patient might have poured water from it over his wounds to keep them moist.

GEORGEANNA M. WOOLSEY

Volunteer Nurse, U.S. Sanitary Commission

Georgeanna and her mother, Jane, were directed by Frederick Law Olmsted, of the New York Sanitary Commission, "to take charge of a feeding station and lodge for the wounded men." Woolsey recalled the process of dispersing the wounded to permanent military hospitals after the battle.

This is the way the thing was managed at first: The surgeons, left in care of the wounded three or four miles out from the town, went up and down among the men in the morning, and said, "Any of you boys who can make your way to the cars, can go to Baltimore." So off start all who think they feel well enough, anything being better than the "hospitals," so called, for the first few days after a battle. . . .

For the first few days the worst cases only came down in ambulances from the hospitals; hundreds of fellows hobbled along as best they could, in heat and dust, for hours, slowly toiling, and many hired farmers' wagons, as hard as the farmers' fists themselves, and were jolted down to the railroad at three or four dollars the man. . . . No men were turned back. You fed and you sheltered them just when no one else could have done so; and out of the boxes and barrels of good and nourishing things, which you, people at home, had supplied, we took all that was needed. Some of you sent a stove (that is, the money to get it), some of you the beef-stock, some of you the milk and fresh bread; and all of you would have been thankful that you had done so, could you have seen the refreshment and comfort received through these things. . . .

Twice a day the trains left for Baltimore or Harrisburg, and twice a day we fed all the wounded who arrived for them. Things were systematized now, and the men came down in long ambulance trains to the cars: baggage cars they were, fitted with straw for the wounded to lie on, and broken open at either end to let in the air. A government surgeon was always present to attend to the careful lifting of the soldiers from ambulance to car. Many of the men could get along very nicely, holding one foot up, and taking great jumps on their crutches. The latter were a great comfort: we had a nice supply at the lodge, and they travelled up and down from the tents to the cars daily. Only occasionally did we dare let a pair go on with some very lame soldier, who begged for them: we needed them to help the new arrivals each day, and trusted to the men being supplied at the hospitals at the journey's end. Pads and crutches are a standing want—pads particularly. We manufactured them out of the rags we had, stuffed with sawdust from brandy boxes; and with half a sheet, and some soft straw. . . .

When the surgeons had the wounded all placed, with as much comfort as seemed possible under the circumstances, on board the train, our detail of men would go from car to car, with soup made of beef-stock or fresh meat, full of potatoes, turnips, cabbage, and rice, with fresh bread and coffee, and, when stimulants were needed, with ale, milk punch, or brandy. Water pails were in great demand for use in the cars on the journey, and also empty bottles, to take the place of canteens. All our whiskey and brandy bottles were washed and filled up at the spring, and the boys went off, carefully hugging their extemporized canteens, from which they would wet their wounds, or refresh themselves, till the journey ended.

"To many mothers, sisters, and wives I penned the last message of those who were soon to become the 'beloved dead.' "

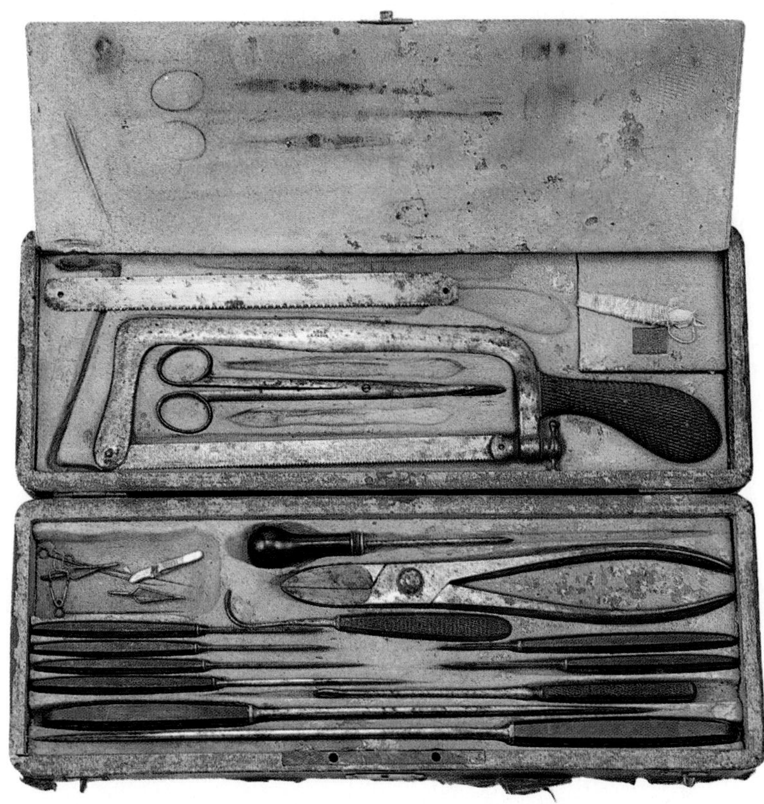

The surgical kit belonging to Dr. John C. Jones, assistant surgeon of the 4th Texas, saw plenty of action at the Battle of Gettysburg. Shown are a bone saw, amputating knives, scalpels, forceps, clips, needles, a probe, a tenaculum, and silk thread.

PRIVATE ANDREW W. REESE

Troup Artillery, Georgia

Confederate artilleryman Andrew Reese of Captain Henry H. Carlton's Georgia Battery recalled that the strict discipline that characterized relationships between the Confederate army and Pennsylvania residents during the early stages of the campaign became increasingly lax during the grim retreat to Virginia.

On Saturday night the 4th, Gen. Lee withdrew his army, and about dark we commenced our retreat. It was pouring rain and dark as Erebus. I sat on my horse all night, getting no sleep, whatever, save a few brief "nods" now and then, when we halted. Hagerstown, Md., was reached Sunday night, and there, for three or four days we offered the enemy battle, which he declined. He had been too terribly punished to risk another combat, and the fact of his having commenced to fall back at Gettysburg twenty-four hours before we did, as we afterwards learned, was additional proof of it.

. . . Orders were very strict in regard to private property, but the track of a large army is marked by ruin and desolation, and there was no exception to the rule in this case. I think Fredericksburg was avenged at Gettysburg and that so far as we went, we had satisfaction for the ravaged fields of Stafford and other counties in Virginia. We burnt the iron works of that old scoundrel Thed. Stevens, and took some 40 horses from him. If $100,000 covers the damages I will be much surprised. I did not do any plundering myself, but am compelled to say that our bill of fare was wonderfully improved. Chickens, butter, "apple-butter," buttermilk, honey, vegetables and the delicious "black heart" cherry were no rarities, as Confederate money was abundant, and the people very patriotic. Some have been so cynical as to say that it was Hobson's choice—that or nothing—but of course that is slander.

Confederate artillerymen stand by their guns along part of the nine-mile line of earthworks that were built between Hagerstown and the Potomac River to cover Lee's retreat.

On July 6, 1863, 34-year-old Alfred R. Waud, artist for Harper's Weekly, and photographer Timothy O'Sullivan found themselves at Devil's Den, where Confederate sharpshooters had proved so effective against Federal officers on Little Round Top. Wearing jackboots, armed with a revolver, and with sketchbook in hand, Waud posed gazing northward toward the Slaughter Pen for O'Sullivan's benefit. Waud's sketch of distant Little Round Top (below) was drawn from a boulder beyond the bushes seen in the left background.

"Where are you, my dear husband what are you doing and what is going on."

FANNY CARTER SCOTT

Wife of Captain R. Taylor Scott—Staff, Major General George E. Pickett

Fanny Carter Scott wrote from her home, "Glen Welby," in Loudoun County, Virginia, seeking news of her husband and her brother, Captain Edward Carter, an officer in the same division. When she learned that her brother had been severely wounded during Pickett's Charge, she secured passes from Federal authorities to go to Chester, Pennsylvania, to nurse him.

Glen Welby - Monday 6th July 1863

Where are you, my dear husband what are you doing and what is going on. We live in utter ignorance of everything and everybody, outside our immediate neighborhood. We rarely see a Southern paper and never hear anything definite of our army. Yesterday, we heard there had been a fight in Pennsylvania and that we had whipped the enemy. Of course, we are all anxiety to hear more. I live daily and hourly in dread of a battle. Has Longstreet been engaged? Is Edward safe?

MAJOR GENERAL GEORGE E. PICKETT

Division Commander, Army of Northern Virginia

Shortly before he marched off with his division to Pennsylvania, General George Pickett was engaged to a young Virginia beauty, Miss LaSalle Corbell. He made no secret of his deep affection toward "Sally," and his fellow generals often chided him during the campaign for his maudlin behavior. After the near destruction of his command on the third day, he joined the long, painful retreat back to Virginia. While waiting to cross back over the Potomac River, he penned this letter to his fiancée.

Williamsport, July 8, 1863

I am crossing the river to-day, guarding some four thousand prisoners back to Winchester, where I shall take command and try to recruit my spirit-crushed, wearied, cut-up people. It is just two months this morning since I parted from you, and yet the disappointments and sorrows that have been crowded into the interval make the time seem years instead. My grand old division, which was so full of faith and courage then, is now almost extinguished. But one field-officer in the whole command escaped in that terrible third of July slaughter, and alas! alas! for the men who fearlessly followed their lead on to certain death.

We were ordered to take a height. We took it, but under the most withering fire that I, even in my dreams, could ever have conceived of, and I have seen many battles. Alas! alas! no support came, and my poor fellows who had gotten in were overpowered. Your uncle, Colonel Phillips, behaved most gallantly—was wounded, but not seriously. Your cousins, Captain Cralle and C. C. Phillips, are among the missing. But for you, I should greatly have preferred to answer reveille on the fourth of July with the poor fellows over there, and how I escaped it is a miracle; how any of us survived is marvelous, unless it was by prayer.

My heart is very, very sad, and it seems almost sacrilegious to think of happiness at such a time, but let my need of your sweet womanly sympathy and comfort in these sad hours plead extenuation, and be prepared, I beseech you, at a moment's notice to obey the summons that will make you my wife.

Confederate prisoners trudge away from Gettysburg as they begin the long journey to prison camps such as Johnson's Island in Lake Erie and Old Point Comfort in Maryland. Many of the 12,000 or so prisoners taken at Gettysburg were not freed until the winter of 1865.

Artillerymen of the Federal siege train haul their 4.5-inch Ordnance rifle through a driving rainstorm as they make their tedious way south toward Frederick in pursuit of Lee's Army of Northern Virginia. The heavy guns, with their massive carriages, were slow to deploy in action, and the two batteries armed with the big rifles, Batteries B and M, 1st Connecticut Heavy Artillery, sat out the Battle of Gettysburg in reserve.

CAPTAIN HENRY L. ABBOTT

20th Massachusetts Infantry, Hall's Brigade

In 1861 Abbott, the scion of a prominent Lawrence, Massachusetts, family, joined the 20th Massachusetts, dubbed the Harvard Regiment for its many officers who were Harvard graduates. On July 3 one of Abbott's close friends, Lieutenant Henry Ropes, was seated under a tree reading Dickens when he was killed by the premature detonation of a Federal shell.

Near Gettysburg, July 6, 1863

My Dear Papa,

When our great victory was just over the exultation of victory was so great that one didn't think of our fearful losses, but now I can't help feeling a great weight at my heart. Poor Henry Ropes was one of the dearest friends I ever had or expect to have. He was one of the purest-minded, noblest, most generous men I ever knew. His loss is terrible. His men actually wept when they showed me his body, even under the tremendous cannonade, a time when most soldiers see their comrades dying around them with indifference.

Killed by friendly fire from a New York battery, Lieutenant Henry Ropes of the 20th Massachusetts Infantry was a combat veteran, having fought in the Seven Days', Second Manassas, and Fredericksburg battles.

COLONEL DAVID W. AIKEN

7th South Carolina Infantry, Kershaw's Brigade

The hard marches and desperate fighting of the Gettysburg campaign exacted a heavy physical toll on Robert E. Lee's Army of Northern Virginia and inevitably eroded morale. In a letter to his wife, Colonel Aiken confided both his discouragement and his determination to fight on.

Near Williamsport July 13 Noon

Only because it is raining very steadily, my dearest wife, and I can do nothing else, do I now attempt to drop you a few lines. I have not one word of news to write, except that we are resting here behind breastworks, in constant hearing of the enemy's guns. We will not attack them it seems, and they are evidently afraid to attack us. We have been here four days, with the Potomac swimming behind us, with our rations cut down to less than half flour, a plenty of fresh beef, no grease, & no salt. Men are exhausted, hungry, dirty, ragged & in many instances barefooted. Orders were issued this AM at daylight to rouse our troops & prepare for action, as the enemy were about to attack us, but I suppose the rain will prevent. If they come upon us they will be whipt; if we go upon them, I rather anticipate a similar fate. No one can tell what the next few days may reveal here. We are now somewhat depressed at the news of the fall of Vicksburg, but I believe it will only make our men fight the harder, & of course whip the enemy easier. Our waggon train began this morning to ford the river, but I fear this rain will put a stop to it by raising the river. We are building, however, a pontoon bridge over the river, which I am told will be done today. By tomorrow night our waggons may be across, & if the enemy does not then attack us I think, or rather hope, we will take up our line of march for Virg soil. This would be cheering news to this army. I don't think Genl Lee or anyone else will ever get it back into Maryland again. I never want to try it over certain.

In an attempt to thwart General Lee's escape into Virginia, Major Peter Weber of the 6th Michigan Cavalry led two companies in a brilliant charge (above) against Heth's division (right). The encounter at Falling Waters on July 14 was one of the last skirmishes of the Gettysburg campaign. Within minutes of the attack, many Michigan troopers, including Weber, lay dead. One of Lee's most promising officers, General Johnston Pettigrew, commander of Heth's rear guard, was mortally wounded.

General Lee's army makes its way over the Chesapeake and Ohio Canal, preparing to cross the rain-swelled Potomac River near Williamsport, Maryland (left). Before a pontoon bridge could be rebuilt, wagons and pack animals were swept away by high water; the slow and dangerous crossing was further complicated by the threat of Union cavalry in pursuit.

Three Confederate captives stand beside a rail and timber breastwork on Seminary Ridge as they await transport to a prison camp. They were among the 5,425 unwounded soldiers taken prisoner by Meade's army; another 6,802 wounded fell into Federal hands.

PRIVATE ZACK LANDRUM

4th Texas Infantry, Robertson's Brigade

Private Landrum was wounded in the leg during the fighting on Little Round Top on July 2 but was able to elude capture by the Federals. After the battle he was evacuated with the wagon trains back to Virginia.

Winchester Va. July 15th 1863
Dear Mother

After so long a silence I once more will try and write you a few lines. I would have answered your letter that you wrote me by Jimmie Cartwright, but we have been on the move ever since, and in that trip, to Pennsylvania where I received a slight check in my farther propertys from a Yankee, you have no doubt before now received through the papers an account of the fight at Gettysburg. It was one of the severest battles that has been fought during this war. We had to fight the Yankees on a Mountain, where it was very steep and rocks as large as a meeting house. . . . I had gone a considerable distance up the Mountain when one of the rascals put me to a stand still, by the means of a Minnie ball through the thigh just above the knee and across the top of my thigh going in my left thigh and out striking the other, bruising it a good deal but not going in. . . .

. . . I was carried to the Hospital one morning and sent on in a wagon to Williamsport Md. and from there here in an ambulance, they are sending the wounded from here to Staunton as fast as they can. I think I will get off in a few days and then I will get a transfer to Richmond. I intend to try and get a furlough and come home if I can cross the Mississippi River but we hear here that Vicksburg has surrendered. I don't believe a word of it, if it is so I will get a furlough and go to Ala. My wound is doing very well. I think I will be able to travel in two or three weeks. I had no paper or anything to write on, but there is a wounded Georgian by my side kindly furnished me with them and says if I can't go home I must go with him. I do not know but I shall if I can't go home. You must excuse such bad writing as I have to write on an old cartridge box. I will write to you as often as I can, write to me at Richmond. I must close as the flies are very bad. Write soon but I hope to be with you all soon.

My love to all—
Your Affectionate Son
Zack Landrum

LIEUTENANT JOHN C. L. MOUNGER

9th Georgia Infantry, G. T. Anderson's Brigade

In May 1863, Lieutenant Colonel John C. Mounger of the 9th Georgia drafted a letter resigning his commission, citing pain from old wounds and concern that his wife could not "manage and control" his slaves. The colonel never submitted the letter, however, and was mortally wounded at Gettysburg. His two sons, John and Thomas, also serving in the 9th Georgia, buried their father and sent the mournful news home to their mother in Brooks County, Georgia. Lieutenant John Mounger survived his father by only a year. He was killed in the Battle of the Wilderness in 1864.

Camp Near Martinsburg Va
July 18th 1863
Dear Mother:

I wrote you a few days ago concerning the death of our dear father, he was killed on the 2nd of July about one hour by sun, He was buried in a family grave yard 1/2 miles below Gettysburg, Pennsylvania, on the Chambers and Baltimore Turnpike, Capt Sutlive had a good coffin made for him and we put him away as well as could be expected, I have the dimensions of his coffin so when we get a chance to move him we can get a box for him without any trouble, Pa died very easy Tom says, I was not with him when He died, I was detailed and sent off after cattle some three or four days before the fight, Tom took good care of dear dear Pa until he died, but he only lived a few minutes after he was shot, He was shot with a minie ball through the right breast and a grape shot from cannon through the bowels Dear Mother we tried to carry him to Virginia before we burried him but it was impossible as the Yankeys were all around us and we could not get across the river without being captured, Dear Mother let us all try and meet him in Heaven, Tom & myself will try and be better boys Tom kept the stars on his coat and a lock of his hair, I wrote you a few days ago but I was in so much trouble that I do not recollect what I wrote, Dear Mother Pa has his horse here I would like to know what to do with him as I cannot draw feed for him, I can sell him but he will not bring more than 3 or 4 hundred dollars in the condition he is in and as for getting him home it will be impossible.

SURGEON DANIEL M. HOLT

121st New York Infantry, Bartlett's Brigade

In 1862 Holt passed the New York examination for military surgeons and joined the 121st New York. After the Battle of Salem Church in May 1863, Holt remained behind with the wounded and fell briefly into Rebel hands. He served until October 1864, when tuberculosis forced his resignation.

But while I thus encouragingly write, believing that I shall soon see home, our work being done, I cannot but feel impressed that we have not yet done with them, however much they now suffer and are demoralized: The shattered, flying mass, will preserve a nucleus around which they will gather, and at some subsequent period will offer battle. Too momentous are the results of this rebellion to the hearts and purposes of the lights of Southern Chivalry to thus quietly witness the extinction of the brightest hopes of a misguided ambition. No, they will some day turn up in some quarter of the globe, but never, never again upon free soil of the Nation.

In this painting by David Blythe, troops of the Federal I Corps ford the Potomac River around Williamsport on July 18 in pursuit of Lee's escaping army.

"Never were a people so high in hope . . . cast down so suddenly and so low."

Battered by the fighting and exhausted from forced marches, the Federal army failed to confront Lee's Confederates. Here a Federal wagon train crosses the Potomac River at Berlin, Maryland, around July 19—five days after the Rebels slipped into Virginia.

LIEUTENANT COLONEL SAMUEL W. MELTON

Staff, Confederate Adjutant & Inspector General's Office

Melton, a South Carolinian, held an appointment in Richmond on the staff of General Samuel Cooper, the Confederacy's chief administrative officer. In a letter to his wife, Melton confided his hopes and fears for the Confederate cause after the defeat at Gettysburg.

Richmond, Va July 22, 1863
My dear Wife:

. . . We have all been much cast down by recent events. Never were a people so high in hope, with such reliable assurances of final success, cast down so suddenly and so low. The blows which have recently been given us by the enemy are terrible—the more so that they came when we were in our highest tide of successes, and expecting at every moment the advent of peace. But we are by no means in despair. Profoundly conscious of the fact that they have us now at a serious disadvantage, our people have girded themselves up all the more bravely, and are even the more determined just as more determination is required. We are obliged to succeed. These reverses but defer the day of triumph, if indeed, they have any serious effect at all.

THE GREAT BATTLES.

Splendid Triumph of the Army of the Potomac.

ROUT OF LEE'S FORCES ON FRIDAY

The Most Terrible Struggle of the War.

TREMENDOUS ARTILLERY DUEL.

Repeated Charges of the Rebel Columns Upon Our Position.

Every Charge Repulsed with Great Slaughter.

The Death of Longstreet and Hill.

Our Cavalry Active on the Enemy's Flank.

THE REBEL RETREAT CUT OFF.

Chambersburgh in Our Possession.

Advance of the Militia under Gen. Smith to Important Positions.

The Rebel Pontoon Bridge at Williamsport Destroyed.

The Contents of the Captured Dispatches from Jeff. Davis to Lee.

CHARLESTON, S. C.

NEWS FROM THE SEAT OF WAR IN PENNSYLVANIA.

THE BATTLE RENEWED AT GETTYSBURG—THREE DAYS' FIGHTING—THE BATTLE STILL RAGING—DESPERATE FIGHTING—SEVERAL YANKEE OFFICERS KILLED—SICKLES HAS A LEG SHOT OFF—DETAILS OF THE BATTLE—EXCITEMENT IN PENNSYLVANIA, ETC.

We have received Northern dates of the 4th. The news is important, and brings intelligence of a renewal of the bloody work in Pennsylvania. We compress the news in the following summary:

THE BATTLE AT GETTYSBURG RENEWED—A TERRIBLE BATTLE—SEVERE LOSS ON BOTH SIDES—THE CONFEDERATES THE ATTACKING PARTY—DETAILS OF THE BATTLE.

The accounts we gave yesterday from the Northern papers of the 3d, brought up the battle at Gettysburg to the morning of Thursday, the 2d instant, when the fighting ceased, for the time, on both sides. It appears that on Thursday, about half-past four o'clock in the evening, the battle was renewed, our forces making the attack on the enemy with terrific force, and the fighting had been continuous, and was still going on up to the latest advices, the battle having raged for three successive days—Wednesday, Thursday and Friday. A correspondent of the New York *Times*, writing from the battle field near Gettysburg, thus describes the battle of Thursday:

The position of our forces after the fight of Wednesday was to the eastward and southward of Gettysburg, covering the Baltimore Pike, the Taneytown and Emmettsburg roads, and still being nearly parallel with the latter. The formation of the ground on the right and centre was excellent for defensive purposes. On our extreme left the ground sloped off until the position was no higher than the enemy's. The ground in front of our line was a level, open country, interspersed here and there with an orchard or a very small tract of timber, generally oak, with the underbrush cut away. During the day a portion of the troops threw up temporary breastworks and an abattis. General Meade's headquarters were at an old house on the Taneytown road, immediately in rear of the centre.

On Thursday morning there were strong premonitions of an early engagement with the enemy in force, but the day wore away and no positive exhibition was made by the enemy. At 3½ o'clock General Meade had received sufficient assurances to justify him in the belief that the rebels were concentrating their forces on our left flank, which all felt to be secure under the protection of the invincible Third corps. Our line was immediately strengthened on that flank, General Sickles' corps being sent to its support, and several batteries from the reserve being brought out and placed in position. At 4½ o'clock, p. m., the enemy sent his first compliments by a salvo of artillery, his first shells falling uncomfortably near General Meade's headquarters. From this hour forth to 8½ o'clock, occurred by

Accounts of the three-day battle in Pennsylvania reached the people of the divided Republic belatedly through newspaper reports. On July 6 the New York Times trumpeted the Union victory at Gettysburg while a few days later, on July 10, a less decisive account of the action appeared in the Charleston Mercury. News traveled slowly in the Confederacy. The Union blockade of the South had wrought stringent conditions—as evidenced by the poor imprint of the Mercury story, a product of worn-out type and wafer-thin paper.

THE GETTYSBURG ADDRESS

Four score and seven years ago our fathers brought forth on this continent, a new nation, conceived in Liberty, and dedicated to the proposition that all men are created equal.

Now we are engaged in a great civil war, testing whether that nation, or any nation so conceived and so dedicated, can long endure. We are met on a great battle-field of that war. We have come to dedicate a portion of that field, as a final resting place for those who here gave their lives, that that nation might live. It is altogether fitting and proper that we should do this.

But, in a larger sense, we can not dedicate— we can not consecrate— we can not hallow— this ground. The brave men, living and dead, who struggled here, have consecrated it, far above our poor power to add or detract. The world will little note, nor long remember what we say here, but it can never forget what they did here. It is for us the living, rather, to be dedicated here to the unfinished work which they who fought here have thus far so nobly advanced. It is rather for us to be here dedicated to the great task remaining before us— that from these honored dead we take increased devotion to that cause for which they gave the last full measure of devotion— that we here highly resolve that these dead shall not have died in vain— that this nation, under God, shall have a new birth of freedom— and that government of the people, by the people, for the people, shall not perish from the earth.

At the dedication of the Gettysburg National Cemetery on November 19, 1863, President Lincoln—bareheaded and to the left of center—delivered his unforgettable message.

The enormity of the Battle of Gettysburg and its part in turning the tide of war that summer of 1863 spawned countless commemorations in the years to come. In 1889, at a gathering of the 20th Maine Infantry to dedicate their monuments on the battlefield, General Joshua Lawrence Chamberlain (sitting at center, right) joins members of the regiment he so steadfastly led in the defense of Little Round Top. Later, in a 50th reunion photograph (above), two old enemies are reunited in the brotherhood of the battlefield to ponder once again the cataclysm of those three days in July.

From an address given at the Gettysburg battlefield October 3, 1889:

"In great deeds something abides. On great fields something stays. Forms change and pass; bodies disappear; but spirits linger, to consecrate ground for the vision-place of souls. And reverent men and women from afar, and generations that know us not and that we know not of, heart-drawn to see where and by whom great things were suffered and done for them, shall come to this deathless field, to ponder and dream, and lo! the shadow of a mighty presence shall wrap them in its bosom, and the power of the vision pass into their souls."

GENERAL JOSHUA LAWRENCE CHAMBERLAIN
FORMER COLONEL OF THE 20TH MAINE INFANTRY

GLOSSARY

battery—The basic unit of artillery, consisting of four to six guns.

bivouac—A temporary encampment, or to camp out for the night.

breastwork—A temporary fortification, usually of earth and about chest high, over which a soldier can fire.

caisson—A two-wheeled vehicle with large chests for carrying artillery ammunition; it is connected to a horse-drawn limber when moved.

canister—A tin can containing lead or iron balls that scatter when fired from a cannon. Used primarily in defense of a position as an antipersonnel weapon.

Coffee Cooler—A shirker or malingerer. One who will begin work when the coffee cools.

echelon—A staggered or stairstep-like formation of parallel units of troops.

enfilade—Gunfire that rakes an enemy line lengthwise, or the position allowing such firing.

flank—The right or left end of a military formation. Therefore, to flank is to attack or go around the enemy's position on one end or the other.

grapeshot—Iron balls (usually nine) bound together and fired from a cannon. Resembling a cluster of grapes, the balls break apart and scatter on impact. Although references to grape or grapeshot are numerous in the literature, its use was rare on Civil War battlefields.

limber—A two-wheeled, horse-drawn vehicle to which a gun carriage or a caisson is attached.

Minié ball—The standard bullet-shaped projectile fired from the rifled muskets of the time. Designed by two French army officers, Henri-Gustave Delvigne and Claude-Etienne Minié, the bullet's hollow base expands, forcing its sides into the grooves, or rifling, of the musket's barrel. This causes the bullet to spiral in flight, giving it greater range and accuracy. Appears as minie ball, minnie ball, Minnie ball, and minnie bullet.

Napoleon—A smoothbore, muzzleloading field artillery piece so named because it was developed under the direction of Napoleon III. It fires a 12-pound projectile (and therefore sometimes is called a 12-pounder). The basic light artillery weapon of both sides, Napoleons were originally cast in bronze; when that material became scarce in the South, iron was used.

Parrott guns—Muzzleloading, rifled artillery pieces of various calibers made of cast iron with a unique wrought-iron reinforcing band around the breech. Patented in 1861 by Union officer Robert Parker Parrott, they are more accurate at longer range than their smoothbore predecessors.

picket—One or more soldiers on guard to protect the larger unit from surprise attack.

Pioneers—Construction engineers.

prolonge—A stout rope on a gun carriage used to manuever an artillery piece over short distances without having to attach it to a limber.

red legs—See *Zouaves*.

salient—That part of a fortress, line of defense, or trench system that juts out toward the enemy position.

skirmisher—A soldier sent out in advance of the main body of troops to scout out and probe the enemy's position. Also, one who fights in a skirmish, a small fight usually incidental to action.

solid shot—A solid artillery projectile, oblong for rifled pieces and spherical for smoothbores, used primarily against fortifications and matériel.

Zouaves—Regiments, both Union and Confederate, that model themselves after the original Zouaves of French Colonial Algeria. Known for their spectacular uniforms featuring bright colors—usually reds and blues—baggy trousers, gaiters, short and open jackets, and a turban or fez, they specialize in precision drill and loading and firing muskets from the prone position.

ACKNOWLEDGMENTS

The editors wish to thank the following for their valuable assistance in the preparation of this volume:
Margie K. Bachman, University of Pittsburgh Press, Pittsburgh; Holly T. Bailey, The Reeves Center, Washington & Lee University, Lexington, Va.; Carl Becker, Miamisburg, Ohio; Petie Bogen-Garrett, Picture Collection, The Library of Virginia, Richmond; Ellen R. Callahan, New Jersey State Archives, Trenton; Elwood W. Christ, Adams County Historical Society, Gettysburg, Pa.; Eileen F. Conklin, Smithsburg, Md.; Laura Costello, South Caroliniana Library, University of South Carolina, Columbia; Kelly DeBrine, Old State House, Little Rock, Ark.; Tom DuRant, National Park Service, Harpers Ferry Center, Harpers Ferry, W.V.; Eileen Flanagan, Chicago Historical Society, Chicago; Bonnie Gibbs, Nottoway County Library, Nottoway, Va.; Paul Glass, Brooklyn; Charles H. Glatfelter, Adams County Historical Society, Gettysburg, Pa.; Randy W. Hackenburg, U.S. Army Military History Institute, Carlisle Barracks, Pa.; Mary Ellen Hayward, Maryland Historical Society, Baltimore; Jonathan Heller, National Archives, College Park, Md.; Lance J. Herdegen, Public Relations Office, Carroll College, Waukesha, Wis.; Cory Hudgins, The Museum of the Confederacy, Richmond; Kathleen Lyons Jakubowski, Solon, Ohio; Gregory Johnson, Alderman Library, University of Virginia, Charlottesville; Megan Lodge, Rochester Historical Society, Rochester, N.Y.; Mary Lohrenz, Mississippi State Historical Museum, Jackson; Clair P. Lyons, Erie, Pa.; Lisa McCown, Special Collections, Leyburn Library, Washington & Lee University, Lexington, Va.; Maurey Meador, Old State House, Little Rock, Ark.; Julia J. Morton, Kent State University Press, Kent, Ohio; Carolyn Parsons, Picture Collection, The Library of Virginia, Richmond; Mary Ellen Pearl, University of Pittsburgh Press, Pittsburgh; Jon K. Reynolds, Lauinger Library, Georgetown University, Washington, D.C.; Hyman Schmartzberg, National Park Service, Richmond Battlefield, Richmond; Paul M. Shevchuk, Gettysburg National Military Park, Gettysburg, Pa.; James W. Slack, Washington, D.C.; Michail J. Winey, U.S. Army Military History Institute, Carlisle Barracks, Pa.; Linda Ziemer, Chicago Historical Society, Chicago.

PICTURE CREDITS

The sources for the illustrations are listed below. Credits from left to right are separated by semicolons; from top to bottom by dashes.
Dust jacket: Front, National Archives Neg. No. 165-SB-41; rear, courtesy Fanny Keith Day, photographed by Steve Tuttle. 6: Map by Nicholas Schrenk. 8: Courtesy D. Mark Katz. 9: Calligraphy by Mary Lou O'Brian/Inkwell, Inc. 15: Map by Walter W. Roberts. 16, 17: Courtesy Special Collections, James Graham Leyburn Library, Washington & Lee Univ., Lexington, Va.; Library of Congress. 18: Courtesy Kathleen Lyons Jakubowski, Solon, Ohio, photographed by Ed Bernik; Clair P. Lyons, Erie, Pa. 19: Courtesy U.S. Army Military History Institute (USAMHI), Carlisle Barracks, Pa., copied by A. Pierce Bounds. 20: Library of Congress No. B813 6785. 21: Gettysburg National Military Park; from *Yankee Rebel: The Civil War Journal of Edmund DeWitt Patterson,* ed. by John G. Barrett, © 1966 Univ. of North Carolina Press. Used by permission of the publisher. 22: South Caroliniana Library, Univ. of South Carolina. 23: Pennsylvania Capitol Preservation Committee. 24, 25: Massachusetts Commandery of the Military Order of the Loyal Legion of the United States and the U.S. Army Military History Institute (MASS-MOLLUS/USAMHI), copied by A. Pierce Bounds; courtesy USAMHI, Carlisle Barracks, Pa., copied by A. Pierce Bounds. 26: From *History of the Eleventh New Jersey Volunteers: From Its Organization to Appomattox,* by Thomas D. Marbaker, MacCrellish & Quigley, Trenton, 1898—courtesy USAMHI, Carlisle Barracks, Pa., copied by A. Pierce Bounds. 27: Frank and Marie Therese Wood Print Collection, Alexandria, Va.; Library of Congress. 28: Culver Pictures, Inc. 29: The Library of Virginia, Richmond. 30: Reprinted from *The Cormany Diaries: A Northern Family in the Civil War,* by James C. Mohr, ed., by permission of the Univ. of Pittsburgh Press, © 1982 Univ. of Pittsburgh Press; Southern Historical Collection, Library of the Univ. of North Carolina at Chapel Hill. 31: From *Confederate Chaplain: A War Journal of Rev. James B. Sheeran, c.ss.r., 14th Louisiana, C.S.A.,* ed. by Joseph T. Durkin, The Bruce Publishing Co., 1960. 32: Courtesy Robert E. Lee Memorial Association, Stratford Hall, Stratford, Va., photographed by Larry Sherer. 33: Library of Congress No. BH 83478—courtesy USAMHI, Carlisle Barracks, Pa., copied by A. Pierce Bounds. 34: Library of Congress No. B-815-264-A, copied by Philip Brandt George. 35: James M. Jordan; courtesy Georgetown Univ. Library. 36: Archive Photos. 37: Calligraphy by Mary Lou O'Brian/Inkwell, Inc. 39: Map by Walter W. Roberts. 40: Library of Congress No. B813 6785; MASS-MOLLUS/ USAMHI. 41: Library of Congress. 43: Lance J. Herdegen; Wisconsin Veterans Museum. 44, 45: Library of Congress. 46: Courtesy Mississippi State Historical Museum, Jackson, photographed by Gib Ford; Dearborn Historical Museum, Dearborn, Mich. 47: Wisconsin Veterans Museum. 48: From *Battles and Leaders of the Civil War* (Vol. 3), The Century Co., New York, 1884-1887. 50: National Archives Neg. No. B-3516, copied by Evan Sheppard; courtesy USAMHI, Carlisle Barracks, Pa., copied by A. Pierce Bounds. 51: Library of Congress No. B811-2393. 53: National Archives Neg. No. B-260, copied by Evan Sheppard—courtesy New York State Div. of Military and Naval Affairs, photographed by Randall Perry. 54: Society for the Historical Preservation of the 26th Regiment N.C. Troops, Inc. 55: Courtesy Mark Sherman, photographed by Larry Sherer. 56: From *Women at Gettysburg, 1863,* by Eileen F. Conklin. 57: Painting by Alfred R. Waud, The Historic New Orleans Collection 1977.137.2.7. 58, 59: Chicago Historical Society; National Archives. 60, 61: National Park Service, Harpers Ferry Center; courtesy National Archives Neg. No. 111-B-17, copied by Evan Sheppard. 62: Courtesy Adams County Historical Society, Gettysburg, Pa., photographed by Larry Sherer. 63: Gregory Coco; courtesy USAMHI, Carlisle Barracks, Pa., copied by A. Pierce Bounds. 64: From *Women at Gettysburg, 1863,* by Eileen F. Conklin; Civil War Library and Museum. 65, 66: Library of Congress. 67: Calligraphy by Mary Lou O'Brian/Inkwell, Inc. 68: Map by Walter W. Roberts. 70: Library of Congress. 71: Old State House, Little Rock, Ark. 73: Map by William L. Hezlep, overlay by Time-Life Books. 74: Rochester Historical Society; courtesy USAMHI, Carlisle Barracks, Pa., copied by A. Pierce Bounds. 75: From *The War between the Union and the Confederacy and Its Lost Opportunities,* by William C. Oates, Neale Publishing Co., New York, 1905. 76: Library of Congress. 77: Alabama Dept. of Archives and History, Montgomery. 78: Courtesy USAMHI, Carlisle Barracks, Pa., copied by A. Pierce Bounds—courtesy Gettysburg National Military Park, NPS, photographed by Larry Sherer. 79: Courtesy Adams County Historical Society, Gettysburg, Pa. 80: Library of Congress No. 3538 Plate 44. 82, 83: Maps by William L. Hezlep, overlay by Time-

Life Books. 84, 85: Library of Congress. 86: Courtesy New York State Div. of Military and Naval Affairs, photographed by Randall Perry. 87: The J. Howard Wert Gettysburg Collection and Civil War Antiquities, copied by Larry Sherer; Private Collection, photographed by Larry Sherer—courtesy Don Troiani, photographed by Al Freni. 88: Library of Congress. 89: LTC Kenneth H. Powers, 69th Regiment Archives. 90, 91: Library of Congress. 92: Courtesy USAMHI, Carlisle Barracks, Pa., copied by A. Pierce Bounds. 93: Library of Congress. 94, 95: Library of Congress No. 3538 Plate 42; courtesy Gettysburg National Military Park, Eisenhower National Historic Site, photographed by Larry Sherer. 96: Library of Congress. 97: Courtesy Stametelos Brothers Collection, Cambridge, photographed by Larry Sherer. 98, 99: New Jersey State Archives, Dept. of State; Library of Congress No. 3538 Plate 36. 101: Map by R. R. Donnelley & Sons Co., Cartographic Services, overlay by Time-Life Books. 102, 103: Courtesy the N.C. Division of Archives and History (2); Library of Congress. 104: Courtesy Don Troiani, photographed by Larry Sherer; Wright State Univ. 106: Library of Congress No. USZC4-971. 107: Calligraphy by Mary Lou O'Brian/Inkwell, Inc. 109: Map by William L. Hezlep, overlay by Time-Life Books. 110: Hampton National Historic Site, National Park Service. 111: Courtesy Museum of the Confederacy, photographed by Larry Sherer—Library of Congress. 112: From *Confederate Veteran Magazine* (Vol. 11, no. 9), Nashville, Sept. 1903, copied by Philip Brandt George—courtesy Jenny Wade House Museum, Gettysburg, Pa., photographed by Larry Sherer. 113: From *The True Story of "Jennie" Wade: A Gettysburg Maid,* by J. W. Johnston, published by J. W. Johnston, Rochester, N.Y., 1917. 114: Library of Congress—Rhode Island State House, photographed by Mark Sexton. 115: National Archives Neg. No. B-4625, copied by Evan Sheppard; Library of Congress No. BH83-475. 116: Courtesy Roger Hunt. 117: From *The Story of a Confederate Boy in the Civil War,* by David E. Johnston, Glass & Prudhomme Co., Portland, Oreg., 1845; Thomas D. Gable. 118-120: Library of Congress. 121: Special Collections Dept., Univ. of Virginia; painting by W. G. Browne, courtesy Southern Historical Collection, Manuscripts Dept., Wilson Library, UNCCH, copied by Fred Stripe. 122: Library of Congress—courtesy Gettysburg National Military Park, Eisenhower National Historic Site, copied by Larry Sherer. 123: From *Pictorial History of the 13th Regiment Vermont Volunteers,* by R. O. Sturtevant, published by The Self-Appointed Committee of Three, Burlington, Vt., 1911 (2)—courtesy James C. Frasca, Croton, Ohio, photographed by Bill Patterson. 124: National Archives Neg. No. 111-B-2022; National Archives Neg. No. BA-636, copied by Evan Sheppard. 125: Courtesy USAMHI, Carlisle Barracks, Pa., copied by A. Pierce Bounds—from *The Photographic History of the Civil War* (Vol.9), by Francis Trevelyan Miller, The Review of Reviews Co., New York, 1911-1912. 126, 127: Library of Congress; Larry T. Jones. 128: Courtesy USAMHI, Carlisle Barracks, Pa., copied by A. Pierce Bounds. 129: Courtesy New York State Div. of Military and Naval Affairs, photographed by Randall Perry; The Museum of the Confederacy, Richmond, photographed by Katherine Wetzel; The Museum of the Confederacy, Richmond, photographed by Larry Sherer. 130: National Archives Neg. No. B-3293, copied by Evan Sheppard. 131, 132: Library of Congress. 134: Library of Congress No. B811-2391. 136, 137: Library of Congress. 138: Courtesy Phyllis Woestemeyer. 139: Courtesy Andy Larson, Gettysburg, Pa., copied by Larry Sherer. 140: Library of Congress No. 353C B8171 259. 141: Calligraphy by Mary Lou O'Brian/Inkwell, Inc. 144: National Archives Neg. No. 165-SB-41, copied by Evan Sheppard. 146: Atlanta History Center/DuBose Collection, photographed by Larry Sherer. 147: Courtesy USAMHI, Carlisle Barracks, Pa., copied by A. Pierce Bounds; courtesy Andy Larson, Gettysburg, Pa., photographed by Larry Sherer. 148: The Museum of the Confederacy, Richmond, photographed by Larry Sherer; courtesy James C. Frasca, Croton, Ohio, photographed by Bill Patterson. 149: The J. Howard Wert Gettysburg Collection and Civil War Antiquities, photographed by Larry Sherer—Archive Photos. 150: Courtesy Don Troiani, photographed by Larry Sherer. 151: National Archives Neg. No. 111-BA-28. 152: Courtesy Don Troiani, photographed by Larry Sherer; from *Women at Gettysburg, 1863,* by Eileen F. Conklin. 153: Col. T. A. Wheat, Gloucester Point, photographed by Katherine Wetzel. 154: Library of Congress No. USZ62-14377. 155: Library of Congress No. B8171-254—Library of Congress. 156: Fanny Keith Day, photographed by Steve Tuttle. 157, 158: Library of Congress. 159: Courtesy USAMHI, Carlisle Barracks, Pa., copied by A. Pierce Bounds. 160: Library of Congress No. USZ62-14376. 161: Library of Congress. 162: National Archives Neg. No. 200-(S)-CC-2288, copied by Evan Sheppard. 164, 165: Painting by David Blythe, National Baseball Hall of Fame and Museum, Inc./Cooperstown, N.Y., photographed by Frank Rollins; Illustration from James M. Geiner, Janet L. Coryell, and James R. Smither, eds., *A Surgeon's Civil War: The Letters and Diary of Daniel M. Holt, M.D.,* Kent State Univ. Press, 1994. 166: Courtesy USAMHI, Carlisle Barracks, Pa., copied by A. Pierce Bounds. 167: Courtesy New York Times; courtesy the Charleston Library Society, Charleston, S.C. 168, 169: National Archives Record Group 111; from *The Face of Lincoln,* comp. and ed. by James Mellon, © 1979 Viking Penguin Inc., published by Viking, New York. 170: Brown Brothers—courtesy Theodore S. Johnson.

BIBLIOGRAPHY

BOOKS

Alexander, E. P. *Military Memoirs of a Confederate.* Dayton: Morningside Bookshop, 1977 (reprint of 1907 ed.).

Barrett, John G., ed. *Yankee Rebel: The Civil War Journal of Edmund DeWitt Patterson.* Chapel Hill: University of North Carolina Press, 1966.

Beaudot, William J. K., and Lance J. Herdegen. *An Irishman in the Iron Brigade.* New York: Fordham University Press, 1993.

Becker, Carl M., and Ritchie Thomas, eds. *Hearth and Knapsack: The Ladley Letters, 1857-1880.* Athens: Ohio University Press, 1988.

Bigelow, John. *The Peach Orchard.* Minneapolis: Kimball-Storer, 1910.

Boatner, Mark Mayo, III. *The Civil War Dictionary.* New York: David McKay, 1959.

Broadhead, Sarah M. *The Diary of a Lady of Gettysburg, Pennsylvania, from June 15 to July 15, 1863.* Hershey, Pa.: Gary T. Hawbaker, no date (reprint of 1864 ed.).

Butts, Joseph Tyler, ed. *A Gallant Captain of the Civil War.* New York: F. Tennyson Neely, 1902.

Caldwell, J. F. J. *The History of a Brigade of South Carolinians.* Philadelphia: King and Baird, 1866.

Clark, Walter, ed. *Histories of the Several Regiments from North Carolina in the Great War, 1861-'65.* Vols. 1-4. Wendell, N.C.: Broadfoot's Bookmark, 1982 (reprint of 1901 ed.).

Coco, Gregory A. *War Stories: A Collection of 150 Little Known Human Interest Accounts of the Campaign and Battle of Gettysburg.* Gettysburg, Pa.: Thomas Publications, 1992.

Coddington, Edwin B. *The Gettysburg Campaign: A Study in Command.* New York: Charles Scribner's Sons, 1968.

Conklin, Eileen F. *Women at Gettysburg, 1863.* Gettysburg, Pa.: Thomas Publications, 1993.

Crumb, Herb S., ed. *The Eleventh Corps Artillery at Gettysburg: The Papers of Major Thomas Ward Osborn, Chief of Artillery.* Hamilton, N.Y.: Edmonston Publishing, 1991.

Crute, Joseph H., Jr. *Confederate Staff Officers: 1861–1865.* Powhatan, Va.: Derwent Books, 1982.

Curtis, O. B. *History of the Twenty-Fourth Michigan of the Iron Brigade.* Detroit: Winn & Hammond, 1891.

Dannett, Sylvia G. L., ed. *Noble Women of the North.* New York: Thomas Yoseloff, 1959.

Davis, William C., ed. *Touched by Fire: A Photographic Portrait of the Civil War.* Vol. 1. Boston: Little, Brown, 1985.

Dawson, Francis W. *Reminiscences of Confederate Service, 1861–1865.* Ed. by Bell I. Wiley. Baton Rouge: Louisiana State University, 1980.

Dickert, D. Augustus. *History of Kershaw's Brigade.* Dayton: Morningside Bookshop, 1976 (reprint of 1899 ed.).

Dooley, John. *John Dooley: Confederate Soldier, His War Journal.* Ed. by Joseph T. Durkin. Washington, D.C.: Georgetown University Press, 1945.

Durkin, Joseph T., ed. *Confederate Chaplain: A War Journal of Rev. James B. Sheeran, c.ss.r., 14th Louisiana, C.S.A.* Milwaukee: Bruce, 1960.

Fox, William F. *New York at Gettysburg.* Vol. 2. Albany: J. B. Lyon, 1900.

Frassanito, William A. *Gettysburg: A Journey in Time.* New York: Charles Scribner's Sons, 1975.

Freeman, Douglas Southall. *Lee's Lieutenants: A Study in Command.* Vol. 3. New York: Scribner, 1944.

Fuller, Charles A. *Personal Recollections of the War of 1861.* Sherburne, N.Y.: News Job Printing, 1906.

Glass, Paul, and Lewis C. Singer. *Singing Soldiers: A History of the Civil War in Song.* New York: Da Capo Press, 1994 (reprint of 1964 ed.).

Hall, Isaac. *History of the Ninety-Seventh Regiment New York Volunteers, ("Conkling Rifles,") in the War for the Union.* Utica, N.Y.: L. C. Childs & Son, 1890.

Hancock, Cornelia. *South after Gettysburg: Letters of Cornelia Hancock from the Army of the Potomac, 1863–1865.* Ed. by Henrietta Stratton Jaquette. Philadelphia: University of Pennsylvania Press, 1937.

Hoke, Jacob. *The Great Invasion.* New York: Thomas Yoseloff, 1959.

Holt, Daniel M. *A Surgeon's Civil War: The Letters and Diary of Daniel M. Holt, M.D.* Ed. by James M. Greiner, Janet L. Coryell, and James R. Smither. Kent, Ohio: Kent State University Press, 1994.

Irby, Richard. *The Captain Remembers: The Papers of Captain Richard Irby.* Ed. by Virginia Fitzgerald Jordan. Blackstone, Va.: The Nottoway County Historical Association, 1975.

James, Bushrod Washington. *Echoes of Battle.* Philadelphia: Henry T. Coates, 1895.

Johnston, J. W. *The True Story of "Jennie" Wade: A Gettysburg Maid.* Rochester, N.Y.: J. W. Johnston, 1917.

Jones, Katharine M., ed. *Heroines of Dixie: Winter of Desperation.* New York: Bobbs-Merrill, 1955.

Krick, Robert K. *Lee's Colonels.* Dayton: Press of Morningside Bookshop, 1979.

Lasswell, Mary, ed. *Rags and Hope.* New York: Coward-McCann, 1961.

Marbaker, Thomas D. *History of the Eleventh New Jersey Volunteers.* Trenton: MacCrellish & Quigley, 1898.

Minnigh, Henry N. *History of Company K, 1st Penn'a Reserves.* Duncansville, Pa.: Homeprint Publisher, 1891.

Mohr, James C., ed. *The Cormany Diaries.* Pittsburgh: University of Pittsburgh Press, 1982.

Moore, Frank. *Women of the War: Their Heroism and Self-Sacrifice.* Hartford: S. S. Scranton, 1866.

Morrison, James L., Jr., ed. *The Memoirs of Henry Heth.* Westport, Conn.: Greenwood Press, 1974.

Muffly, J. W., ed. *The Story of Our Regiment: A History of the 148th Pennsylvania Vols.* Des Moines: Kenyon, 1904.

Nesbitt, Mark. *35 Days to Gettysburg.* Harrisburg, Pa.: Stackpole Books, 1992.

Oates, William C. *The War between the Union and the Confederacy and Its Lost Opportunities:* New York: Neale, 1905.

Pfanz, Harry W.:
Gettysburg: Culp's Hill and Cemetery Hill. Chapel Hill: University of North Carolina Press, 1993.
Gettysburg: The Second Day. Chapel Hill: University of North Carolina Press, 1987.

Pierce, Tillie Alleman. *At Gettysburg or What a Girl Saw and Heard of the Battle.* New York: W. Lake Borland, 1889.

Ramey, Emily G., and John K. Gott. *The Years of Anguish: Fauquier County, Virginia, 1861–1865.* Fauquier, Va.: Fauquier County Civil War Centennial Committee, 1965.

Rollins, Richard, ed. *Pickett's Charge: Eyewitness Accounts.* Redondo Beach, Calif.: Rank and File Publications, 1994.

Scott, Robert Garth, ed. *Fallen Leaves: The Civil War Letters of Major Henry Livermore Abbott.* Kent, Ohio: Kent State University Press, 1991.

Small, Cindy L. *The Jennie Wade Story.* Gettysburg, Pa.: Thomas Publications, 1991.

Small, Harold Adams, ed. *The Road to Richmond.* Berkeley: University of California Press, 1939.

Souder, Emily Bliss. *Letters from a Field Hospital.* Philadelphia: Canton Press, 1864.

Stewart, George R. *Pickett's Charge.* Dayton: Press of Morningside Bookshop, 1980.

Sturtevant, Ralph O. *Pictorial History of the 13th Regiment Vermont Volunteers.* Burlington, Vt.: The Self-Appointed Committee of Three, 1911.

Trulock, Alice Rains. *In the Hands of Providence: Joshua L. Chamberlain and the American Civil War.* Chapel Hill: University of North Carolina Press, 1992.

Turner, Charles W., ed. *Ted Barclay, Liberty Hall Volunteers: Letters from the Stonewall Brigade, 1861–1864.* Berryville, Va.: Rockbridge, 1992.

United States War Department. *The War of the Rebellion: A Compilation of the Official Record of the Union and Confederate Armies.* Series 1, Vol. 27, Part 1-Reports. Washington, D.C.: Government Printing Office, 1889.

Warner, Ezra J.:
Generals in Blue: Lives of the Union Commanders. Baton Rouge: Louisiana State University Press, 1964.
Generals in Gray: Lives of the Confederate Commanders. Baton Rouge: Louisiana State University Press, 1959.

Wheeler, Richard. *Witness to Gettysburg.* New York: Meridian, 1987.

Woodward, Harold R., Jr. *Major General James Lawson Kemper, C.S.A.: The Confederacy's Forgotten Son.* Natural Bridge Station, Va.: Rockbridge, 1993.

PERIODICALS

Bowen, Edward R. "Collis' Zouaves: The 114th Pennsylvania Infantry at Gettysburg." *Philadelphia Weekly Press,* June 22, 1887.

Bowen, George A. "The Diary of Captain George A. Brown 12th Regiment New Jersey Volunteers." *Valley Forge Journal,* Dec. 1984.

Braun, Robert A. "The Fight for Devil's Den: 124th New York vs. Texas Infantry." *Military Images,* July-Aug. 1983.

Cowan, Andrew. "Cowan's New York Battery." *National Tribune,* Nov. 12, 1908.

Early, John Cabell. "A Southern Boy's Experiences of Gettysburg." *The Journal* (Military Service Institution, New York), May-June 1911.

Easley, Dennis B. "With Armistead When He Was Killed." *Confederate Veteran,* 1912, Vol. 20.

Farley, Porter. "Reminiscences of the 140th Regiment New York Volunteer Infantry." *Rochester Historical Society,* 1944, Vol. 22.

Gearhart, Edwin R. "In the Years '62 to '65: Personal

Recollections of Edwin R. Gearhart, a Veteran." *Daily Times* (Stroudsburg, Pa.), Mar. 19-Aug. 6, 1900.
Gladstone, William. "The Children of the Battlefield." *Military Images,* Mar.-Apr. 1981.
Hadden, R. Lee. "The Deadly Embrace: The Meeting of the Twenty-Fourth Regiment, Michigan Infantry and the Twenty-Sixth Regiment of North Carolina Troops at McPherson's Woods, Gettysburg, Pennsylvania, July 1, 1863." *Gettysburg,* July 1991.
Houston, Thomas D. "Annals of the War." *Philadelphia Weekly Times,* Oct. 21, 1882.
Howard, David Ridgely. "Left on the Field." *The Telegram* (Baltimore), 1879, No. 16.
Long, Roger. "A Mississippian in the Railroad Cut." *Gettysburg,* Jan. 1991.
Lumbard, Joseph A. "History of the 147th Pennsylvania Volunteers." *Snyder County Tribune,* no date.
McNeily, John S. "Barksdale's Mississippi Brigade at Gettysburg." *Publications of the Mississippi Historical Society,* 1914, Vol. 14.
Maust, Roland R. "The Union Second Corps Hospital at Gettysburg, July 2 to Aug. 8, 1863." *Gettysburg: Historical Articles of Lasting Interest,* Jan. 1, 1994.
Moore, John H. "Annals of the War." *Philadelphia Weekly Times,* Nov. 4, 1882.
Moran, Frank E. "Annals of the War." *Philadelphia Weekly Times,* Apr. 22, 1882.
Olds, Fred A. "Brave Carolinian Fell at Gettysburg." *Southern Historical Society Papers,* Vol. 35.
Owen, Henry T. "Annals of the War." *Philadelphia Weekly Times,* Mar. 26, 1881.
Reese, Andrew. Letter in the *Southern Banner,* Aug. 26, 1863.
Storch, Marc, and Beth Storch. "'What a Deadly Trap We Were In': Archer's Brigade on July 1, 1863." *Gettysburg,* Jan. 1992.
Taylor, Oliver. "The War Story of a Confederate Soldier Boy." *Bristol Herald Courier,* 1863.
Tout-le-Monde. Letter to the editor. *The Savannah Republic,* July 22, 1863.
Troutman, Charles E. "Three Days at Gettysburg." *Philadelphia Weekly Times,* June 17, 1882.
Winschel, Terrence J.:
"The Colors Are Shrouded in Mystery." *Gettysburg,* Jan. 1992.
"The Gettysburg Diary of Lieutenant William Peel." *Gettysburg,* July 1993.
"Part II: Heavy Was Their Loss: Joe Davis' Brigade at Gettysburg." *Gettysburg,* July 1990.
Wright, Steven J. "'Don't Let Me Bleed To Death': The Wounding of Maj. Gen. Winfield Scott Hancock." *Gettysburg,* Jan. 1992.

OTHER SOURCES

Aiken, David Wyatt:
Letter, June 22, 1863. Columbia, S.C.: South Caroliniana Library.
Letter, June 28, 1863. Columbia, S.C.: South Caroliniana Library.
Letter, July 13, 1863. Columbia, S.C.: South Caroliniana Library.
Blanchard, C. H. Unpublished personal account. Regimental Files. Gettysburg, Pa.: Gettysburg National Military Park Library, no date.
Cavada, Adolfo. "Adolfo Cavada Diary." Unpublished personal account, 1861-1863. Philadelphia: Historical Society of Pennsylvania.
Coles, Robert T. "History of the Fourth Regiment, Alabama Volunteer Infantry, C.S.A., Army of Northern Virginia." Unpublished manuscript. Montgomery: Alabama Department of Archives and History, no date.
Daniel, John Warwick. Unpublished personal account. Charlottesville: Alderman Library, University of Virginia, no date.
Daniel, William L. Letter, June 28, 1863. Columbia, S.C.: South Caroliniana Library.
Fite, John A. "Short and Uninteresting History of a Small and Unimportant Man." Unpublished manuscript. Nashville: Tennessee Archives, no date.
Funk, Jacob B. Unpublished personal account. John S. Patton Papers. Pittsburgh: Historical Society of Western Pennsylvania, 1863.
Landrum, Zack. Letter, July 15, 1863. Regimental Files. Gettysburg, Pa.: Gettysburg National Military Park.
McNeill, Alexander. Letter, July 7, 1863. Columbia, S.C.: South Caroliniana Library.
Melton, Samuel W. Letter, July 22, 1863. Columbia, S.C.: South Caroliniana Library.
Mounger, John, and Tom Mounger. Letter, July 18, 1863. Atlanta: Georgia Department of Archives and History.
Park, Andrew. "Some of My Recollections of the Battle of Gettysburg." Unpublished manuscript. Little Rock, Ark.: State Archives, no date.
Richardson, Sidney J. Letter, July 8, 1863. Atlanta: Georgia Department of Archives and History.
Taylor, William B. Letter, July 29, 1863. Gettysburg, Pa.: Gettysburg National Military Park Library.
Turner, John McLeod. Unpublished letter to the editor, Oct. 10, 1877. Grimes Papers, Southern Historical Collection. Chapel Hill: University of North Carolina Library.
Wilkerson, John A. "My Experience at Gettysburg, 1863." Unpublished manuscript. Little Rock, Ark.: State Archives, 1863.

INDEX

Numerals in italics indicate an illustration of the subject mentioned.

A

Abbott, Henry L.: *159;* letter by, 159
Aiken, David W.: *22;* letter by, 22-23, 29, 160
Alexander, Edward Porter: 10
Anderson, George T.: 72, 82
Anderson, Richard H.: 69, 98
Angle: 109, 129; Confederate breakthrough at, *122*
Archer, James J.: 37, 38, *40,* 61
Armistead, Lewis A.: 108, 115, 120, *127,* 128
Army of Northern Virginia: 9-10, 141, 143; battalion pin, *111;* burial of dead, 136, *147,* 148, 163; cavalry screen for, 11, 142; deserters, 35; order of battle, 14; reorganization into three corps, 10; retreat from Gettysburg, 141-143, 148, *154,* 157, *160, 161,* 163
Army of the Potomac: Artillery Reserve, 93; burial details, 136, 141-142, *147,* 149; and captured Confederates, 41, *132,* 133, 145, *146, 157, 162;* casualties at Chancellorsville, 9; casualties at Gettysburg, 141, 143; civilian assistance to wounded, 60-61, 62, 64, 79, *149,* 150; corps badges, 47, 150; headquarters detachment, *24-25;* order of battle, 14; Napoleon howitzer (12-pounder), *114;* Ordnance rifle, *158;* Parrott rifle, *125;* shoes, *148;* siege train of, *158*
Avery, Isaac E.: *102*

B

Baltimore, Md.: 19; defensive measures in, *27*
Baltimore Pike: Federal reserves along, *106*

Barclay, Alexander T.: *16;* letter from, 16
Barksdale, William A.: 83, 91, 98
Barlow, Francis C.: 38, 57, 58
Barlow's Knoll: artillery action at, *57*
"Battle Cry of Freedom": 28; sheet music cover, *28*
Baxter, Henry: 38
Bayly, William H.: account by, 105
Benedict, George G.: *124,* account by, 124
Benning, Henry L.: 72
Berlin, Md.: Federal wagon train at, *166*
Beverly's Ford: 11
Bigelow, John: 94; account by, 93-96; map by, *95*
Big Round Top: *66,* 70, 72, 73, 81
Birney, David B.: 97
Blackford, Charles Minor: 11
Black Horse Tavern: 64
Blanchard, C. H.: account by, 136
Bliss farm: 100-101
Blue Ridge Mountains: 11, 21, 22
Blythe, David: painting by, *164-165*
Bowen, Edward R.: *92;* account by, 92, 120
Bowen, George A.: account by, 40, 147
Branch, Sanford: *146*
Brandy Station: cavalry battle at, 10-11
Brewer, W. S.: 55
Broadhead, Joseph: 18, 105
Broadhead, Mary: 18
Broadhead, Sarah M.: *18;* diary entries of, *18,* 105
Brockenbrough, John: 48
Bryan, Abram: 128
Bryan house: *128*
Buford, John: 12, 13, 37
Bulger, Michael J.: 75
Burgwyn, Henry King: 38, 55
Burnside, Ambrose E.: 69
Bushman, Louis A.: 78

C

Caldwell, John C.: 82, 83
Carlisle, Pa.: Confederate occupation of, 12
Carter, Edward: 156
Carter, Robert G.: 9, 11, 12
Cashtown, Pa.: 37; Confederate concentration at, 12, 13
Cashtown Pike: 50, 52
Cavada, Adolfo: *64;* account by, 64, 97
Cavada, Frederic: 64, 97
Cemetery Hill: *58-59,* 61, 65, 67, 107; first day's fighting at, 38-39, 58-59; second day's fighting at, 69, 98, *map* 99, *102-103,* 104; third day's fighting at, 109, *114*
Cemetery Ridge: 67, 69, 81, 83, *106,* 107; bombardment at, 108, 112, 115, 116, 118-119, 120, *131,* 141; July 2 assault on, 98; Pickett's Charge, 108, *map* 109, 110-133, *126-127*
Centreville, Va.: 20; Union concentration at, 11
Chamberlain, Joshua Lawrence: 72, 143, *170;* address given by, 171
Chambersburg, Pa.: Confederate occupation of, 12, 28, 29, 30
Chambersburg Pike: 37, 38, *58-59;* action at, 43, *48*
Chancellorsville, Va.: and beginning of Gettysburg campaign, 9
Charleston Mercury: account of Gettysburg, *167*
Cheek, William M: account by, 55
Chesapeake and Ohio Canal: *160*
Clarke, Willie: 42
Coles, Robert T.: *77;* account by, 77, 133-134
Colvill, William: 98
Comfort, Maria: *113*
Cooke, Sidney: 39
Cooper, Samuel: 166
Copse of trees: *120*
Corbell, LaSalle "Sally": 157
Corby, William: absolution for Irish Brigade, *88*
Cormany, Rachel: *30;* letter by, 30
Cormany, Samuel: 30
Coulter, Richard: *116*
Cowan, Andrew: *125;* account by, 125, 130
Crennell, William H.: 78
Culp, William: 104
Culpeper, Va.: Confederate concentration at, 10, 11
Culp's Hill: 47, *58-59,* 67, *134,* 135, 136; July 2 assault on, 69, 98, *map* 99; July 3 assaults on, 107, 110-*111,* 117
Curtis, Orson B.: account by, 46-47
Cushing, Alonzo H.: 108, 128

D

Daily Richmond Examiner: news item from, *29*
Daniel, John W.: account by, 65
Daniel, Junius: 117
Daniel, William L.: account by, 31
Davis, Jefferson: war strategy, 10
Davis, Joseph R.: 37, 38, 40, 42
Dawes, Rufus: 43
Dawson, Francis W.: account by, 33, 115
Democratic Party: Northern peace advocates, 10
De Trobriand, Regis: 82
Devil's Den: *155;* fighting in, 69, *70,* 71, 72, *map* 73; sharpshooter's nest in, *144;* target rifle found in, *78*
Dickert, D. Augustus: 10
D'Ivernois, Bourry: 34
Dix, Dorothea: 152
Dooley, John: *35;* account by, 35, 112, 145
Doubleday, Abner: 38; and staff, *50*
Durboraw, Isaac N.: *138, 139;* account by, 138-139

E

Early, John Cabell: account by, 54
Early, Jubal A.: 12, 38, 54, 57, 65, 99, 141
Early, Samuel H.: 54, 65
Easley, Dennis B.: account by, 127
Edward's Ferry: Union crossing at, 12
Ellis, Augustus Van Horne: 70, 72
Emmitsburg, Md.: 18, 34, 35
Emmitsburg road: 40, 69, 82, 83, 92, 93, 96, 97, 108, 121, 133
Erickson, Christopher: *96*
Evans, Clement A.: 12
Evergreen Cemetery: 56, 113, 142; gatehouse of, *61*
Ewell, Richard Stoddert: 10, 15, 38, 39, 69, 99, 107

F

Fairfax Court House, Va.: Meade's headquarters at, *25*
Falling Waters: Confederate rearguard action at, 121, 142, *161*
Falmouth, Va.: Union army headquarters at, 11
Farley, Porter: *74;* account by, 74-75, 78
Farnsworth, Elon J.: 133
Fisk, Wilbur: 11
Fite, John A.: account by, 133
Flags: 3d Ark., *71;* 24th Mich., *46;* 2d Miss., *46;* 11th Miss., *129;* 69th N.Y., *89;* 104th N.Y., *53;* 28th N.C., *129;* 147th Pa., *23;* 6th Wis., *43*
Forbes, Edwin: painting by, *122;* sketches by, *27, 90-91, 120*
Frank Leslie's Illustrated Newspaper: front page of, *27*
Franklin's Crossing: artillery action at, *16-17*
Franks, Rufus: 77
Frederick, Md.: 26; Union concentration at, 12
Fredericksburg, Va.: Confederate concentration at, 11
Fremantle, Arthur: 32
Fuger, Frederick: 108
Fuller, Charles A.: *86;* account by, 86
Funk, Jacob B.: account by, 85

G

Garlach, Anna Louise: *63;* account by, 63
Garnett, Richard B.: 108, 115, 122
Gearhart, Edwin A.: account by, 49-50
George, Newton J.: 133
Gerald, George B.: account by, 90-91
Gettysburg, Pa.: 19; armies converge at, 13, 37-38; Carlisle Street, *58;* field hospitals in, 130, 142, *146, 149,* 150, *151,* 152-153; removal of dead to military cemeteries, 148; sharpshooting fire in, *65,* 105, 138; transfer of wounded to

permanent hospitals, 152-153; Wagon Hotel, *19*
Gettysburg Address: *168-169*
Gettysburg anniversary commemorations: *170*, 171
Gettysburg campaign: battlefield, *panorama map* 6-7; chronology of, 13; Confederate and Union routes of march, *map* 15; first day's fighting, *map* 39; orders of battle for, 14; Pickett's Charge, *map* 109; second day's fighting, *maps* 68, 82, 83, 99
Gettysburg National Cemetery: dedication ceremony for, *168-169*
Gibbon, John: 115
Giles, Valerius C.: account by, 81
Goldsborough, W. W.: 142-143
Goodrich, F. C.: grave marker for, *147*
Gordon, John B.: 38
Grant, Ulysses S.: 10

H

Hagerstown, Md.: 33, 65, 154
Hagerstown road: 36, *60-61*
Haley, John: 11, 82
Hall, Isaac: *129;* account by, 129
Halleck, Henry W.: 142
Hamilton, William H.: sword of, *123*
Hancock, Cornelia: account by, 152
Hancock, Winfield Scott: 38-39, 67, 69, 82, 98, 108, *124*
Harper's Weekly: 127, 155
Harrisburg, Pa.: 19; Confederate threat to, 12
Hays, Alexander: 109, 128, 129
Hays, Harry Thompson: 98
Hazlett, Charles E.: 72, *74*, 75, 78
Herr Ridge: 37, 69
Heth, Henry: 12-13, 37, 38, *40*, 121; account by, 40
Hill, Ambrose Powell: 10, 11, 13, 37, 38, 39, 40
Hill, David J.: account by, 44
Holstein, Anna Morris: account by, 149
Holstein, William: 149
Holt, Daniel M.: *165;* letter by, 165
Hood, John Bell: 69, 72
Hooker, Joseph: 9, 10, 11, 15, 26, 40; relieved of command, 12, 23
Howard, David R.: *110;* account by, 110-111
Howard, Oliver O.: 38, 56, 67
Humiston, Amos: ambrotype belonging to, *149*
Humphreys, Andrew A.: 64, 83, 97
Hyde, Peter S.: shirt of, *148*

I

Imboden, John D.: 141
Indiana troops: 19th Infantry, 46
Irby, Richard: *35;* account by, 35
Iverson, Alfred: 38

J

Jackson, Thomas J. "Stonewall": death of, 9-10
Jacobs, Michael: 142
James, Bushrod W.: account by, 150
James, John T.: account by, 118-119, 121
Jeffords, Harrison: 83
Johnson, Edward: 99, 107, 110
Johnston, David E.: *117;* account by, 117
Jones, John C.: surgical kit of, *153*
Jones, John T.: *54*, 55
Jones, Marcellus: 37

K

Kelly, Patrick: 89
Kelly's Ford: 11
Kemper, James L.: 108, *121*
Kershaw, Joseph B.: 82
Kidd, George: 129
Kilpatrick, Hugh Judson: 133
King, William T.: tailor shop sign of, *62*

L

Ladley, Oscar D.: *104;* account by, 104
Landrum, Zack: letter by, 163
Law, Evander M.: 72, 81
Leaves from the Battlefield of Gettysburg: 150
Lee, Robert E.: 9, 28, 30, *32*, 39, 160; arrival at Gettysburg, 38, 40; civilian admirers, 33; invasion plans of, 10, 11, 12, 15; orders for July 2 attacks, 67-69, 98; orders prohibiting looting, 12, 29, 154; and Pickett's Charge, 107, 108, 110; retreat from Gettysburg, 141, 142, 143, 158, 161
Leister farmhouse: *140*
Liberty Hall Volunteers: 16
Lincoln, Abraham: 10; and Gettysburg Address, *168-169*
Little Round Top: *66*, 69, 70, 71, 98, 107, *136-137*, 143, *155;* breastworks on, *76;* fighting on, 72, *map* 73, 74-75, 77, 81, 163
Livermore, Charles: 12
Longstreet, James: 10, 11, 30, 32, *33*, 40, 92, 115; and July 2 attacks, 69, 71, 98; and Pickett's Charge, 107, 108, 110
Lumbard, Joseph A.: letters by, 23, 41
Lutheran Theological Seminary: 18, 19, 38, 50, *51*

M

McAllister, Mary: account by, 60-61
McClellan, George: 23
McDermott, Anthony: account by, 128
McLaws, Lafayette: 69, 82, 83
McNeill, Alexander: letter by, 148
McPherson farm: *48*
McPherson's Ridge: 37, 38, 42, 43, 46, 48, 49, 54
McPherson's Woods: 38, 40, 41
Mahoney, Patrick: 38
Manassas Junction, Va.: 22; Union concentration at, 11
Marbaker, Thomas D.: *26;* account by, 26, 145
Marks, Thomas Elisha: *117*
Marshall, Charles: 9
Marsh Creek: 37
Meade, George, Jr.: 12
Meade, George Gordon: 34, 38, 39, 40, 72, 115, 142; arrives at Gettysburg, 67; assumes command of Army of the Potomac, 12, 23, 26; defensive deployments by, 67, 69, 107; headquarters at Fairfax Court House, *25;* headquarters at Gettysburg, 116, *140;* reliance on subordinates, 98, 107, 142; with staff, *26*
Melton, Samuel W.: letter by, 166
Meyer, Henry: account by, 89
Meyer, Thomas: 141-142
Middleburg, Va.: cavalry action at, 11
Miller, Hugh R.: 42
Milroy, Robert H.: 11
Minnigh, Henry M.: *139*
Moore, John H.: *112;* account by, 112
Moran, Francis E.: account by, 92
Morrow, Henry: 38, 47, 61
Mounger, John C.: 163
Mounger, John C. L.: account by, 163
Mounger, Thomas: 163
Murphy, William B.: 46
Myers, Elizabeth Salome "Sallie": *64;* account by, 64

N

New York Times: 130, 142; account of Gettysburg victory, *167*
Norris, Sherman R.: 136

O

Oak Ridge: 38
Oates, William C.: 72, *75;* account by, 75
Olmstead, Frederick Law: 152
Orange & Alexandria Railroad: 11
O'Rorke, Patrick H.: 72, 74
Osborn, Thomas W.: account by, 57, 115
O'Sullivan, Timothy: photographs by, *144*, *147*, *155*
Owen, Henry T.: *122;* account by, 110, 122

P

Park, Andrew: account by, 42
Parks, V. A. S.: 71

Patrick, Marsena R.: 25
Patterson, Edmund D.: 12, *21;* journal entries by, 21-22, 28
Paul, Gabriel R.: *53,* 116
Peach Orchard: 101, 136; artillery fire near, *136-137;* fighting in, 69, 82, *map* 83, 87, *90-91,* 92, 93, *94,* 98
Peel, William: account by, 129
Pender, William D.: 38
Pennsylvania College: 19, 142
Pettigrew, James Johnston: 12-13, 38, 108, 161
Phillips, Charles A.: *93*
Pickett, George E.: *33,* 107, 108, 110, 121, 156; letter by, 157
Pierce, Elliot C.: kepi of, *150*
Pierce, Tillie: *79;* account by, 62, 70, 79
Pierson, Charles: field glasses of, *87*
Pile, George C.: account by, 135
Pleasonton, Alfred: and Brandy Station, 10-11
Plum Run Valley: Confederate advances in, *66,* 72, 73, 98
Potomac River: 10; Confederate movement across, 11, 141, 142, 154, 157; Union movement across, 12, *164-165, 166*
Prey, Gilbert G.: account by, 53
Prince, Henry: 135

R

Randall, Francis: *123*
Rappahannock River: 9, 21; artillery action at, *16-17;* Federal pontoon bridges at, *8;* fords at, 11
Reed, Charles W.: illustrated letter by, *20;* sketches by, *88, 118-119*
Reese, Andrew W.: account by, 154
Revere, Paul J.: *87;* field glasses of, *87*
Reynolds, John F.: 12, 13, 37, 50, 64, 115; death of, 38, *41*
Richardson, Sidney J.: letter by, 65
Richmond, Va.: 10
Robertson, Jerome B.: 72
Robinson, John: 52, 53
Rodes, Robert E.: 11, 38, 40
Rogers, Jefferson C., 81
Root, George F.: 28
Ropes, Henry: *159*
Rose farm: 72, 82; Confederate graves near, *147*
Rose Woods: fighting in, 71

S

Saint Joseph's Academy: *34*
Savannah Republican: 71
Schimmelfennig, Alexander: *63*
Schreiner, Hermann L.: 28
Scott, Fanny Carter: *156;* letter by, 156
Scott, R. Taylor: 156
Sedgwick, John: 98, 142
Seminary Ridge: 18, 38, 49, 50-51, 58, 69, 108; bombardment at, 117, 118-119, 120; Confederate prisoners at, *162;* forming for Pickett's Charge, *118-119*
Sheeran, James B.: *31;* account by, 31
Shenandoah River: 11, 21-22
Sherfy farm: 83, 90, 91, 92
Sickles, Daniel E.: 64, 69, 83
Sisters of Charity of Saint Vincent de Paul: 34
Skelly, Johnston "Jack" Hastings, Jr.: *113*
Slaughter Pen: 77, 155; Confederate dead in, *80*
Small, Abner: *50;* account by, 50-52, 116
Smith, James E.: 71, 72
Souder, Emily Bliss: letter by, 150-151
Stannard, George J.: 108, 124
Steuart, George H.: 135
Stewart, Alexander: 64
Stewart, Robert: 12
Stiles, Robert: 141
Stone, Henry H.: *97;* jacket of, *97*
Stuart, James Ewell Brown "Jeb": 40, 142; and Brandy Station, 10-11; raid around Union army, 12, *map* 15
Sturtevant, Ralph O.: *123;* account by, 123
Sullivan, James P.: *43;* account by, 43, 130

T

Tate, Samuel M.: 102
Taylor, William B.: *21;* letter by, 21
Thorn, Elizabeth M.: *56,* 142; account by, 56
Thorn, Peter: *56*
Tiffany and Co.: 53
"Tout-le-Monde": account by, 71
Trimble, Issac R.: 108
Trostle farmhouse: Union artillery positions in, *93, 95, 96*
Troutman, Charles E.: *100;* account by, 100-101
Tucker, Henry: *125*
Turner, John M.: account by, 121

U

Uhlster, William E.: *125*
U.S. Christian Commission: 150; assistance to wounded, *149*
U.S. Regular Army: 2d Infantry, 147; 8th Infantry, *24-25;* 4th Artillery (Wilkeson's Battery G), *57;* 5th Artillery (Hazlett's Battery D), 72, 74, 75
U.S. Sanitary Commission: 142, 152; tin cup issued by, *152*
Upperville, Va.: cavalry action at, 11

V

Vicksburg, Miss.: fall of, 160, 163; siege of, 10
Vincent, Strong: 72, 74
Von Fritsch, Frederick: account by, 34-35, 58-59
Von Gilsa, Leopold: 34

W

Wade, Ga.: *113*
Wade, Mary Virginia "Jennie": *113;* bread dough tray, *112*
Wadsworth, Craig Wharton: *115*
Wadsworth, James S.: 115
Wagon Hotel (Gettysburg): *19*
Waller, Ashby: 46
Ward, J. H. Hobart: 70, 72
Ware, Thomas L.: diary entries of, *30*
Warren, Gouverneur Kemble: 72
Waud, Alfred R.: *155;* sketches by, *44-45, 126-127, 136-137, 155*
Webb, Alexander S.: 108, 127
Weber, Peter: *161*
Weed, Stephen H.: 72, 74, 75, *78,* 79
Weikert farm: 62, 70, 79
Wheat Field: fighting in, 69, *map* 82, *84-85,* 86, *88,* 89
Whittier, Edward N.: *104;* account by, 104
Whitworth, Sam: 133
Wilcox, Cadmus M.: 98
Wilkerson, John R.: account by, 71
Wilkeson, Bayard: *57,* 130, 142
Wilkeson, Samuel: *130,* 142
Willard, George L.: 98
Williamson, Amzi L.: jacket and cap of, *55*
Williamsport, Md.: 11, 35, 157, 160; Confederate earthworks covering Potomac River crossings near, 142, *154;* Union army crosses Potomac River at, *164-165*
Williford, James H.: hat of, *87*
Willoughby Run: 40, 42
Wilson, Lawrence: account by, 135
Winchester, Va.: capture of Union forces at, 11
Winslow, George B.: 85
Woolsey, Georgeanna M.: *152;* account by, 152-153
Woolsey, Jane: 152
Wright, Ambrose R.: 98
Wright, Edwin B.: 47
Wright, Philander: hat of, *47*

Y

York, Pa.: Confederate occupation of, 12
Young, John: 77

Z

Ziegler's Grove: *120*
Zouaves: 64, 92, 97

VOICES OF THE CIVIL WAR

SERIES EDITOR: Henry Woodhead
Administrative Editor: Philip Brandt George
Picture Editor: Paula York-Soderlund

Editorial Staff for *Gettysburg*
Deputy Editor: Harris J. Andrews
Associate Editors Research/Writing: Kirk Denkler, Gemma Villanueva, Mark H. Rogers
Senior Copyeditor: Donna D. Carey
Picture Coordinator: Paige Henke
Editorial Assistant: Christine Higgins
Design: Studio A—Antonio Alcalá, David Neal Wiseman

Special Contributors: Brian C. Pohanka, Gerald P. Tyson (text); Patricia Cassidy, Jennifer Clark, Charles F. Cooney, Kristin A. Dittman, Ruth Goldberg, Timothy Krapf, Jennifer Mendelsohn, Henry Mintz, Barry Wolverton (research); Roy Nanovic (index).

Correspondents: Christina Lieberman (New York). Valuable assistance was also provided by Elizabeth Brown, Daniel Donnelly (New York).

General Consultants
Brian C. Pohanka, a Civil War historian and author, spent six years as a researcher and writer for Time-Life Books' Civil War series and Echoes of Glory. He is the author of *Distant Thunder: A Photographic Essay on the American Civil War* and has written and edited numerous works on American military history. He has acted as historical consultant for projects including the feature film *Glory* and television's *Civil War Journal.* Pohanka participates in Civil War reenactments and living-history demonstrations with the 5th New York Volunteers, and he is active in Civil War battlefield preservation.

Dr. Richard A. Sauers is a historian specializing in the Civil War. As chief historian for the Pennsylvania Capitol Preservation Committee he directed the research and documentation of more than 400 Civil War battle flags and authored *Advance the Colors!,* the two-volume study of Pennsylvania's Civil War flags. He is active in Civil War and local historical societies and is involved in battlefield preservation. He is assistant editor of *Gettysburg* magazine. His published works include *A Caspian Sea of Ink: The Meade-Sickles Controversy* and *"The Bloody 85th": A Supplement to the History of the 85th Pennsylvania.* He has also compiled a critical bibliography of the Gettysburg campaign.

Paul Smith is a researcher and historian of Civil War campaigns and the roles played by individuals in the war. A student of early photography, he is currently preparing a book on the first war photographs. He is a member of the Society of the Old Greek Cross (Federal VI Corps) and the Daguerrian Society.

Time-Life Books is a division of Time Life Inc.

PRESIDENT AND CEO: John M. Fahey Jr.

TIME-LIFE BOOKS

MANAGING EDITOR: Roberta Conlan

Director of Design: Michael Hentges
Director of Editorial Operations: Ellen Robling
Director of Photography and Research: John Conrad Weiser
Senior Editors: Russell B. Adams Jr., Dale M. Brown, Janet Cave, Lee Hassig, Robert Somerville, Henry Woodhead
Special Projects Editor: Rita Thievon Mullin
Director of Technology: Eileen Bradley
Library: Louise D. Forstall

PRESIDENT: John D. Hall

Vice President, Director of Marketing: Nancy K. Jones
Vice President, Director of New Product Development: Neil Kagan
Associate Director, New Product Development: Elizabeth D. Ward
Marketing Director, New Product Development: Wendy A. Foster
Vice President, Book Production: Marjann Caldwell
Production Manager: Marlene Zack
Quality Assurance Manager: James King

Third printing. Printed in U.S.A.
Published simultaneously in Canada.
School and library distribution by Time-Life Education, P.O. Box 85026, Richmond, Virginia 23285-5026.

Library of Congress Cataloging-in-Publication Data
Gettysburg / by the editors of Time-Life Books.
p. cm.—(Voices of the Civil War)
Includes bibliographical references and index.
ISBN 0-7835-4700-5
1. Gettysburg (Pa.), Battle of, 1863. I. Time-Life Books. II. Series.
E475.53.B33 1995S
973.7'349—dc20 94-42303
CIP

OTHER PUBLICATIONS

The Time-Life Complete Gardener
The New Home Repair and Improvement
Journey Through the Mind and Body
Weight Watchers® Smart Choice Recipe Collection
True Crime
The American Indians
The Art of Woodworking
Lost Civilizations
Echoes of Glory
The New Face of War
How Things Work
Wings of War
Creative Everyday Cooking
Collector's Library of the Unknown
Classics of World War II
Time-Life Library of Curious and Unusual Facts
American Country
Voyage Through the Universe
The Third Reich
Mysteries of the Unknown
Time Frame
Fix It Yourself
Fitness, Health & Nutrition
Successful Parenting
Healthy Home Cooking
Understanding Computers
Library of Nations
The Enchanted World
The Kodak Library of Creative Photography
Great Meals in Minutes
The Civil War
Planet Earth
Collector's Library of the Civil War
The Epic of Flight
The Good Cook
World War II
The Old West

For information on and a full description of any of the Time-Life Books series listed, please call 1-800-621-7026 or write:

Reader Information
Time-Life Customer Service
P.O. Box C-32068
Richmond, Virginia 23261-2068